# ESL Study Guide

to accompany

Gerow

# ESSENTIALS OF PSYCHOLOGY

# ESL Study Guide

to accompany

Gerow

# ESSENTIALS OF PSYCHOLOGY

Prepared by

Glenda Streetman Smith, Ph.D.
*North Harris College*
*North Harris Montgomery Community College District*

HarperCollins*CollegePublishers*

ESL Study Guide to accompany Gerow ESSENTIALS OF PSYCHOLOGY



ISBN: 0-673-99257-8

93 94 95 96 97 9 8 7 6 5 4 3 2 1

# CONTENTS



*This special section features Key Terms and their defintions from each chapter in a flashcard format. Tear them out and test yourself!*

## PREFACE

You are beginning a wonderful adventure, an introductory psychology course. This study guide is designed to help you succeed. You will benefit most by familiarizing yourself with the design of the study guide and then working through each chapter as you read the chapters in your text.

Each chapter contains learning objectives, a chapter outline, lessons on learning the vocabulary of psychology, practice tests in true-false, fill-in, and multiple choice formats, a section that explains idioms and difficult phrases, a set of questions to check your understanding of the learning objectives, and helpful study tips.

The **learning objectives** suggest what you should know when you have finished studying a chapter. However, don't limit your knowledge or interest to the objectives.

The **chapter outline** provides you with a fairly detailed summary of each chapter in outline form. This will serve as a good review of the main points, but is not intended to replace the more detailed content of your textbook chapter.

One of the most difficult tasks in an introductory psychology course is learning the considerable terminology. The section titled **Learning Vocabulary** is designed to help you with the new terms and definitions that you will encounter, not only in future psychology courses, but in many other courses and in many different contexts. The exercises are in a familiar matching format.

The section called Idioms and Difficult Phrases should be especially helpful. In this section, we have defined slang, informal speech, idioms, and cliches that non-native speakers of English often find difficult. The phrases are all page referenced so that you may locate them in context as they are used in your book.

The **practice tests** consist of true-false, fill-in, and multiple choice questions. Do not limit your studying to the information in these questions. They are intended to be just a sampling of the information in the chapter, not a comprehensive test. The answers to all the practice tests and the matching exercises are presented for all chapters at the end of the study guide.

For each chapter, we've included a series of questions to test your knowledge of the learning objectives. Try answering these in a few sentences, then check your responses by looking up the answers in your textbook. Page references are provided. Your answers will show you areas that you may wish to review and identify areas that you have mastered. Working on this section should leave you well-prepared for short-answer and essay exams.

Finally, **Dr. G's Best Study Tips** are ideas that my students have proven to be effective and efficient. I suggest that you read through the study tips in all fifteen chapters as soon as possible so that you may apply any or all of them right from the beginning of the course.

Use this study guide faithfully, and you will enjoy your successful adventure through psychology.

# ESL Study Guide

to accompany

Gerow

# ESSENTIALS OF PSYCHOLOGY

# HOW TO SUCCEED IN THIS COURSE

**Factors Affecting The Learning Process**

The learning process is an important area of concern for psychologists. You will find this out as you study the principles of learning in your psychology course. The purpose of this book is to help you to improve your learning of psychology. As you read the sections below, you will see how the principles of learning apply not only to your psychology course, but to your other courses as well.

Remember, effective study habits are developed not for their own sake, but to make learning more efficient. You don't go to college to study; rather you go to learn. A good college student is one who knows how to maximize opportunities to learn. You can be a good student if you can put the principles of learning to work for you. In this first section, we'll preview some of these concepts so you can begin to use them right now. We have put these principles in the form of six pieces of advice. If you take this advice, we believe you'll be pleased with the results.

**Set Goals and Motivate Yourself to Reach Them**

We are all aware that we can learn some things "by accident" without really intending to do so. We may not set out to learn the numbers on the uniforms on the players of our favorite team, but after attending a number of games, we discover that we can identify the players without a scorecard. Our most efficient learning, however, takes place when we intend to learn, when we make a conscious effort to acquire new information. However, to learn more efficiently, we need to be motivated to learn. And we can motivate ourselves to learn through establishing goals.

Difficulties in learning in college tend to arise when students do not have clear goals, do not know why they are there, and do not have the motivation to do well. Therefore, it's a good idea to clarify in your own mind why you are in college—it will help you to make the commitment necessary to be a successful college student. Doing well in college is probably too general a goal. To be most effective, goals and motives should be as specific and concrete as possible. "Doing well" must, therefore, be broken down into manageable pieces. Familiarize yourself with your instructor's requirements and set reasonable goals. Set a schedule for your studying and learning and stick to it.

**Practice, Practice, and Practice Some More**

Learning is defined as a relatively permanent change in behavior that occurs as the result of practice or experience. Practice is an integral part of the learning process. Acquiring new information or developing a new skill involves working with the material, studying it, and practicing. The more you practice the material, the longer it will be retained.

In addition, how you distribute your practice over time is extremely important. Experiments have shown that more learning occurs when material is studied in four 15-minute sections separated by breaks than when the same material is studied in a one-hour session, even though overall study time is the same in each case. So take short breaks. Get up and stretch, walk to the window and look out, get a drink of water, and so on. But be careful; don't overdo it—15 minutes of study followed by a four-hour break is not going to work for you!

**Get Feedback On Your Learning**

A very important concept to efficient learning is knowledge of results, or feedback. A person who has little knowledge of how their learning is progressing is at a distinct disadvantage when compared to the person who is informed. Imagine learning how to shoot basketball foul shots while blindfolded. With little information about how you are doing or where the ball is really going, you can hardly expect to improve your shooting skill. The same argument holds true for any kind of learning.

Some of the feedback you receive in college comes when your instructor evaluates your work. Use your returned exams and papers as feedback. Review them. Note errors you have made. Decide how your study/learning habits need to be changed. You can also get valuable feedback by discussions with other students, by constantly appraising and testing yourself, and by using the Study Guide that accompanies your textbook.

**Make The Material You Learn Meaningful To You**

If you have never studied French, you would certainly find it easier to memorize a list of twelve common English words than to memorize a list of twelve common French words. The reason is quite clear: you know what the English words mean; you associate them with other things; you can imagine some use of them. The French words, on the other hand, strike you as nonsense. You cannot relate to them in a meaningful way.

This example can be generalized about many other areas. The learning of any information is made easier to the extent that the information can be made meaningful, personal, or useful. This implies fitting the new information in with your past experience and future plans. The Study Questions in your Study Guide make you think about concepts and relate them to familiar situations. They help you learn how to relate psychological concepts to everyday life.

### Give Yourself Rewards For Learning

One of the major foundations of the psychology of learning is the Law of Effect. This law holds that behavior will be repeated (that is, learned) or will be dropped (that is, forgotten) depending on the effect that behavior has on the individual. Quite simply, what the law says is that we tend to continue with those activities that make us feel good and tend not to continue with those that provide no satisfaction. This observation, or law, can be applied in many situations.

We all know the satisfaction that comes when our goals are attained. As with anything in life, that great exhilarating feeling of doing well on a quiz, term paper, or laboratory report will do more to insure your doing well again than anything else. Many rewards will also come from instructors, friends, and members of your family, like praise and tokens for a job well done. These rewards provide reinforcement for your behavior from others you care about.

However, you can't always depend on rewards from others to maintain your studying. You should develop the habit of providing meaningful rewards for yourself. Study hard for 50 minutes. Then, reward yourself for putting in the effort. Get something to eat or drink. Watch television. Do something to make yourself feel good—to reward yourself for a job well done. It is likely you will be surprised at how something so simple could have such a significant impact on your behavior.

### Work To Improve Your Performance

We must now make a distinction between two related processes. Learning is a process that takes place inside an individual. We cannot see learning take place. We cannot plot its course. We cannot directly observe knowledge increasing. What we must do is infer that learning has taken place by measuring the individual performance. You may think that because your little nephew can play a tune on the piano, that he has learned to play. But if he cannot (for whatever reason) demonstrate his new skill to you, how are you to know whether he has learned anything? In order to demonstrate that learning has taken place, he must perform. Much the same situation exists in the college classroom.

You may have learned a great deal about a subject, but if you cannot demonstrate what you have learned, as on an examination, why should anyone assume that learning has taken place? Put rather simply, learning involves acquiring new information; performance involves retrieving that information when it is needed. It is your performance that is evaluated. Your performance, not your learning, earns your grades in the classroom, or your raise or promotion in the workplace.

The experience of any college course involves two phases of information processing. In the first phase, information must be acquired or learned, which involves practice. In the second phase, learned information must be retrieved from memory, a process which also takes practice. It is this latter kind of practice that too many students neglect. Practice your performance by self-testing before your instructor tests your performance on an exam. The many items on the Practice Tests in your Study Guide perform this function very well. Take them as you would a real exam. Then find the correct answers in the book; this will help you determine whether you are on the right track.

In the sections that follow we will elaborate on these general principles by giving you specific advice on how to get more out of class, how to use your textbook more effectively, and how to prepare better for examinations.

## LEARNING IN THE CLASSROOM

"But I never missed a class!" is the claim teachers often hear from students who have not done well on an exam, and who have not yet learned the difference between simply attending a class and taking an active part in class. The difference has a great effect on how well students learn. Just going to class, although a step in the right direction, seldom does anyone very much good.

It is important that you go to class with some expectations about what is going to take place there. No two classroom experiences in college are going to be exactly the same. Instructors will handle their classrooms according to their own individual designs and desires. Even so, classes tend to have more in common than you might expect. In this section we will outline some of the common denominators of classroom instruction and point out some steps you can take to maximize the benefits derived from going to class. Try to put the following advice into practice; you'll be pleasantly surprised.

**Prepare For Class**

It is extremely important to be prepared for class. It is always easier to listen and understand information you are somewhat familiar with than it is to listen and understand totally unfamiliar information. To be sure, few lectures and class activities are designed to be about something you knew before you took the class. The material will be new; that is what you are paying for. But if you carefully plan and prepare, lectures or class discussions will not sound alien to you.

Once the term is underway, preparing for class will become relatively easy. You will have had time to "feel out" your instructor. You will find that some instructors lecture from the book, which means that they will spend most of the class time reviewing and expanding on the material found in your textbook. If topics are covered in order, then preparing for class largely amounts to keeping ahead of your instructor in the book so that you know beforehand what will be happening. Even those instructors who do not lecture from the book may lecture on materials related to the assigned text (or to another available text) so that you should be able to anticipate a good deal of the class activities for any given day. Instructors who use class discussion expect you to listen to what is going on and to make contributions. Your task here is essentially the same as for lectures—be ready.

Remember, for any class, and for any instructor, the important thing is to avoid going to class unprepared. At least you should have reviewed recent lecture notes and previewed the textbook so that you are familiar with most of the vocabulary words that your instructor will use. The content of introductory psychology courses is largely devoted to learning new vocabulary. If you are familiar with terms before going to class, listening for new ideas and concepts will be easier because you will not have to think about new words. You will have a chance to think, organize what is being said, and summarize your thoughts in coherent notes.

Most good listening is a matter of attitude. To be an effective listener and user of information, you must be in the proper frame of mind. As you enter the classroom and take your seat, try to rid your mind of all the trivial activities of the day. You cannot listen well to a lecture if you are thinking about last night's date and this afternoon's lunch. You can't contribute to a discussion if all you want to talk about is last weekend's game. You must be thinking about psychology. Get your mind warmed up. What's the instructor going to talk about? What contributions will you be expected to make? How will the discussion fit with material you already know? How can you relate this to your own experience?

The importance of preparing adequately for discussion/recitation classes and seminars should be especially apparent to you. You should be prepared not only to listen intelligently, but also to participate and carry your weight in the discussions. Having assignments completed is a necessity for participation. It is bad enough not knowing what your instructor is talking about; however, not understanding a discussion among your classmates is a frustrating and potentially embarrassing experience. When you find yourself surprised at what is being said in class, you have not prepared correctly.

**Develop Your Listening Skills**

Listening is essentially an active process in which you relate what is being said to what you have already stored in your memory. It is a process of taking in new information, organizing it, and storing it in such a way that it can be used at some later time. Given the large amount of information in the classroom, this active process will require considerable concentration on your part.

We do not often think of it as such, but listening is a skill, a skill that can be developed just like typing, bicycle riding, or reading. Proficiency in listening can be increased through practice. Listening in class for new information is different from listening in casual conversation or listening to a hard-rock radio station. This is because a larger portion of the information will involve new or technical vocabulary terms, and you will be expected to recall the information (on examinations) at some later time. Every time you listen in class you are practicing a very basic skill.

**Take Useful Notes**

Class attendance and careful listening are important in lecture classes because lectures are presented to you only once. You will, therefore, need some written record of the information presented orally in class to study and review later. You will need a record of this information to integrate with material found in your textbook and outside readings. Good lecture notes written in your own words are as valuable as a summarized and organized compilation of classroom information.

**Principle 1: Select and Organize the Material Presented to You**

It will soon become apparent to you, if it is not already, that there is no way you can write down everything your instructor says in class. This can be an advantage. Notetaking should be an active process in which you select and organize the material you write down. Although it is generally better to take too many notes than to take too few, you must be an active listener who participates in class—not just a mechanical writer.

Good notetaking can be enhanced by good preparation. Get ready for class. Know what to expect. Familiarize yourself with vocabulary terms from the textbook. Your class notes will be the tangible product of good listening habits.

The notes will be *your* notes. Put them in a form that you can use. Except for technical terms and new vocabulary, use your own words. Relate what your instructor is saying to your own experiences. In this way, your notes will become more meaningful to you when you review them later. Copying information is not learning it.

In the course of taking notes, you should develop some shortcuts, some alternatives to writing everything out in longhand. The key here, once again, is flexibility. Feel free to abbreviate, but only if you will be able to understand your own symbols when you go back to your notes for study at some later time. Illegible or incoherent notes are worse than useless: you have wasted valuable listening time taking them.

You should also be aware that there will be times when it is best not to take notes at all. Participating in a classroom discussion or asking questions may provide you with the sort of information you will remember best. The reason for this involves your being an active participant in the proceedings as opposed to a passive notetaker sitting on the sideline. Once again, one of the best ways to learn new material is to get involved, work with it, and make it personal.

**Principle 2: Edit and Review Your Notes**

When the class is over and the instructor has left the room, only part of your work is done. During the class period you have been listening, selecting, organizing, participating, thinking and writing. Now you must go back over your written record of the class, edit, and review your notes. This should be accomplished in three stages.

**Stage 1** Immediately after class, while the material is still fresh in your mind, review your notes, fill in gaps, underline for emphasis, note unclear sections that will require further work, and generally prepare the notes for further use. You should use your margins to add information from the lecture that you simply did not have time to record. By rereading your notes immediately after class, you should be able to spot sources of possible difficulty; that is, places in your notes that are hard to understand. If your notes are hard to understand right after you have written them, they will probably be impossible to interpret later.

**Stage 2** Several times a week as part of your study for each course, continue the editing process. Use your textbook, other notes, outside readings, or consult with your instructor and other students to check spellings, complete lists, note relationships with other lectures, and clarify sections that are not readily understandable. The outlines that appear in each chapter of this book should help you with this. Use them to put your notes together in a meaningful whole.

Because you will be participating in classroom discussion, and what is said will usually be fragmented, stages one and two are particularly important for discussion, recitation, and seminar classes. As you continue to work with your notes and other sources, you will build an integrated set of study resources. If this is done, you are ready to begin reviewing several days before each exam. Final preparation for the exam is done in an orderly and calm fashion. You are not frantically searching and cramming, thus you avoid a primary reason for test anxiety.

**Stage 3** A very important stage in reviewing your notes should occur following each examination in a course. After taking an exam, you should go back and critically evaluate your notebook. To what extent did your notes help? How might they be improved? Did you write too much? Too little? Was the format the best you could have used? Did you spend too much or too little time on your notes?

Always remember, good notes can be the difference between success and failure in class. Don't depend on other students' notes; they were written for someone else and may not make much sense to you. At any rate, they will be less useful to you because good notes are not separable from all the other things a good student does to learn class material.

## Importance of Textbook Study

There is more information about psychology in your textbook than you could ever get in class. Since this is the case, learning how to get information from your textbook is one of the most important lessons you can learn in college. This is not to de-emphasize the role of your instructor or lessen the value of attendance. In many cases instructors will update textbook material, interject personal experience and points of view, and emphasize what they feel are the most important sections of assigned readings. Your instructor, having studied widely in psychology, is aware of more points of view than those presented in your text and is available to answer questions and discuss ideas that result from your textbook study.

Even after you graduate from college, you will find textbook study skills useful in your daily life. Much of the information you will need can be gained through reading. Whether you are reading a cookbook, an operator's manual for a piece of equipment, a business report, or a weekly news magazine, the textbook study skills you develop and practice in college can be applied. Use the following techniques to make your textbook study more efficient and productive.

## Read Your Textbook Differently From Other Books

Perhaps the most significant insight about textbook study is the realization that it is quite different from casual reading. "Reading the chapter" or "moving your eyes over the page" is not studying.

Studying is an active process. It is the active accumulation of information. Studying a text involves a great deal more concentration and mental effort than reading fiction for pleasure. You should look for major ideas and evidence to support those ideas. What is the author trying to say? How are the conclusions supported? You should look for ways to relate what you are reading to your previous experience. How does the information pertain to what you have read elsewhere, to what was said in lecture, or to your own personal experience? How can you make the information in the text relevant and meaningful?

There are times while studying when you should look up from the book, pause, and consider what you have read. You should be able to quickly summarize in your own words the paragraphs you have just read. Stop and think about the significance of the material you have just read. Just getting through a given number of pages or chapters in an allotted amount of time is not studying. Speed may be fine, but speed without comprehension is a waste of time.

Works of fiction are rarely accompanied by extensive illustrations. Perhaps this accounts for why pictures, drawings, figures, graphs, and tables are often overlooked in textbook study. Ignoring textbook illustrations is a mistake, since these drawings, figures, and graphs are constructed with great care and are included in the text to provide a pictorial summary. Very often a passage in a textbook cannot be understood without referring to accompanying illustrations. Imagine trying to understand the structure of the nervous system without having the illustrations, too. Don't be surprised if you have to refer back and forth between the written text and the illustrations a number of times before you can fully understand either. This is what study is: an active search for understanding.

To prepare for an examination through effective textbook study, you should study your assignment at least once from your instructor's point of view. That is, imagine that it is your job to write an examination covering the material you are studying. What sorts of questions would you ask? And, more importantly, could you provide adequate answers? This is one of the most effective techniques for self-evaluation.

Effective textbook study is a skill that can be learned by anyone. It will not be learned automatically. It takes hard work and practice to develop textbook study skills. The rewards for your work, however, should be almost immediate. You should be able to feel the difference in your reading efficiency. Your test grades should improve and your understanding should increase.

## Prepare For Textbook Study

Because textbook study is so important, it is an activity that you should think about before beginning. Develop some expectations about the material that you are going to read by reading through the chapter summary and by glancing at the headings, subtitles, and illustrations. From this preview, you should be able to assess the content of the chapter. How important does the material appear to be? How does it compare with material read elsewhere? Does the assigned reading contain considerable detail, perhaps requiring more study time than you had originally planned? How much do you plan to cover in your allotted time? Very basically, you should begin your textbook study by surveying the assignment and developing a feeling for what you are going to read.

Before you actually begin studying your text, you should have a series of questions in mind. Preview the chapter summaries and headings and pay particular attention to the learning objectives for each chapter that appears in the Study Guide, which was written to help you study your textbook. In addition to providing you with hints about what the chapter will cover in detail, they often give rise to a number of questions. Your questions may be very simple ones. For example, if a chapter heading makes no sense to you at all, your questions may be "What in the world is that all about?" Often, however, the summary, headings, italicized terms, or illustrations will remind you of points raised in class, covered in some other reading, or related to your own experience. A very basic question in this case may be, "What are the relationships between what I know about this and what the textbook says?" The more you know about any chapter covered in the text, the more detailed your questions. Developing a set of questions about the material you are going to read and thinking about these questions before you begin your reading will give you a framework for evaluating and understanding the assignment.

**Make Textbook Study An Active Process**

When we say textbook study is an active process, we mean that it is a mental activity. You must be mentally active and alert while studying so that you can search, question, and think. The textbook and its accompanying Study Guide are designed to facilitate this active process. Use the features built into them; they are based on proven principles from the psychology of learning.

A simple and effective way to make textbook study an active process is to turn chapter and unit headings into questions. For example, by using the heading "Make Textbook Study an Active Process," questions can be formulated. What is active textbook study? What are the individual elements that make textbook study active? Another example in your text includes material on the autonomic nervous system. Here the questions become: What is the autonomic nervous system? What does "autonomic" mean? How does this system function? What parts make up this system? How is it related to other systems studied? You would typically begin this process as you prepare for textbook study. The study questions in the Study Guide that accompanies your textbook should help you with this process. They identify key issues by relating psychological concepts to your experience.

As you become more familiar with the subject matter, your questions will become more specific. This process becomes enhanced when you distribute your allotted study time over days and weeks. You begin moving from the general to the specific, building understanding. This process cannot take place in a short time. For this reason, cramming seldom works because you have to deal with the general and specific all at once, often resulting in confusion rather than understanding.

One of the most helpful study aids you can devise for yourself is an accurate vocabulary list. This can be of two types. You should certainly make a practice of looking up the meanings of all words that you don't understand. Making a list of these and practicing their use will add to your personal working vocabulary. In addition, you might find it helpful to make a listing of important or technical terms, their meanings, and/or significance for inclusion in your notebook. If you do not know the meaning of the words used to explain an important concept, you are certainly going to have difficulty understanding the concept itself. Pay attention to the terms defined in the margin of your textbook and use the Glossary at the back of your textbook—both are valuable resources for understanding the terminology of psychology. The psychology vocabulary exercises in your Study Guide are designed to help you to learn the over 500 terms contained in your textbook. Use them.

Underlining in textbooks is a common practice. Unfortunately, this practice is often misused. The purpose of underlining is to highlight or emphasize a particular passage of the text so that the essential points of a chapter can be quickly reviewed by simply rereading the underlined passages. The mistake that many students make is to underline too much. When 80 percent of a page is underlined for emphasis, the remaining 20 percent usually appears more striking. Remember that you are underlining major areas so that you can review your textbook without having to read it all again. Underlining is a summarizing process and should not be used indiscriminately.

You can increase the value of your textbook for studying by using the margins of the pages for your own personal notation. Make your text a storehouse of references. Cross reference textbook material with information in your notebook by jotting down in the margin the date of the lecture covering the same material that is found on the particular page of the book. Similarly, note any other sources of related information you are familiar with, such as library readings or laboratory manuals. Any questions that arise in your reading should also be noted in the margin. It's your book—use it; write in it. For library books, which are not your property, such notations cannot be made in the book. In this case, taking notes on the reading (in your notebook) will be the best method of preserving information.

Your textbook includes "Before You Go On Questions" in each chapter. By thinking about these questions, you slow down your reading and give yourself time to learn better. This helps you to discover what you know and what you don't know about the reading assignment. The Study Guide contains practice test questions for each chapter. They are designed to help you check your knowledge of textbook material. These questions provide a method of self-evaluation that is particularly useful when preparing for examinations. We next consider examinations—what students typically dread most about college.

**Examinations**

Almost everyone associated with the college experience finds examinations distasteful. Graduates commonly list exam taking among their most unpleasant memories of college. Exams call for hard work and a lot of preparation, and they often generate a great deal of anxiety. Even instructors rarely find much enjoyment in trying to formulate and grade an honest, comprehensive test of students' learning. But no matter how "progressive," "modern," or "liberal" the college you attend, you can probably count on taking examinations. They have become a fact of educational life. It is our hope that by following the suggestions presented here, you can make taking examinations a useful, meaningful learning experience. Exams can be viewed in a positive light. They may provide you with new information or help you view information in new and different ways. Moreover, exams give students feedback about their progress.

**Preparing For Examinations**

Few occasions are quite as pleasant as the one you experience when you walk into class to take a big exam fully prepared, confident that you know the material and that you are going to do well. We also know from personal experience how absolutely miserable you feel when you face an exam unprepared, doomed before you begin, unable even to understand, much less answer the first question. The key lies in being fully prepared. Proper preparation for examinations helps to furnish the kind of positive reinforcement that education is supposed to provide. Preparing for exams is not an easy, automatic process; it involves scheduling your time, self-testing your progress, and continuous active reviewing.

Before we deal with how to prepare for examinations it is important to consider briefly how information is acquired and what "study" really means. Study is an active process, not significantly different from acquiring new information and new skills in daily life. Simply spending time with your books, and notes, and passively sitting in class is not learning. You learn things by listening to experts, watching others perform, reading, and practicing. All of these require active thought and application on your part.

If you want to learn how to tune your car's engine or how to sew, you will probably watch and ask questions of those who can already sew or tune engines. You will read about the task, even if what you read is just the owner's manual to your new car or sewing machine. Then you will practice, making some errors at first, but sooner or later you will acquire the skill and simultaneously develop a certain understanding of the principles of auto mechanics or sewing. This means that you have "passed the exam." As you continue to listen, read, and practice, you will be able to undertake more difficult or complex tasks and your understanding will deepen.

The very same processes are involved in acquiring academic skills and understanding. You have to take an active role in the process. You should listen carefully to your instructor, ask questions, and seek additional information from your textbook. You should try to relate the new information to what you already know. Once you understand the principles involved, you should be able to answer exam questions. In fact, you should be able to apply psychological information to a wide range of situations, but the only way to know if you can is by practicing. If you discover that you do not understand a concept, you will have to go back to your notes, books, or instructor for insight into the solution. Again, you will have to be actively involved. You will have to think about the information presented.

**Rule 1: Prepare on a Daily Basis - Don't Cram.** In almost every case, you will be notified of an upcoming examination well in advance. Often, scheduled exams are noted on the course outlines distributed on the first day of class. Most of your exams should then come as no surprise to you. We often hear students complain that they have two, or even three final exams scheduled for the same day, which they feel allows them only one day to study for each. Nothing could be more untrue. The students have had the whole term to prepare for each of the exams. What they fail to realize is that daily preparation is needed. They should have begun preparing (studying) for their examinations on the first day of class.

To be truthful, preparing daily is not an easy task. It is difficult to sit down today to study for an examination that won't take place for three more weeks. With so much time before the exam, it seems that there will be plenty of opportunities for studying later.

Daily preparation for examinations is exactly what was discussed earlier about gaining understanding, developing new skills, and forming new concepts. To prepare for exams, you do not have to do anything new. Preparing for and carefully listening in class is daily preparation, as well as taking good class notes and reviewing and editing them soon after class. A crucial step in preparing for exams is to make and adhere to a realistic schedule. If you study your textbook on a regular schedule, you will avoid the need for cramming. Using the library when necessary will also help you prepare. A more practical way of viewing these procedures is to consider them as ways of getting ready to do the best possible job of taking an examination. Doing all of these things throughout the term will enable you to sidestep the unpleasant effects of cramming: loss of sleep, anxiety, missed work, cancellation of social activities, and poorer grades.

**Rule 2: Find Ways to Test Yourself.** As examination day approaches, you will want some indication of how well your studying has been progressing. To be effective, the process of self-testing must begin well in advance of the examination date. If you wait until the night before and find you are having trouble, there is little time to study the areas you do not know well. There are many different techniques for evaluating your own achievement, all of which involve constructing, taking, and grading your own test on the assigned material. For example, if you think that you may have to identify the important structures of the eye, draw a picture of one, labeling all of the structures you can think of and then check your drawing with the one in your book. Did you leave out any parts? Did you put in any that don't belong? If know that your next exam will ask you for the definitions of all the new terms in a chapter, see if you can write out a definition for the terms in your own words and then simply check to see if you have made errors. Even for an essay exam you should test yourself on the factual information involved. It will be help to work out a few practice outlines without referring to your book or notes. Having the factual information in mind and thinking through several different answers to anticipated questions should make writing the essay itself relatively easy.

Self-testing means that you test yourself before your instructor does. The Practice Tests for each Chapter in this study guide are a good way to get started. Use them to get a feel for what your instructor's examinations will be like. The practice test items in the study guide, were developed from the same material your instructor will be testing you on. Your instructor will likely phrase the questions differently and might emphasize some material more than other material, but your instructor will probably not ask you anything greatly different. If you find yourself struggling to come up with reasonable questions on your own, you certainly need more studying. Go back to your notes, textbook, study guide, the library, your instructor; study some more and try again until you can construct your own test—and pass it.

**Rule 3: Build Learning by Reviewing.** If you have maintained a schedule of daily preparation and have consistently evaluated your own performance, you should be able to approach the examination day with confidence. There is no way that everything you need to know for an exam can be assimilated on the night before. You cannot digest and understand large amounts of difficult material in a few hours. Attempting to do so will only result in confusion and in a poor performance on the exam. However, it is well worth your time to review the material to be covered. Review means "look at again." You should certainly review just before each examination. But a more helpful procedure is to review on a regular basis; that is, throughout the term. You should be constantly reviewing what you have learned. You should look back over material either on a weekly basis or at the completion of a meaningful unit, such as the assigned topic. Experimental evidence and common sense suggest that most forgetting takes place soon after learning. Frequent review, however can significantly improve retention over a period of time. By definition, review will not introduce new material to be learned, it will simply refresh your memory of familiar material.

**A Final Word** One final word about preparing for exams. When you take an examination, you are being asked to perform on the basis of what you have learned. Although the effects of anxiety on learning are often subtle, the effects of anxiety on performance are evident and well-known. Your performance will be poor if you become overly anxious, upset, and uptight—even if you have learned the material reasonably well. Just realizing that anxiety may reduce your efficiency does little to reduce anxiety. Anxiety is one of those things that is very difficult to eliminate by sheer force of

willpower. The most effective way to reduce anxiety is to deal with its cause. If you have conscientiously applied yourself to the job of preparing for an exam, you should have reduced, if not eliminated the most common cause of anxiety. If being overly nervous about taking exams becomes a source of concern for you, you should consider talking to someone in the counseling center or the psychology department who can help you overcome this problem.

**Types of Examinations**

During your college years you will experience a wide variety of examinations. If you really know and understand the material to be examined, the type of test you are given should be of small consequence. Nonetheless, each different type of exam should be approached with a slightly different method of preparation. You should find out early in the term what type of exams you will be taking in your psychology course so that you can prepare properly from the outset.

As a rule of thumb, you will probably discover that in a large class the exam will be objective tests. In such tests, you indicate your answer by circling a number or a letter or by writing one or two words. These exams are objective because there is little doubt about the correctness of your answers. They are right, or they are wrong. The advantage of such tests is that they can be easily and quickly scored (often by machines), which makes their use in large classes virtually mandatory. Subject areas with a great deal of terminology, such as introductory psychology, are most often tested by objective examinations.

Subjective exams, where your answer will be interpreted and evaluated by a grader, seldom have just one correct answer to a question. Factors such as clarity of expression, logic of organization, and accuracy of factual information all play a part in determining your grade. With subjective examinations, you will be expected to organize, criticize, analyze, interpret, explain, and define. More writing is called for with subjective exams than with objective exams. Because of the time required to grade subjective examinations, you can expect a greater number of these exams in small classes. A few examples of objective and subjective exams are described below.

**Objective Examinations.** Obtaining a complete understanding of the material to be tested is surely the best way to prepare for any examination. However, if you know that you will be given an objective exam, the questions that you ask yourself while studying your notes and your text should be the same type that you might expect to find on the exam. Try actively to anticipate your instructor's questions. Most of the questions on objective exams are geared toward facts. A good examiner, however, can ask about all sorts of things in an objective way. Objective test items are generally of the following varieties.

**True/False** A true/false test is simply a listing of statements that you must judge as being either true or false. Occasionally, you will have a space to justify your answer. True/false items should generally be considered at face value. That is, do not try to over-interpret a statement; do not read into an item more than what is there. For example, the statement "The sun rises in the east" should probably be considered true, even if you understand that the sun does not rise but rather the earth's rotation makes the sun appear to rise. You should also be on the lookout for some key words in true/false tests. In general, words like "only," "never," and "always" are clues that the statement is probably a false one. Unless you know you will be penalized for incorrect responses, never leave an item unanswered. If all else fails, guess. A rule of thumb, developed through the experience of taking and constructing true/false examinations, is that unusually long statements are more often than not true, while short statements tend to be false ones. (The rationale here is that instructors don't like to waste time writing a long untrue statement about their subject matter.)

**Multiple Choice** Multiple choice items present the examinee with a number of alternative ways of completing the statement. One of the alternatives will result in a correct statement. Multiple choice questions appear easier than true/false questions because the correct answer is included among the alternatives and may be discovered by the process of eliminating the incorrect choices. On the other hand, multiple choice items are more difficult than true/false items because there are more ways to make an error.

There are several "tricks" to taking multiple choice tests. We'll consider five. First, even if you're not really sure which of the choices provides the best answer you can usually narrow your choice to two or three alternatives. If all else fails, you should then guess; and unless you remember something that suggests you have guessed incorrectly, you are generally best off sticking with your first guess. Second, if you have absolutely no other information to go on, experience suggests that the longest alternative in a multiple choice item is often the correct one. Third, avoid the two common mistakes students make in taking multiple choice exams. These are reading too much into the question (the same as with true/false exams) and choosing the first alternative that seems reasonable without even reading the other choices. Your job will be to indicate the best alternative, something you cannot do without reading all of them. Fourth, as is true with all objective tests, you are well advised to skip over those items you cannot answer at first reading. You may well find that the answer to an item is revealed to you in a question appearing later in the test. Finally, before handing in your paper, check to be sure that you have supplied an answer to every question.

**Completion** A completion, or "fill-in-the-blank," exam item is somewhat similar to a multiple choice item except that you must provide the word or phrase that best completes a statement. There is little substitute here for knowing the correct answer. Be sure to put something reasonable in each blank and check to see that the answer you provide is grammatically correct; that is, it results in a complete sentence. If you can think of nothing at all to put in a blank, you might be better off skipping the item. Inserting a word or phrase that is utterly ridiculous will only serve to flaunt your ignorance of that item.

**Matching** Matching questions may take on a number of forms, but all questions of this type call for you to put complementary items together. You are to associate items on one list with items on another list. Material found in matching questions almost always involves specific factual material, such as matching names with dates, events with dates or names, words with definitions, and so forth. It is particularly important with this type of exam to read and understand the directions. For example, you will need to know if any of the alternatives can be used more than once. Again, be sure to match all the items unless there is a penalty for guessing incorrectly.

**Subjective Examinations** As stated above, subjective exams will involve interpretation and evaluation by a grader. These exams are subjective because there is not just one correct answer to each question. A grader will have to interpret and evaluate your response by the organization of information, the clarity of expression, and the accuracy of the facts you supply.

**Essay** This is a general term used to describe tests calling for such things as explanation, analysis, criticism, comparison, outline, enumeration, description, and summarization. Notice the differences among these words- each one calls for a distinct approach to the question. For example, explaining something is not the same thing as outlining or describing it. A common error in essay exams is the failure to answer the question in the manner specified. A complete description of a phenomenon in response to a question calling for criticism of that phenomenon will be considered as a wrong answer. If you are not already aware of the subtle differences among the above mentioned key words, it would be worth the time to check and learn the definitions of each.

You might be lucky on a multiple choice test and guess the correct alternative for an item or two. Luck has little to do with essay exams. The only way to do well is to be prepared, and the best way to prepare is obviously to anticipate the exam by studying the material to be covered so that you can describe it, evaluate it, criticize it, or analyze it. If you have completely thought through all of the material in these terms, you should be able to handle any question that appears on the exam. Regardless of the form your answer takes, the quality of your response will be in a large part determined by your understanding of the information. You can hardly evaluate a phenomenon when you do not know the facts involved. Most graders have had enough experience to spot an answer filled with many words and few facts. Padding an answer with excess verbage is more likely to detract from your grade than add to it.

The first thing to do when you get your test paper is to read it carefully. Pay particular attention to the instructions. You may find that you need only answer a percentage of the questions instead of every one. You will seldom be required to answer the questions in the order in which they are asked, so choose what you consider to be an easy item to begin with. Avoid the very common mistake of writing your answer without thinking about it first. If you have time, it would be helpful to sketch a brief outline of your answer before you attempt to write it out. When you have completed your paper, take a minute to read through what you have written. You may think of new information to add or find an error to correct.

**Short Answer** A short answer test is a variety of the common essay exam. The questions are generally more specific and therefore call for shorter, more concise answers. If a question can be answered in a short paragraph of four or five sentences, it would qualify as a short answer question. Preparing for and taking a short answer test is essentially the same as preparing for and taking an essay exam: anticipate questions, read all the questions and directions, think before you write, and review your answers before you hand in your paper.

**Take Home** You may encounter the sort of examination where you will be given a series of questions or problems to complete at home, using whatever resources you can find to help you answer the question. These take-home exams are qualitatively different from the usual in-class subjective exams. Because there is little time constraint, answers will generally be longer. Because you will have your books to use, a higher degree of precision and accuracy will be expected in your answers. The examiner is looking for a unique, personalized response to a question that does not have a specific solution. Copying or paraphrasing from your books or notes will not be sufficient. You will have to demonstrate that you understand the material that you find in these sources. Preparation should be the same as for other subjective examinations, with the added dimension that you must be familiar enough with the resources at your disposal that you can quickly find whatever information you don't know.

**Open Book** These exams are given in class, but you have the opportunity to bring some resource material with you to consult during the exam. Too often students get the impression that because they can bring their books to the exam that they don't have to prepare for the test. Nothing can be further from the truth. Open-book exams are usually constructed so that you will have little time to spend looking through your book. Preparation for this exam is virtually the same as for other essay exams. In addition, you must be familiar enough with your book so that your information can be rapidly retrieved. The less time you have to spend referring to your book, the better off you-will be. Your answers to an open-book exam should be different from simple essay exam answers. You cannot expect to gain much credit for simply restating the facts found in your book. You must analyze, interpret, and organize these facts, perhaps with examples, in ways that are not spelled out in your text. The factual information you present will have to be complete and precise.

**After The Examination**

Independent of the grade you earn, you should consider every examination as a potential learning experience. This may be difficult to do. A natural reaction to a low grade on an exam is to throw it away and forget it. But a low grade implies that you haven't adequately learned the material. The first thing to do is to note which questions you have missed and do whatever is necessary to discover the correct answer. You may "correct yourself" by simply referring to your notes or your textbook. If, after trying on your own, you still do not understand your error, see your instructor. Before you put an exam away, be sure that if you were given the very same exam again that you would be able to answer every question correctly. Failure to review each exam may lead to future errors because some questions on subsequent exams may presuppose your understanding of material on which you were previously tested.

You should also use your examinations to help you evaluate your study habits. If you consistently do well on exams for your psychology course, you should continue to do whatever you are doing, or you may even want to reduce the time spent on psychology to devote more time to another course. (But, of course, it can be dangerous to mess with success.) If you are not achieving the grades you want on your exams, you should certainly change the way you are studying. The first and the simplest thing you should do is to provide yourself with more time to study and to schedule that time accordingly. You will need to evaluate each and every aspect of your study habits. Perhaps you will discover that you have been spending too much time studying your text and not enough time studying your notes or vice versa. Perhaps you should develop a different style of notetaking. There are any number of changes which you can make in the ways you study. Failing to change your study habits when you are not doing well in a course is the worst mistake you can make.

**A Final Word About Sitting Down To Study Psychology**

Effective study involves concentration. Anything that interferes with your concentration is a distraction. There are two kinds of distractions. The first is mental. By this we mean that your mental attention must be focused only on the task at hand. You must put out of your mind all irrelevant thoughts and daydreams. You can't effectively study psychology while you are thinking about a poor grade on an English theme. If your mind drifts to a conversation you overhear in the hall, you might be better off joining the conversation than straining to hear what is being said, thereby distracting yourself from your study. If during a study period you find your mind wandering, this is an indication that it is time to take a break.

A second type of distraction is physical. In most instances, physical distractions are easier to avoid than mental distractions. It is best to find a quiet environment to study. Experience has shown that learning is diminished when background noise increases. Maybe you "got by" in high school studying by the sound of your stereo or radio, but the odds are that music playing in the background will interfere with the learning of more difficult material encountered in college. It is a wise practice to face your desk to the wall rather than to the window. If you study at home, see to it that other members of your family understand that you need to be left alone. The same goes for roommates.

Some of the most common distractions are social activities that take you away from your studies during scheduled study periods. It takes willpower to turn down invitations to go to the movies or to join a card game in the lounge. These activities are fine when they are done during your free time. When you are distracted from study time by extracurricular activities you find yourself losing free time, losing sleep, cramming, and performing poorly.

What was said above was basically common sense. To make it possible for you to study, it should be obvious that you need to find yourself a comfortable, quiet place where you can concentrate. Although it is true that you should develop the habit of studying any place, you should establish a home base where most of your work will be done. Wherever it might be, you will want your home base to be well equipped. Once you begin to study, you shouldn't have to get up and search for things you need for studying. If possible, use a desk that can be reserved just for your studying. A desk is designed for studying, as opposed to the kitchen table, which is often used for other purposes. Your desk has a place to keep a sufficient supply of paper, pencils, erasers, pens, and anything else you will need.

Your home base should serve as your own private library. All of your textbooks and assigned reading books should be kept here, as should reference books such as a good dictionary, a thesaurus, and books you have checked out of the library. As was noted above, your term schedule should be clearly in view in your home base. You should get into the habit of using your study area only for studying. Try to avoid using your study environment for paying bills, writing letters, or talking with friends. By so doing, you will immediately establish the proper frame of mind upon entering your home base, thereby fully utilizing the hours you spend there.

As you learn more about psychology you will see that this advice is based on sound psychological theory and research. If you put what you've read here into practice, we believe the results will be positive for you.

# CHAPTER 1—THE NATURE OF PSYCHOLOGY

**Learning Objectives**

1. Know which two points must be demonstrated in order to claim that psychology is a science.
2. Describe the subject matter of psychology and the use of operational definitions.
3. Discuss how Descartes, Locke, Darwin, and von Helmholtz influenced psychology.
4. Describe when and where psychology began and who originated it.
5. Describe behaviorism and psychoanalysis as approaches to psychology.
6. Describe the two approaches that have challenged behaviorism, humanism and gestalt psychology.
7. Describe the different areas of psychology and what sort of work a psychologist in each area would do.
8. List psychology's two major goals.
9. Define naturalistic observation and discuss the potential problems with its use.
10. Explain how surveys and case history studies are used in Psychology.
11. Explain why correlation is used, what data are needed to calculate a correlation coefficient, and the meaning of positive, negative, and zero correlation coefficients.
12. Understand the essence of doing an experiment and be able to identify and define independent, dependent, and extraneous variables.
13. Explain how random assignment and baseline design contribute to control in experiments.
14. Discuss ethics in psychological research.
15. Discuss the interaction of nature and nurture.
16. Define phenomenology.
17. Discuss the claim that psychology is one of the most applied sciences.

**Chapter 1 Outline**

I. Preview
   A. A working definition of psychology is a necessary foundation in order to examine specific issues, concerns, approaches, and methods in the psychology field.
   B. Modern psychology can be more fully appreciated by examining how psychology has changed throughout history.
   C. Psychology consists of many interrelated themes that involve the concerns and interests of modern man.

II. Defining Psychology
   A. Psychology is the scientific study of behavior and mental processes.
   B. Psychology is a science.
      1. A science is composed of an organized body of knowledge.
      2. Psychology's body of knowledge has been gained through scientific methods.
   a. Scientific methods are a set of scientific procedures involving observation, description, control, and replication.
         b. The basic process of the scientific method is as follows:
            i. Psychologists make observations.
            ii. They then formulate hypotheses.
            iii. They explore alternate explanations as needed.
   C. The subject matter of psychology
      1. Psychologists study behavior.
         a. Behavior is what organisms do that is observable and measurable.
         b. Such behavior must be publicly verified by a number of observers.
         c. Events, including behaviors, that can be publicly verified have greater credibility in science.
      2. Psychologists study mental processes, internal activities of consciousness, including cognitions and affect.
         a. Cognitions consist of the mental processes of perceiving, thinking, understanding, and remembering.
         b. Affect refers to the feelings or moods that accompany an emotional reaction.
         c. The **ABC's** that comprise the subject matter of psychology are affect, behavior, and cognitions.
      3. Psychologists use operational definitions.

a. Operational definitions define concepts in terms of the procedures used to measure the concepts.
b. They help to specify how a behavior will be measured, and as a result, they help us communicate accurately with others.

III. Psychological Approaches Past and Present
 A. No two psychologists approach their subject matter in exactly the same way because they include their individual experiences, expertise, values, and prejudices in their study.
 B. The formal roots of psychology can be found in both philosophy and science.
  1. The philosophers suggested that it is reasonable to seek explanations of human behaviors at a human level.
   a. René Descartes (1596-1650), a French philosopher, saw the body as a complicated machine.
    i. He believed the body and mind (or soul) are separate entities that interact.
    ii. He called this interaction interactive dualism.
   b. British empiricism focused on how the contents of the mind are acquired through experience.
    i. John Locke (1632-1704) believed that people are born with empty minds (tabula rasa or blank slate).
    ii. Empiricists speculated about how the mind is filled with ideas, thoughts, and memories.
  2. Science progressed in many ways during the nineteenth century.
   a. Charles Darwin's work had a significant influence on psychology as he confirmed that humans are part of the animal world.
   b. Hermann von Helmholtz (1821-1894) pioneered in areas of physiology related to psychology.
    i. He was a physician/surgeon.
    ii. He studied sensation, perception, and the operation of the nervous system.
 C. Psychology begins: The early years
  1. Wilhelm Wundt (1832-1920) founded his psychological laboratory at the University of Leipzig in 1879.
   a. This event marks the "beginning" of psychology.
   b. Wundt was interested in consciousness.
   c. Wundt's variety of psychology was called structuralism because of his interest in the structure of the human mind.
  2. Edward Titchener (1867-1927) opened a psychology laboratory at Cornell University and refined introspection, a technique in which one examines one's own mental experiences and reports them in the most fundamental way.
  3. William James (1842-1910) at Harvard took issue with the structuralists.
   a. He thought of himself as a philosopher.
   b. He taught a course in psychology.
   c. He defined psychology as the "science of mental life."
   d. He believed the mind could not be broken into parts and structures but that the emphasis should be on the adaptive functions of the mind, a philosophy called functionalism.
  4. Functionalism focused on consciousness or mental life.
   a. The functionalists relied on experimental methods and introduced the study of animals to psychology.
 D. Psychoanalysis is a Freudian approach to psychology.
  1. It emphasizes the influence of the unconscious and instincts.
  2. Sigmund Freud (1856-1939) has had a profound impact on how we think about ourselves.
   a. He was a practitioner.
   b. He had profound insights despite a lack of scientific rigor.
   c. He studied his patients and himself.
   d. From him comes psychology's concern with diagnosis and treatment.
 E. Behaviorism is an approach to psychology emphasizing the overt, observable, measurable behavior of organisms.

1. John Watson (1878-1958) at Johns Hopkins University developed the approach to psychology known as behaviorism.
    a. He argued that psychology must concentrate on the observable and measurable.
    b. He felt that overt behavior was the appropriate study of psychology.
2. B. F. Skinner (1904-1990) epitomizes the behavioristic approach.
    a. He attempted to demonstrate that behavior can be predicted by studying relationships between responses and their consequences.
    b. He avoided reference to internal states.
    c. He focused on observable events.
    d. He argued that psychology should be defined as the science of behavior.

F. Humanistic psychology is an approach emphasizing the person or self as a central matter of concern.
1. Humanism arose as a reaction against behaviorism and psychoanalysis.
    a. The leaders were Carl Rogers (1902-1987) and Abraham Maslow (1908-1970).
    b. Humanists argue that the individual or the self should be the central issue in psychology.

G. Gestalt psychology was begun in the first quarter of this century by a group of German scientists.
1. Gestalt means whole or totality.
2. Gestalt psychology was established by Max Wertheimer (1880-1943).
3. Gestaltists argued against studying perception in terms of separate units.
4. They argued that the whole is greater than the sum of its parts.
5. They believed some ways of perceiving the world are innate.

H. Modern approaches to psychology are divided into major areas.
1. Psychological/biological psychology is concerned with the interactions among bodily activity, behavior, and mental processes.
2. Developmental psychology is concerned with the physical and psychological development of the individual from conception through death.
3. Educational/instructional psychology is devoted to the processes of learning and memory and their application.
4. A clinical psychologist diagnoses and treats persons with psychological disorders.
    a. Clinical psychologists usually have Ph.D.s.
    b. This is the largest subfield in psychology.
    c. Sixty percent of all psychologists are in the clinical area.
5. Counseling psychology involves treating individuals with less severe and less chronic disorders than those clinicians treat.
6. Health psychologists study the relationship between psychological variables and physical health.
    a. This is a new subfield in psychology.
    b. Health psychologists are interested in prevention.
7. Cognitive psychology involves the investigation of the basic processes of the mind.
    a. Psycholinguists study language.
    b. Some study artificial intelligence with computers.
8. Psychometrics involves test development and statistical interpretation.
9. Social psychology reflects how the behavior of an individual affects others, and vice versa.
10. Industrial/organizational psychologists work in many areas related to business and industry.
11. One goal of psychology is to discover and understand the scientific laws of behavior and mental processes.
12. Another goal of psychologists is to apply what is learned about mental processes and behavior in real-world settings.

IV. Observational Methods in Psychology

A. Naturalistic observation involves watching behaviors as they occur naturally.
1. Observer bias may occur with this method.
2. Behaviors may not occur when the observer is watching.
3. The behaviors that the observer wants to watch may not occur when desired.

4. The method of naturalistic observation does not help explain behaviors, only describe them.

B. Surveys are a means of collecting observations from a large number of subjects by interview or questionnaire.
   1. Surveys ask a sample of respondents the same question or set of questions.
   2. Surveys can provide a general data base.
   3. The size and representativeness of the sample is critical.

C. A case history provides in-depth information on one or a few persons studied over a long period of time.
   1. It examines a wide range of variables.
   2. It is usually retrospective.
   3. Interviews and/or tests may be used to gather data.
   4. Its major advantage is that it provides much detail.
   5. Its chief disadvantage is that it may be difficult to generalize case study findings.

V. Correlational Methods in Psychology

A. Correlation is a statistical procedure that can be used to assess the nature and degree to which sets of observations are lawfully related.
   1. The difficult part of this study is devising acceptable operational definitions for the responses.
   2. Two sets of data must then be collected.
   3. A correlation coefficient may range from -1.00 to +1.00.
      a. A positive correlation means that high scores on one measure are related to high scores on the other or vice versa.
      b. A negative number means that high scores on one response are related to low scores on the other.
      c. Zero correlations indicate the two sets of observations are not related to each other.
      d. As correlations approach zero, predictability decreases.
      e. The closer to + 1.00 or - 1.00, the stronger the relationship.
      f. Cause-effect conclusions are inappropriate for correlational studies.
      g. Even when two responses are highly correlated with each other, predictions cannot be made for individual cases.

VI. Experimental Methods in Psychology

A. Experimental methods involve a set of operations that investigate relationships between controlled and manipulated events.
   1. Independent variables are the conditions the experimenter manipulates.
   2. Dependent variables are measured by the experimenter and depend on the manipulation of the independent variable.
   3. Extraneous variables are all other variables that might influence the dependent variables.

B. Exercising control is essential to have confidence in experimental results.
   1. The entire experimental group must receive the same treatment.
   2. The control group does not receive the experimental treatment.
   3. Random assignment means that each participant in the research has an equal chance of being assigned to any one of the groups in the experiment.
   4. In a baseline design, each subject receives both the experimental and control conditions.

VII. Ethical Considerations in Psychological Research

A. Ethical considerations are often central to the gathering of information.

B. Subject risk must be assessed in research.
   1. Subjects' confidentiality must be guaranteed.
   2. Participation must be entirely voluntary.
   3. Subjects must give their informed consent.
   4. Subjects should be debriefed after the research.

C. Animal guidelines are also stringent.
   1. They should have trained and experienced care.
   2. Discomfort, illness, and pain should be minimized.
   3. Subjecting animals to stress and pain is acceptable only if no other procedure is available.

VIII. Some Important Themes and Threads

A. An organism's nature and nurture interact.

1. Early in psychology's past it was realized that questions about one's nature and nurture were not either/or questions.
2. Behaviors and mental processes result from an interaction of inherited, genetic influences and environmental influences.

B. Things are not always as they seem.

1. Phenomenology is the study of events as they are experienced by the individual; that experience is reality.
2. Individuals select, attend to, interpret, remember, and hence, experience different aspects of the very same world.

C. For many questions in psychology there are no simple answers.

1. Complex phenomena often have complex explanations.
2. Behaviors and mental processes generally have multiple causes.

D. Psychology has practical application in the real world.

1. The subject matter of psychology is the behavior and mental processes of organisms.
2. Psychology is concerned with the study of health and environmental issues.

**Learning Chapter 1 Vocabulary**

Write the definition for each of the following terms on the lines provided at the right. Then fold the paper vertically so you can see only the term and try to say the definition. Practice like this until you can say them all correctly.

PSYCHOLOGY ________________

SCIENCE ________________

SCIENTIFIC METHODS ________________

HYPOTHESIS ________________

BEHAVIOR ________________

PUBLICLY VERIFIABLE ________________

MENTAL PROCESSES ________________

COGNITION ________________

AFFECT ________________

OPERATIONAL DEFINITION ________________

INTERACTIVE DUALISM ________________

BRITISH EMPIRICIST ________________

INTROSPECTION

STRUCTURALISM

FUNCTIONALISM

BEHAVIORISM

PSYCHOANALYSIS

HUMANISTIC PSYCHOLOGY

GESTALT

NATURALISTIC OBSERVATION

OBSERVER BIAS

SURVEY

SAMPLE

CASE HISTORY

CORRELATION

CORRELATION COEFFICIENT

EXPERIMENT

INDEPENDENT VARIABLES

DEPENDENT VARIABLES

EXTRANEOUS VARIABLES

EXPERIMENTAL GROUP

CONTROL GROUP ______________________

RANDOM ASSIGNMENT ______________________

BASELINE DESIGN ______________________

DEBRIEF ______________________

PHENOMENOLOGY ______________________

**IDIOMS AND DIFFICULT PHRASES**

**did not just spring forth, full blown, a few years ago** (p. 14) refers to the fact that psychology did not begin suddenly in its current, advanced form, instead, it developed slowly taking many years

**themes and threads** (p. 14) similar ideas

**taken as a matter of faith** (p. 14) accept without concrete proof, we just believe

**skimming through** (p. 15) turning the pages quickly and not reading every word

**on the other hand** (p. 16) another way to think about this subject
This phrase, "on the other hand," indicates that the writer may be presenting a different or contrasting idea. This can be a clue to a style of writing that is used often in psychology, comparing and contrasting. Comparing tells how two of more things are alike. Contrasting tells how two or more things are different.

**The ABCs** (p. 16) the basic ideas

**approach their subject matter** (p. 17) work on psychology

**traced to the beginnings of history** (p. 17) followed to the beginnings of history, the idea is that these questions have existed for a very long time

**formal roots of psychology** (p. 17) psychology was influenced by philosophy and science almost as if it grew or developed from a combination of these two

**HMS Beagle** (p. 18) the name of a ship. HMS is a British term and stands for Her Majesty's Service, to indicate that the ship belongs to England.

**physician by trade** (p. 19) his job was being a doctor. A person's job is also referred to as their trade.

**someone with a vision** (p. 19) someone good at planning for the future

**championed the cause of** (p. 20) believed in and publicly supported

**began to take issue with** (p. 20) disagreed with

**off base** (p. 20) working on the wrong idea

**Freud was struck** (p. 21) he noticed

**nearly single-handedly changed** (p. 22) did it alone

**behavior fits the bill** (p. 22) is appropriate

**big picture of perception** (p. 23) the entire idea

**from here on out** (p. 29) from this moment of time into the future

**as it happens** (p. 29) it is so

**more often than not** (p. 31) most of the time

**by and large** (p. 31) usually

**in the long run** (p. 31) generally

**that's quite a mouthful** (p. 31) that is a lot to say or communicate, a complex idea

**terribly simple** (p. 32) very simple

**she weaves the terms together** (p. 32) she relates the ideas to each other

**the short of it is** (p. 33) the main point is

**to keep an eye out for** (p. 37) pay attention

**the same size as a quarter** (p. 38) about the size of a U.S. 25 cent coin

**for the moment** (p. 39) now

**and so it goes** (p. 39) it is the same

**consumer** (p. 40) user

**Matching**

Match the following key terms from your text with the appropriate definition.

| | | | |
|---|---|---|---|
| ______ | 1. psychology | ______ | 2. baseline design |
| ______ | 3. extraneous variable | ______ | 4. case history |
| ______ | 5. scientific methods | ______ | 6. observer bias |
| ______ | 7. hypothesis | ______ | 8. affect |
| ______ | 9. random assignment | ______ | 10. operational definition |
| ______ | 11. interactive dualism | ______ | 12. psychoanalysis |
| ______ | 13. British Empiricists | ______ | 14. humanistic psychology |
| ______ | 15. introspection | ______ | 16. gestalt |
| ______ | 17. functionalism | ______ | 18. phenomenology |
| ______ | 19. behaviorism | ______ | 20. structuralism |
| ______ | 21. independent variables | ______ | 24. sample |
| ______ | 25. debrief | ______ | 26. naturalistic observation |

a. The method of observing and noting behaviors as they occur naturally.
b. When one's own motives, expectations, and past experiences interfere with the objectivity of one's observations.
c. The portion of a larger population systematically chosen for study.
d. An intensive, retrospective, and detailed study of some aspects of one (or a few) individual(s).
e. A number that indicates the nature (+ or -) and the strength (0.00 to +1.00 or -1.00) of the relationship between measured responses.
f. Those events in an experiment that are manipulated by the experimenter that are hypothesized to produce changes in responses.
g. Those factors in an experiment that need to be minimized or eliminated so as not to affect the dependent variable.
h. Those participants in an experiment who do not receive any experimental treatment or manipulation.
i. The selection of members of a population in such a way that each has an equal opportunity to be assigned to any one group.

j. A method in which subjects' performance with an experimental treatment is compared with performance without that treatment (the baseline).
k. To fully inform a subject about the intent and/or hypotheses of one's research once data have been collected.
l. Descartes' position that a separate body and mind influence each other and are thus knowable.
m. The scientific study of behavior and mental processes.
n. An approach to psychology emphasizing the person or self as a central matter of concern.
o. A technique in which one examines one's own mental experiences and reports them in the most fundamental, basic way.
p. The feelings of mood that accompany an emotional reaction.
q. A tentative proposition or explanation that can be tested and confirmed or rejected.
r. The study of events as they are experienced by the individual; that experience is reality.
s. Philosophers (including Locke) who claimed, among other things, that the contents of the mind come from experience.
t. Whole (gestalt) totality, configuration; where the whole is seen as more than the sum of its parts.
u. An approach to psychology emphasizing the study of the mind and consciousness as they help the organism adapt to the environment.
v. The form of psychotherapy associated with Freud, aimed at helping the patient gain insight into unconscious conflicts.
w. An approach to psychology emphasizing the overt, observable, measurable behavior of organisms.
x. A definition of a concept given in terms of the methods (or operations) used to measure that concept.
y. An approach to psychology (associated with Wundt and Titchener) that sought to discover the elemental structures of the mind, how they were formed, and how they were combined and organized.
z. Systematic procedures of discovery that include observation, description, control, and replication.

**True-False Practice Test 1**

____ 1. Psychology has its formal roots in the fields of philosophy and history.
____ 2. One might say that the followers of Locke and the followers of Descartes would differ significantly in the emphasis placed on the role that experience plays in our thinking.
____ 3. In the mid 1800s, both physicists and physiologists made significant contributions to the field of psychology.
____ 4. Child psychology, educational psychology, and industrial psychology all have a common origin in structuralism.
____ 5. Though popular in the early years of psychology, both structuralism and behaviorism are virtually nonexistent in the current study of psychology.
____ 6. A real strength of Sigmund Freud was his research ability as a laboratory scientist.
____ 7. Carl Rogers and Abraham Maslow founded the humanistic approach to psychology.
____ 8. Humanism focuses on the self, whereas behaviorism focuses on the unconscious.
____ 9. The gestalt psychologists focused their study on perception.
____ 10. An industrial psychologist is likely to be involved as a consultant to an advertising company.
____ 11. One advantage of the case history method is that it can provide a wealth of information about a few individual cases.
____ 12. A second advantage of the case history method is that the information learned can be easily generalized to other cases.
____ 13. The actual value of a correlation coefficient can never be zero.
____ 14. Correlation studies are widely used to demonstrate cause-effect relationships.
____ 15. Predictions cannot be made for individual cases even when two responses are highly correlated.
____ 16. One advantage of using laboratory animals such as rats is that control of extraneous variables is often easier.
____ 17. Most of what we know in psychology has been learned by conducting experiments.

____ 18. There is no problem with using animals in research either in terms of generalizing results or in terms of ethical considerations.
____ 19. Ethical considerations are so important in the field of psychology because the subjects for research are usually living organisms.
____ 20. In psychological research, safety is of great concern, but confidentiality does not really matter.

**Fill-in Practice Test 1**

1. The founder of British Empiricism was ____________ ________________.
2. Descartes suggested that the mind and the body influence each other. This position became known as ____________ ____________.
3. Psychology has its roots in two other disciplines, ______________ and ______________.
4. One's feelings, mood, or emotional state are referred to as ______________.
5. One's perceptions, thoughts, and memories are referred to as ________________.
6. Psychologists study mental processes and ________________.
7. ________________ definitions define concepts in terms of the procedures used to measure them.
8. The man we would most likely credit as being the first psychologist is ________ ______________.
9. ____________ ____________ was the psychologist who shifted the focus from the structure of the mind to the function of the mind.
10. The psychologist who was responsible for psychology shifting from the study of the mind to the study of behavior was ____________ ______________.
11. Freud founded an approach to psychology that became known as ______________.
12. The best meaning for the word "gestalt" is ______________.
13. ______________ is a statistical procedure that can be used to assess the nature and degree to which sets of measured responses are related.
14. In a ______________ correlation, high scores on one set of responses are associated with high scores on the other.
15. The research method intended to discover cause/effect relationships is ____________.
16. The variable that the researcher manipulates is called the ______________ variable.
17. Variables that should be eliminated from consideration are referred to as ____________ variables.
18. Subjects who receive some treatment or manipulation are said to be members of the ______________ group.
19. ____________ ________________ means that each research participant has an equal chance of being assigned to the control group or any of the experimental groups.
20. ____________ occurs when the participants in an experiment are told the true nature and intent of the research.

**Chapter 1 Multiple Choice Practice Test**

1. The beginning of psychology is generally linked to the work of
   a. Sigmund Freud
   b. John Locke
   c. William James
   d. Wilhelm Wundt
2. The study of animals was introduced to psychology by the
   a. functionalists
   b. British Empiricists
   c. structuralists
   d. followers of Charles Darwin

3. The psychologist who was responsible for psychology shifting from the study of the mind to the study of behavior was
   a. William James
   b. John Watson
   c. Wilhelm Wundt
   d. Edward Titchener

4. The psychological approach that focuses on the individual and suggests that the self should be the central concern of psychology is
   a. functionalism
   b. behaviorism
   c. humanism
   d. psychoanalysis

5. Which of the following approaches in psychology would most likely be associated with this statement, "the whole is more than the sum of its parts?"
   a. humanism
   b. psychoanalysis
   c. gestalt
   d. structuralism

6. The telephone company has decided to make its offices "smoke-free" environments and wants a psychologist to teach smoking cessation classes for its employees. The type of psychologist most likely to do this job is a/an
   a. developmental psychologist
   b. educational psychologist
   c. clinical psychologist
   d. counseling psychologist

7. Jose and Maria are having marital difficulties. They are most likely to seek help from a/an
   a. health psychologist
   b. clinical psychologist
   c. counseling psychologist
   d. social psychologist

8. Which of the following best describes the subject matter of psychology?
   a. perceptions, behavior, mental health
   b. affect, behavior, cognition
   c. thoughts, feelings, sensations
   d. behavior, cognition, perception

9. Trang's son is almost two years old and is not yet talking. Which of the following psychology specialists would she most likely consult about this problem?
   a. physiological psychologist
   b. clinical psychologist
   c. health psychologist
   d. developmental psychologist

10. The difference between clinical psychologists and counseling psychologists is primarily in
   a. the severity of the problems they encounter
   b. the different methods that each employs
   c. their graduate training
   d. the work settings where they are employed

11. The psychological approach that emphasizes the role of the unconscious and instincts is
   a. humanism
   b. interactive dualism
   c. phenomenology
   d. psychoanalysis

12. A significant contribution of the behaviorist approach was the emphasis placed on
   a. measurable observations
   b. unconscious motives
   c. interpreting experience
   d. sensations and perceptions

13. The Gestalt approach to psychology was founded by
   a. Wundt
   b. Wertheimer
   c. Watson
   d. James

14. The work of Dianne Fossey, the researcher who studied gorillas in their own environment, is an example of
   a. experimentation
   b. correlation
   c. case history
   d. naturalistic observation

15. In which type of research is observer bias more likely to present a problem?
   a. naturalistic observation
   b. case history
   c. experimental design
   d. correlation

16. The best research method for gathering information about a large group of subjects is a/an
   a. experiment
   b. survey
   c. case history
   d. correlation

17. Correlation coefficients may range in value from _____ to ____
   a. 0 to 2
   b. -1 to + 1
   c. 0 to + 1
   d. -1 to 0

18. As a person's cholesterol level increases, the risk for heart disease also increases. This is an example of
   a. case study
   b. naturalistic observation
   c. negative correlation
   d. positive correlation

19. The research method responsible for most of our knowledge in the field of psychology is
   a. experiment
   b. case history
   c. correlation
   d. survey

20. A researcher conducts a study in which she exposes women to different fear conditions and then measures their desire to affiliate. In this experiment, the various fear conditions would be the
   a. dependent variables
   b. independent variables
   c. extraneous variables
   d. effect

21. You conduct a study in which you wish to determine the effects of blood-doping on athletes. You have the athletes run a five mile course without the blood-doping. The following week, they run the same course after blood-doping. The method you have used for controlling extraneous variables is
   a. random assignment
   b. matching
   c. correlation
   d. baseline design

22. Which of the following is/are ethical considerations for psychological research?
   a. The subjects' confidentiality must be guaranteed.
   b. Participation in research should be totally voluntary.
   c. Subjects must give advised consent.
   d. All of the above.

**Check Your Knowledge of the Learning Objectives**

The following questions are examples of what you should know when you have finished studying this chapter. Write the answers to these questions. Use your book to verify the answers. Page references are provided.

1. Which two points must be demonstrated in order to claim that psychology is a science? p. 14

2. What is the subject matter of psychology? p. 15

3. How are operational definitions used in psychology? p. 16

4. How did Descartes influence psychology? p. 17-18

5. How did Locke influence psychology? p. 18

6. How did Darwin influence psychology? p. 18-19

7 How did von Helmholtz influence psychology? p. 19

8 When and where did psychology begin and who should be credited with its origin? p. 19

9. List the main ideas of behaviorism. p. 22

10. List the main ideas of psychoanalysis. p. 21

11. List the main ideas of humanism. p. 23

12. List the main ideas of gestalt psychology. p. 23

13. Describe the different areas of psychology and what sort of work a psychologist in each area would do. p. 24-25

14. List psychology's two major goals. p. 25-26

15. Define naturalistic observation and discuss the potential problems with its use. p. 26-27

16. Explain how surveys and case history studies are used in Psychology. p. 27

17. Explain why correlation is used, what data are needed to calculate a correlation coefficient, and the meaning of positive, negative, and zero correlation coefficients. p. 28-29

18. Explain how random assignment and baseline design contribute to control in experiments. p. 35

19. List four ethical concerns for humans in psychological research. p. 36

20. List the ethical concerns for animals in psychological research. p. 36

21. Discuss the relationship between nature and nurture. p. 37

# Dr. G's Best Study Tips #1

The following questions will help you determine if your study habits are similar to those of successful students. Answer as honestly as you can. Then check your answers to learn which of your habits could be improved.

A = always   U = usually   N = never

**Time Management**

| | | | | DO YOU . . .??? |
|---|---|---|---|---|
| A | U | N | 1. | Study every day including the weekends? |
| A | U | N | 2. | Study at regularly scheduled times? |
| A | U | N | 3. | Know how much time you spend studying? |
| A | U | N | 4. | Turn assignments in on time? |
| A | U | N | 5. | Only study when an exam is near? |
| A | U | N | 6. | Study after 10 o'clock at night? |
| A | U | N | 7. | Review frequently? |
| A | U | N | 8. | Procrastinate and try to get things done at the last minute? |
| A | U | N | 9. | Take short breaks every hour or so? |
| A | U | N | 10. | Find time for fun? |

**Answers**

1. Always or usually are the answers that successful students give. Establishing studying as a part of your regular routine is important for two reasons. First, it helps get you started. As with other positive habits such as exercise, routine creates the attitude of expectation that you will do what has to be done. Second, research tells us that we learn more efficiently if we study for shorter sessions spaced over several days rather than cramming at the last minute.
2. Always or usually are the answers that successful students give.
3. Always know how much time you spend. What other way is there to determine whether your study methods are effective and efficient? As a general rule of thumb, an average student should plan to spend two hours of study time for every hour of class. On a semester hour basis, most introductory psychology courses would consist of three hours of class per week. Therefore, MINIMUM study time should be at least six hours per week.
4. Always turn assignments in on time. It is senseless to turn an assignment in late and risk losing points when you are doing the work anyway. Do it on time.
5. Never. More successful students study well in advance of exams so that their study time can be distributed over many study sessions. Cramming may be reinforced because it works in some cases. However, you will find that as the amount of material increases and the complexity increases, cramming is a less and less effective learning strategy. I believe this is a crucial adjustment that students must make in the transition from high school study skills to college study skills.
6. Either seldom or never unless you have no other choice. For most people, general alertness and mental efficiency decline late at night. Studies have shown that some students can accomplish in one hour earlier in the day what will take them an hour and a half to do later at night.
7. Always. Frequent reviewing is one of the keys to learning large amounts of complex information.
8. Never or seldom. Successful students enjoy getting assignments and studying for exams done ahead of time and then relaxing when they know they are fully prepared.
9. Usually or always. Studies indicate that the most efficient timing is to study for about fifty minutes to an hour and then take a short break of five or ten minutes. There are two exceptions to this: either writing a paper, or solving a complex problem in math or logic will benefit more from periods of continuous work (say two to three hours) without the interruptions of a break.
10. Always. Successful students find time for fun because they use efficient strategies that leave them time to do so and because they know the wisdom of the old adage, "All work and no play makes Jack a dull boy."

# CHAPTER 2 —THE BIOLOGICAL BASES OF BEHAVIOR

**Learning Objectives**

1. Discuss the basic concepts involved in the genetic transmission of physical characteristics.
2. Describe the main structural features of the neuron, and the role of myelin.
3. Discuss the basic process involved when a neuron fires.
4. Explain how neural impulses are transmitted at the synapse.
5. Name four neurotransmitters and indicate some psychological reaction when each is involved.
6. Explain how the nervous systems are structured.
7. Describe the major features of a spinal reflex and explain why spinal cord injury sometimes causes paralysis.
8. Discuss the two brain stem structures, their location, and their functions.
9. Describe the cerebellum, its location, and its major function.
10. List the location and functions of the RAS, limbic system, hypothalamus, and thalamus.
11. Explain the location of the four lobes of the cerebral cortex and the primary sensory, motor, and association areas of the cerebrum.
12. Describe the split-brain procedure and differentiate the functions of the right and left hemispheres.

**Chapter 2 Outline**

I. Preview
  A. We must understand basic biological functions to understand people.
  B. We must understand the nervous system to understand behaviors and mental processes.

II. Genetics and Psychology
  A. The science of genetics studies how traits and characteristics are passed from one generation to the next.
  B. The formal discipline of genetics began about the time of the Civil War.
    1. Gregor Mendel discovered the gene to be the basic mechanism of hereditary transmission.
    2. The genes Mendel assumed to exist can be found on tiny, threadlike structures called chromosomes.
      a. Chromosome literally means "colored body."
      b. The nucleus of each human cell contains 23 pairs except sex cells, which contain only half of the 23 possible pairs.
    3. Genes can be dominant or recessive.
      a. The characteristics of the dominant gene will be expressed, or will show up, regardless of the gene paired with it.
      b. A recessive gene expresses its characteristics only when it is paired with another, similar recessive gene.
    4. Complications exist concerning genes and heredity.
      a. Many genes will express their characteristic, or show their presence, only if other genes are present also.
      b. Genes do not create any physical characteristics directly.
      c. Noticeable effects of some genes require time and development before they are expressed.
      d. Physical characteristics that are primarily determined by genetic transmission require at least some minimal environmental interaction for those traits to be evidenced.
  C. Considerable evidence shows that psychological traits are influenced greatly by genetic factors.

III. The Neuron
  A. Neurons are individual nerve cells.
    1. Neurons are the basic units of the nervous system.
    2. There are approximately 100 billion neurons in the human brain.
  B. The following is the neural structure.
    1. The cell body is the largest mass of the cell.
      a. It contains the nucleus.
      b. It contains genetic information.

2. Dendrites extend out from the cell body.
    a. There may be many dendrites per neuron.
    b. Dendrites receive messages from other neurons.
3. The axon is also a long structure extending away from the cell body.
    a. The axon may be as long as two or three feet.
    b. Neural messages travel down the axon toward other neurons.
4. Myelin is a white, fatty covering or sheath for axons.
    a. It is found on about half of the neurons in adults.
    b. It has not yet developed at birth.
    c. It protects axons by acting as an insulator.
    d. It speeds neural impulses.
    e. It is usually found on neurons that transmit messages over long distances.
5. Axon terminals are the branching end points of axons.
    a. They connect with dendrites, cell bodies, and axons of other nearby neurons.
    b. They make it possible for one neuron to interact with hundreds, even thousands, of other neurons.
6. We are born with more neurons than we will ever have again.
    a. No neurons are generated after birth.
    b. Neurons are not replaced.
    c. Functions of lost neurons may be taken over by surviving neurons.

C. The function of a neuron is to transmit neural impulses from one place in the nervous system to another.
1. Neurons are filled with and surrounded by fluids.
    a. These fluids contain chemical particles called ions.
    b. Ions have a positive or negative charge.
    c. Ions are heavily concentrated in and around the nervous system.
2. The resting potential is the electrical charge of a neuron at rest.
    a. The resting potential of a neuron is -70 mV.
    b. The outside of a resting neuron is positively charged.
    c. The inside of a resting neuron is negatively charged.
    d. The difference in charge creates tension, and the ions are drawn together like poles of a magnet.
3. The action potential is about +40 mV.
    a. The inside of the neuron is momentarily more positive than the outside.
    b. This change in polarity lasts for about 1/1000 of a second.
4. A neural impulse moves down the neuron as the change in polarity occurs along the neuron's membrane.

IV. From One Cell to Another: The Synapse

A. The synapse is the general location where an impulse is relayed from one neuron to another.

B. Axon terminals are at the end of each axon.
1. Axon terminals contain small pockets of chemicals called vesicles.
2. Vesicles contain complex chemicals called neurotransmitters.

C. Neurotransmitters are released into the synaptic cleft.
1. The synaptic cleft is a space between the axon terminals of one cell and the dendrites of the next cell.
2. Release of neurotransmitters by one cell usually stimulates the next cell to fire.
3. Some neurotransmitters inhibit cell firing.
4. There are more than 60 known neurotransmitters.
    a. Acetylcholine is associated with memory function and is being studied concerning memory problems such as those found in Alzheimer's disease.
    b. Norepinephrine and dopamine are related in the sense that both seem to be involved in mood regulation.
        i. Norepinephrine causes arousal and anxiety; the lack of it produces feelings of depression.
        ii. Too much dopamine results in involuntary tremors; too little creates difficulty in voluntary movement.
    c. Endorphins are natural pain suppressors.

V. Nervous Systems: An Overview
   A. The central nervous system (CNS) includes the neurons in the brain and spinal cord.
   B. The peripheral nervous system (PNS) is composed of all other neurons.
      1. The somatic nervous system is part of the PNS.
         a. The PNS serves the skeletal muscles.
         b. The PNS picks up impulses from the major sensory receptors.
      2. The autonomic nervous system (ANS) is largely independent of CNS control.
         a. The ANS activates the smooth muscles and glands.
         b. The ANS provides feedback to the CNS about internal processes.
         c. The ANS is divided into two parts, the sympathetic and parasympathetic divisions.
            i. The sympathetic division is activated during emotional excitement.
            ii. The parasympathetic division is active during relaxation.
   C. The endocrine system interacts with the nervous system to affect behavior.
      1. The endocrine system is a network of glands.
      2. It secretes hormones into the bloodstream.
   D. All of the nerve fibers in each of the different systems have profound influences on each other.

VI. The Spinal Cord
   A. The spinal cord is a massive collection of neurons within the spinal column.
      1. Nerve fibers enter the spinal cord toward the back (on dorsal roots).
      2. Nerve fibers leave toward the front (on ventral roots).
      3. The central portion of the spinal cord is filled with cell bodies and unmyelinated axons.
      4. The outer portion of the spinal cord contains myelinated axons.
   B. The spinal cord has two functions.
      1. The spinal cord rapidly transmits neural impulses to and from the brain.
         a. Impulses to and from different parts of the body leave and enter the spinal cord at different levels.
         b. The higher in the spinal cord that damage occurs, the greater will be the loss of function.
      2. The spinal cord plays an important role in spinal reflexes.
         a. A spinal reflex is an automatic, involuntary response to a stimulus.
         b. Spinal reflexes involve three types of neurons.
            i. Sensory neurons carry impulses to the spinal cord.
            ii. Interneurons carry impulses within the spinal cord.
            iii. Motor neurons carry impulses from the spinal cord to muscles.

VII. "Lower" Brain Centers
   A. These are physically below the cerebral cortex.
   B. They were first to develop both in an evolutionary sense and in a developing brain.
   C. They are the brain structures that are most clearly shared with other animals.
   D. The brain stem is just above the spinal cord.
      1. The lowest part of the stem is the medulla.
         a. It is involved in involuntary reflexes.
         b. Nuclei in the medulla control reflexive eye and tongue movements.
         c. It controls breathing.
         d. It monitors heartbeat.
         e. It controls the level of respiration.
         f. Most brain fibers cross from left to right and vice versa at the medulla.
         g. The process of crossing fibers from one side of the body to the opposite side of the brain is called cross-laterality.
         h. Cross laterality takes place in the brain stem.
      2. The pons, just above the medulla, is a relay station.
   E. The cerebellum smoothes and coordinates body movements.
      1. Voluntary movement originates in higher brain centers.
      2. Some movements such as eye movements ,originate in the cerebellum.
      3. Cerebellum damage disrupts fine, coordinated movement.
         a. Damage to the outer region results in jerky tremors or involuntary trembling during movement.
         b. Damage to the interior results in tremors when the person tries to remain still.

F. The reticular activating system (RAS) is a network of nerve fibers that begins in the brain stem and goes to the top of the brain.
    1. It is involved in the level of activation or arousal.
    2. It acts as a valve for sensory messages from the lower to the higher brain centers.
G. The limbic system is a collection of small structures.
    1. It controls many instinctive, complex behaviors.
    2. It is involved in displays of emotion.
    3. The amygdala produces reactions of rage and aggression when stimulated.
    4. The septum reduces the intensity of emotional responses when stimulated.
    5. The hippocampus processes memories.
H. The hypothalamus is involved in motivational and emotional behaviors.
    1. It monitors critical internal body functions, such as feeding behavior and body fluid level.
    2. It is involved in aggressive and sexual responses.
    3. The hypothalamus has been implicated in the development of homosexual orientations.
I. The thalamus acts like a relay station between the cerebral cortex and lower brain structures.
    1. It integrates sensory messages and directs them to the cortex.
    2. Sensory messages from the lower body and all senses (except smell) pass through the thalamus.

VIII. The Cerebral Cortex
A. The cerebral cortex is the large, convoluted outer covering of the brain that is the seat of cognitive functioning and voluntary action.
B. The cortex is divided into the left and right cerebral hemispheres.
C. Each hemisphere is divided into four lobes.
    1. The frontal lobe is defined by two large crevices.
    2. The temporal lobe is located roughly at the temple.
    3. The occipital lobe is the area in the back of the brain.
    4. The parietal lobe is behind the frontal lobe and in front of the occipital lobe.
D. The cerebral cortex can be divided into three major areas, based on function.
    1. The sensory areas receive information from the sense receptors.
        a. The occipital lobes handle visual information.
        b. Auditory impulses terminate in the temporal lobes.
        c. Body senses send impulses to a strip at the front of the parietal lobes.
    2. Conscious, voluntary cerebral control of muscle activity originates in the motor areas.
        a. The motor areas are strips at the back of the frontal lobes.
        b. The left hemisphere's motor area controls the right side of the body. This is called cross-laterality.
    3. The three association areas are frontal, parietal, and temporal.
        a. The function of these areas is not well understood.
        b. It appears that higher-level mental activities are processed here.
E. The two cerebral hemispheres have different functions.
    1. The two hemispheres are richly interconnected by a network of nerve fibers called the corpus callosum.
    2. It is possible to study hemisphere function through a surgical technique called split-brain procedure.
        a. Information is passed from the right hemisphere to the left, where speech production apparatus is located.
        b. A major task of the left hemisphere is the production of speech and the use of language.
        c. Virtually no behavior or mental process is the simple, single product of just one hemisphere.
        d. The left hemisphere appears to dominate in the processing of analytical information and in calculation tasks.
        e. The right hemisphere is credited with expression and interpretation of emotions, along with the processing of visual information.

**Learning Chapter 2 Vocabulary**

Write the definition for each of the following key terms on the lines provided at the right. Then fold the paper vertically so you can see only the term and try to say the definition. Practice like this until you can say them all correctly.

GENETICS

GENE

CHROMOSOME

DOMINANT GENE

RECESSIVE GENE

NEURON

CELL BODY

DENDRITES

AXON

MYELIN

AXON TERMINALS

NEURAL IMPULSE

ION

RESTING POTENTIAL

ACTION POTENTIAL

SYNAPSE

VESICLES

NEUROTRANSMITTERS

SYNAPTIC CLEFT ______________________

CENTRAL NERVOUS SYSTEM (CNS) ______________________

PERIPHERAL NERVOUS SYSTEM (PNS) ______________________

SOMATIC NERVOUS SYSTEM ______________________

AUTONOMIC NERVOUS SYSTEM (ANS) ______________________

SYMPATHETIC DIVISION ______________________

PARASYMPATHETIC DIVISION ______________________

ENDOCRINE SYSTEM ______________________

HORMONES ______________________

SPINAL CORD ______________________

SPINAL REFLEX ______________________

BRAIN STEM ______________________

MEDULLA ______________________

NUCLEI ______________________

CROSS-LATERALITY ______________________

PONS ______________________

CEREBELLUM ______________________

TREMORS ______________________

RETICULAR ACTIVATING SYSTEM (RAS) ______________________

LIMBIC SYSTEM

HYPOTHALAMUS

THALAMUS

CEREBRAL CORTEX

CEREBRAL HEMISPHERES

FRONTAL LOBES

TEMPORAL LOBES

OCCIPITAL LOBES

PARIETAL LOBES

SENSORY AREAS

MOTOR AREAS

ASSOCIATION AREAS

CORPUS CALLOSUM

SPLIT-BRAIN PROCEDURE

**Idioms and Difficult Phrases**

**taking a building-block approach** (p. 48) presenting information that builds on itself just as bricks are stacked to make a building. In other words, the information is related. Understanding one concept is necessary to understand the next.

**Some dogs have been bred to be lap dogs** (p. 48) A lap dog is a very small dog that someone might hold in their lap. The expression *lap dog* is sometimes used in a mean way to describe a person who is very dependent or is treated without respect, like a pet.

**To some degree it has always been appreciated** (p. 48) To some degree means not totally. Some appreciation has been withheld.

**The science of genetics began at about the time of the U. S. Civil War** (p. 48) The U. S. Civil War was fought from 1861 to 1865.

**some strange mass of gooey tissue** (p. 48) Gooey is a slang word that refers to texture. Very moist bread dough could be described as gooey.

**Roughly, here's what happens.**(p. 46) the word roughly means the without much detail.

**of this gift of heredity** (p. 50) *Gift* is used in a sarcastic sense

**Aunt Tillie's mental illness** (p. 50) The name, Aunt Tillie, is used as an example. It does not refer to a specific person.

**We may not be sure about snowflakes, but it is a sure bet that no two neurons are identical.** (p. 51) Scientists have suggested that no two snowflakes have the same crystal structure. *It is a sure bet* means you can be certain.

**Here's a far-reaching observation** (p. 52) This is an important observation with many implications.

**Here's a related reality**.(p. 52) In this sentence, reality is the same as fact.

**And it's no great mystery where ions come from**.(p. 53) It is well known, or easy to discover.

**in the familiar knee jerk reflex** (p. 61) a reflex of the leg muscles. You can demonstrate this by crossing your legs while in a seated position and lightly hitting your top leg just below the knee (the term knee jerk reflex is sometimes used to describe other spontaneous actions).

**unable to move experiences** (p. 64) the author puts the word *move* in quotes here to remind the reader that these experiences are not being physically moved in the true sense of the word move (like moving your book from the desk to the floor). The way these experiences are moved (or transferred) from one area of the brain to another is not understood.

**we've still got a lot of cortex left over** (p. 68) *Left over* means remaining.

**Matching**

Match the following key terms from your text book with the appropriate definition.

| | | | |
|---|---|---|---|
| ______ | 1. myelin | ______ | 2. neurotransmitters |
| ______ | 3. thalamus | ______ | 4. axon terminals |
| ______ | 5. sympathetic division | ______ | 6. occipital lobes |
| ______ | 7. cross-laterality | ______ | 8. central nervous system |
| ______ | 9. somatic nervous system | ______ | 10. endocrine system |
| ______ | 11. resting potential | ______ | 12. synapse |
| ______ | 13. gene | ______ | 14. brain stem |
| ______ | 15. neuron | ______ | 16. cerebellum |
| ______ | 17. parasympathetic division | ______ | 18. split-brain procedure |
| ______ | 19. peripheral nervous system | ______ | 20. frontal lobes |
| ______ | 21. hormones | ______ | 22. dendrites |
| ______ | 23. neural impulse | ______ | 24. ion |
| ______ | 25. vesicles | ______ | 26. association areas |

a. A network of glands that secrete hormones directly into the bloodstream.
b. The basic mechanism of hereditary transmission; that which gets passed from one generation to the next.
c. The largest of the cerebral lobes, located in front of the central fissure and above the lateral fissure.
d. The cerebral lobes at the very back of the brain.
e. A variety of chemical compounds, secreted by the glands of the endocrine system, many of which have effects on behavior or mental states.
f. A nerve cell, the basic building block of the nervous system that transmits neural impulses.
g. The lowest part of the brain, just above the spinal cord, comprised of the medulla and the pons.
h. Branchlike extensions from a neuron's cell body where most neural impulses are received.
i. The process of nerve fibers crossing over the brain stem so that the left side of the body sends impulses to and receives impulses from the right side of the brain, and vice versa.
j. A white fatty covering found on some axons that serves to insulate and protect them, while increasing the speed of impulses.
k. The series of branching end points of an axon where one neuron communicates with the next in a series.
l. A sudden and reversible change in the electrical charges within and outside the membrane of a neuron, which travels from the dendrite to the axon end of a neuron.
m. An electrically charged (either + or -) chemical particle.
n. The difference in electrical charge between the inside of a neuron and the outside when it is at rest.
o. A spherical structure at the lower rear of the brain involved in the coordination of bodily movements.
p. The last sensory relay station; it sends impulses to the appropriate area of the cerebral cortex.
q. Those neurons involved in the maintenance of the states of calm and relaxation.
r. The general location where an impulse is relayed from one neuron to another by means of neurotransmitters.
s. The small containers concentrated in axon terminals that hold neurotransmitter molecules.
t. Chemical molecules released at the synapse that will, in general, either excite or inhibit neural impulse transmission.
u. Those areas of the frontal, parietal, and temporal lobes in which higher mental processing occurs.
v. Those neurons in the brain and spinal cord.
w. Those neurons not found in the brain or spinal cord, but in the periphery of the body.
x. Sensory and motor neurons outside the CNS serving sense receptors and skeletal muscles.
y. A surgical technique of severing the corpus callosum, allowing the two hemispheres to operate independently.
z. Those neurons involved in states of emotionality.

**True-False Practice Test**

___ 1. Chromosomes are found only in the reproductive cells of organisms.
___ 2. The nucleus of all human cells contains 23 pairs of chromosomes.
___ 3. Our self-image is at least partially determined by genetic factors.
___ 4. The neurons or nerve cells in the brain, although different from other cells in the nervous system, are essentially identical.
___ 5. In the brain, the white matter is composed of myelin, a substance that is not found in the gray matter.
___ 6. Myelinated fibers can carry neural impulses 100 times faster than unmyelinated ones.
___ 7. The longer the nerve fibers in the body, the more likely they are to be myelinated.
___ 8. The time in our lives when we possess the greatest number of neurons is at birth.
___ 9. Alcohol kills brain cells.
___ 10. One unique characteristic of neurons is that lost ones are not replaced.
___ 11. The sole function of neurotransmitters is to excite the transmission of neural impulses.
___ 12. Hórmones are secreted into the bloodstream by the endocrine system.
___ 13. Many hormones and neurotransmitters are similar and can have similar effects.
___ 14. Unlike the nervous system, the endocrine system has no effect on behavior.
___ 15. Sensory impulses that originate below the neck enter the brain through the spinal cord.
___ 16. The higher on the spinal cord that injury takes place, the greater the portion of the body that will lose function.
___ 17. We have no voluntary control over the nuclei in the medulla.
___ 18. Due to cross-laterality, a stroke victim who has suffered damage to the left side of the brain is likely to suffer the results in terms of damage to the right side of the body.
___ 19. The influence of the limbic system on emotional responses is the same for both humans and animals.
___ 20. Patients who have undergone split-brain surgery appear quite normal unless they are engaged in laboratory tests.
___ 21. It is safe to say that in general, language and speech are processed in the left hemisphere.

**Fill-in Practice Test**

1. The ________ is the basic mechanism of hereditary transmission.
2. A ____________ ______ is one whose characteristics will be expressed in the organism.
3. A single nerve cell is called a ________.
4. The cell body contains the __________ of the cell.
5. The ______ is the long thin fiber in the neuron that sends neural impulses to other neurons.
6. _________ is a white, fatty substance found on about half of the neurons.
7. _________ is the feature of neurons that is undeveloped at birth.
8. Axons end in a branching series of points called ______ ___________ that communicate with other neurons.
9. A ________ _________ is a sudden and irreversible change in the electrical charges within and outside a neuron.
10. The tiny chemical particles that carry the electrical charge in the brain are called _____.
11. The small electrical charge present when a neuron is at rest is called _________ ___________.
12. A neural impulse is relayed from one neuron to another at a location called the _________.
13. The complex chemicals in the brain are referred to as ____________________.
14. The natural pain suppressors in the brain are called ____________.
15. Acetylcholine is a neurotransmitter that affects ________.
16. The _________ _________ ________ is made up of all the nerves and nerve fibers in the brain and spinal cord.
17. The endocrine system secretes __________ into the bloodstream.
18. The ________ ______ is a massive collection of neurons within the spinal column that resembles a rope.
19. ________ ___________ are simple automatic behaviors that occur without conscious, voluntary action of the brain.
20. The fact that the left side of the body sends impulses to and receives messages from the right side of the brain is a function of _______ ___________.
21. The ________ ________ controls the instinctive behavioral patterns of animals.
22. The _____________ is the part of the limbic system involved in forming memories.

23. The largest structure in the human brain is the __________.
24. The series of fibers connecting the two hemispheres of the cerebral cortex is called the _______ _________.
25. The surgical technique that separates the two hemispheres in the cerebral cortex is known as _________ __________.

**Chapter 2 Multiple Choice Practice Test**

1. The first person to study genes was
   a. Gregor Mendel
   b. Charles Darwin
   c. René Descartes
   d. Sir Francis Galton
2. A gene whose characteristic is transmitted to the individual regardless of the gene with which it is paired is referred to as a
   a. recessive gene
   b. master gene
   c. dominant gene
   d. trait-bearing gene
3. The function of the dendrites is
   a. receiving neural impulses
   b. sending neural impulses
   c. storing neural impulses
   d. unknown
4. Which of the following is NOT a function of myelin?
   a. speeding the transmission of neural impulses
   b. aiding the production of neurotransmitters
   c. insulating the nerve cell
   d. acting as a protective covering for the axon
5. The time in our lives when we will possess the greatest number of neurons is
   a. at birth
   b. during childhood
   c. in adolescence
   d. in early adulthood
6. Neurotransmitters are contained in the
   a. vesicles
   b. cell body
   c. nucleus
   d. axon terminals
7. Which of the following is the best description of the role of neurotransmitters?
   a. they inhibit the firing of neurons
   b. they enhance the firing of neurons
   c. they have no effect on the firing of neurons
   d. they either enhance or inhibit the firing of neurons
8. The neurotransmitter(s) that influence normal memory function is/are
   a. dopamine
   b. acetylcholine
   c. norepinephrine
   d. endorphins
9. Endorphins are neurotransmitters that affect
   a. motor skills
   b. level of pain
   c. memory function
   d. anxiety and arousal

10. The skeletal muscles and sense organs are served primarily by the
    a. autonomic nervous system
    b. somatic nervous system
    c. central nervous system
    d. peripheral nervous system

11. The endocrine system is primarily related to behavior in the areas of
    a. motivation and emotion
    b. deviance and disorder
    c. violence and depression
    d. memory and mood

12. Kutina has been frightened by a strange noise outside her apartment. Her heart is pounding and her breathing is rapid. Although she may not be aware of it, her body is also producing extra adrenalin. All these changes are in response to the
    a. central nervous system
    b. sympathetic nervous system
    c. parasympathetic nervous system
    d. endocrine system

13. Smooth muscle movements such as a golf swing are controlled by the
    a. cerebellum
    b. pons
    c. medulla
    d. cerebrum

14. Which of the following is NOT monitored by the hypothalamus?
    a. eating
    b. sleeping
    c. shivering
    d. feeling thirsty

15. Knowledge of the two hemispheres of the cerebral cortex has increased tremendously because of
    a. split-brain surgery
    b. animal research using CAT scans
    c. case studies like that of Phineas Gage
    d. the work of researchers like Broca

16. For most right-handed individuals, speech is controlled in the
    a. right hemisphere
    b. left hemisphere
    c. cerebellum
    d. temporal lobes

17. The first split-brain surgical procedures were done to help with the disease of ________.
    a. schizophrenia
    b. Parkinson's disease
    c. autism
    d. epilepsy

18. Reflexes like eye blinks are controlled by the
    a. spinal cord
    b. medulla
    c. pons
    d. cerebrum

19. The staggering walk of a drunk is likely produced by the effects of alcohol on the
    a. cerebrum
    b. pons
    c. medulla
    d. cerebellum

20. Level of arousal and activity is controlled by the
    a. cerebellum
    b. brain stem
    c. reticular activating system
    d. central nervous system

21. If someone tickles your right foot, that sensation would be processed in the
    a. left temporal lobe
    b. right parietal lobe
    c. right occipital lobe
    d. left parietal lobe

22. Which of the following is NOT a correct match in terms of hemispheric dominance?
    a. left hemisphere - speaking
    b. left hemisphere - arithmetic
    c. left hemisphere - drawing
    d. left hemisphere - writing

23. Catherine is outdoors playing and the weather begins to turn cloudy and colder. Since Catherine is without her coat, she will have to rely on part of her brain to initiate some warming responses. The part of the brain that can do this job is the
    a. medulla
    b. hypothalamus
    c. hippocampus
    d. thalamus

**Check Your Knowledge of the Learning Objectives**

The following questions are examples of what you should know when you have finished studying this chapter. Write the answers to these questions. Use your book to verify the answers. Page references are provided.

1. What are the basic concepts involved in the genetic transmission of physical characteristics? p. 48-50

_______________________________________________
_______________________________________________
_______________________________________________
_______________________________________________

2. Describe the main structural features of the neuron. p. 51

_______________________________________________
_______________________________________________
_______________________________________________

3. Explain the role of myelin. p. 51

_______________________________________________
_______________________________________________

4. Discuss the basic process involved when a neuron fires. p. 53

_______________________________________________
_______________________________________________
_______________________________________________
_______________________________________________

5. Explain how neural impulses are transmitted at the synapse. p. 54

_______________________________________________
_______________________________________________
_______________________________________________
_______________________________________________

6. Name four neurotransmitters and indicate some psychological reaction when each is involved. p. 56

_______________________________________________
_______________________________________________
_______________________________________________
_______________________________________________

7. Explain the structure of the nervous system. p. 57-58

8. Describe the major features of a spinal reflex and explain why spinal cord injury sometimes causes paralysis. p. 60-61

9. Discuss the two brain stem structures, their location, and their functions. p. 61-62

10. Describe the cerebellum, its location, and its major function. p. 63

11. List the location and functions of the RAS. p. 63-64

12. List the location and functions of the limbic system. p. 64

13. List the location and functions of the hypothalamus. p. 65

14. List the location and functions of the thalamus. p. 65

15. Explain the location and function of the four lobes of the cerebral cortex. p. 66

16. Describe the functions of the motor, sensory, and association areas. p. 66-69

17. Describe the split-brain procedure. p. 70

18. Differentiate the functions of the right and left hemispheres. p. 70-72

## Dr. G's Best Study Tips #2

The following questions will help you determine if your study habits are similar to those of successful students. Answer as honestly as you can. Then check your answers to learn which of your habits could be improved.

A = always U = usually N = never

**Distractions**

| | | | **DO YOU . . .???** |
|---|---|---|---|
| A | U | N | 1. Eat or chew gum while you study? |
| A | U | N | 2. Watch TV or listen to the stereo while you study? |
| A | U | N | 3. Daydream or lose concentration? |
| A | U | N | 4. Study in the library or other quiet place? |
| A | U | N | 5. Think about other things you should be doing? |

**Answers**

1. Never is the answer that successful students give. Eating or chewing gum while studying is distracting for two reasons. First, the rhythmical chewing creates a physiological interference. You are likely to begin to read in rhythm with the chewing. This reading rate would be much slower than normal and would interfere with your reading comprehension. Remember the old childhood trick of rubbing your stomach and patting your head at the same time. Each activity interferes with the other. Reading and chewing are related in much the same fashion. The second reason for not eating is that the taste and smell of the food may serve as a reminder of a previous experience and thus send you off into a daydream. You will find it much more difficult to concentrate. If you are truly hungry, both the dining experience and your studying will benefit if you just take a break and eat.
2. Never is the best answer. Many research studies have shown that groups not listening to stereo or television perform better on memory and learning tasks than those groups who do listen. Regardless of how well you are now doing, you could improve by turning off these distractions.
3. Hopefully, you can answer never or seldom. Losing concentration causes aloss of study time. Refer to Dr. G's study tips on reading a textbook and the importance of generativity emphasized in study tip #1. In addition, you may want to try the pencil cure. Keep a pencil or pen in your hand as you read or study. After every page, attempt to write a brief summary of what you have read. You may list only key words or phrases. If you can do this, you know you have been concentrating. If not, you have caught yourself quickly and have only one page to reread.
4. Always is the answer that successful students give. The library not only has the advantage of being quiet, it keeps you away from numerous other distractions such as phone calls, roommates, even personal effects that may start you daydreaming or thinking of other things.
5. Successful students would answer never or seldom. If interfering thoughts about realistic concerns do distract you while studying, the best solution is to write them down. You will then have the problem preserved so that you can take care of it at a later time. This way, you have no need to keep mulling the problem over while you try to concentrate on studies.

# CHAPTER 3—HUMAN DEVELOPMENT

**Learning Objectives**

1. List the three stages of prenatal development.
2. Discuss the impact of diet, drugs, and stress on prenatal development.
3. List the reflexes that neonates possess and discuss their importance.
4. Describe the landmarks of early motor development.
5. Describe the basic sensory capacities of the neonate.
6. Describe the cognitive skills that develop during each of Piaget's cognitive stages.
7. Discuss the criticisms of Piaget's theory.
8. Describe Erikson's eight crisis stages of development.
9. Explain Kohlberg's theory of moral development.
10. Describe the physical changes that accompany adolescence.
11. Discuss drug use and abuse in adolescence.
12. Describe sexuality in adolescence and the associated problem of teenage pregnancy.
13. Describe the characteristic developments of early adulthood.
14. Discuss the issues that are typically faced during middle adulthood.
15. Describe the elderly population in the United States and the problems associated with ageism.
16. Discuss Kübler-Ross's theory of death and dying.

**Chapter 3 Outline**

I. Preview
   A. Humans share certain developmental events that unite us as a species.
   B. Physically and psychologically, we experience spurts of growth, periods of leveling off, and times of decline.
   C. Many of the general traits, ideas, attitudes, and habits that are formed in childhood remain with us well into adulthood.
   D. Development actually begins at conception, not at birth.
   E. Development continues throughout adolescence and adulthood.

II. Prenatal Development: Influences before Birth
   A. Human development begins at conception, when the father's sperm cell unites with the mother's ovum.
      1. Twenty-three chromosomes from each parent pair off within a single cell, the zygote.
      2. The period from conception to birth is called the prenatal period of development.
   B. Prenatal development is divided into three stages.
      1. The stage of the zygote is the shortest, lasting from conception until approximately 2 weeks later.
         a. The ovum is generally fertilized in one of the fallopian tubes.
         b. The zygote takes 7 days to move down the fallopian tubes to the uterus.
         c. The zygote takes about another 7 days to become firmly implanted in the wall of the uterus.
      2. The stage of the embryo lasts 6 weeks.
         a. At the beginning of this stage, three types of cells can be differentiated:
            i. Cells that become the nervous system
            ii. Cells that become the internal organs
            iii. Cells that become the muscles, skeleton, and blood vessels
         b. It is during this time that the unborn organism is most sensitive to external or environmental influences.
      3. The stage of the fetus is the longest, lasting until birth.
         a. Organs grow and begin to function.
         b. Arms and legs move by the end of the third month.
         c. By around 7 months, the fetus reaches viability, which means it can survive if born prematurely.
         d. The fetus is ready to be born at about 270 days.
   C. Environmental influences on prenatal development can have serious and lasting consequences.
      1. Maternal malnutrition often leads to increases in miscarriages, stillbirths, and premature births.

a. Deficiencies in specific vitamins and minerals affect the prenatal organism.
b. Calcium deficiencies affect development of bones and teeth in the fetus.

2. Many drugs and chemicals affect the developing organism.
a. Mothers who smoke a pack of cigarettes or more a day double their chances of having a low-weight baby.
b. Mothers who smoke have more miscarriages, stillbirths, and babies who die soon after birth than do mothers who do not smoke.
c. Heavy drinking increases the probability of having smaller babies and babies with retarded physical growth, poor coordination, poor muscle tone, and intellectual retardation.
d. Collectively, these problems are called fetal alcohol syndrome.
e. Psychoactive drugs such as heroin and/or cocaine cause considerable complications for fetuses, who are born addicted to the drug, and who must suffer painful withdrawal.
f. Tetracycline taken during pregnancy colors fetal bones and teeth yellow.
g. Thalidomide cause shortened, malformed limbs and usually mental retardation.
h. DES (diethylstilbestrol), given to reduce miscarriages, is implicated in cervical cancer in daughters and infertility in sons.

3. Maternal stress causes hormone changes and reduces the amount of oxygen available to the fetus.

III. Physical and Motor Development in Childhood
A. Neonates are capable of a wide range of behaviors.
1. Almost all motor responses are reflexive.
2. These responses help the neonate respond to basic needs.
3. Neonates have more than a dozen reflexes that can be measured.
B. The motor development of children is very regular in sequence.
1. Regardless of the rate of one's motor development, there are regularities in the sequence of motor development.
2. Although there is wide variability in children's ages at the onset of each stage, this wide variability of ages is considered normal.
3. The regularity of physical growth and development seems to be guided by two different principles.
a. Cephalocaudal sequencing refers to the fact that a child's growth and bodily control proceed from head to upper torso to lower body.
b. Proximodistal sequencing refers to the observation that a child's growth and bodily control proceed from the internal organs to the arms and legs to the hands and feet to the fingers.

IV. Sensory and Perceptual Development in Childhood
A. All of a human's sensory modalities are functioning at birth.
B. Senses develop in the following order: touch, body position, balance, taste, smell, hearing, and vision.
C. The development of depth and distance perception is of interest to psychologists.
1. Eleanor Gibson and Richard Walk (1960) invented the visual cliff to test depth perception in young children.
2. Research findings indicate that by crawling age, the child seems to perceive depth and judge it to be dangerous.
3. Neonates placed on the Plexiglas over the deep side of the cliff show a decrease in heart rate.
4. Seven-month-old infants show an increase in heart rate, apparently demonstrating fear.
D. Newborns hear very well.
E. Newborns can also respond to differences in taste and smell.
1. They discriminate among the four basic taste qualities.
2. They show a preference for sweet-tasting liquids.
3. Right after birth, neonates respond predictably to a variety of strong odors.

V. Cognitive and Social Development in Childhood
A. The cognitive abilities of neonates have been experimentally demonstrated.
1. Friedman (1972) demonstrated what could be called memory in neonates 1 to 4 days old.

a. A baby was shown a checkerboard pattern repeatedly until he or she appeared bored.
b. When shown a new pattern, the baby stared at it for the full time it was shown.
c. The assumption is that for the baby to recognize the new stimulus as novel, he or she would have to have a memory of the old one.

2. Robert Fantz (1961, 1963) showed babies pairs of visual stimuli.
   a. In every case, the babies preferred to look at more complex stimulus patterns.
   b. Fantz also discovered that neonates show a distinct preference for drawings of the human face.

B. Piaget's theory of cognitive development amounts to acquiring schemas, or organized mental representations of the world.
   1. Organizing and forming mental representations involve two processes.
      a. Assimilation involves taking new information and fitting it into an existing schema.
      b. Accommodation involves changing and revising existing schemas in the face of new experiences or new information.
   2. Piaget proposed that children progress through four stages of development as they assimilate and accommodate.
      a. In the sensorimotor stage (0 to 24 months), children discover by sensing and by doing.
         i. Causality is an important schema learned at this stage.
         ii. Object permanence, whereby objects exist even when they are not in view, develops at this stage.
      b. In the preoperational stage (2 to 6 years), a child's thinking is self-centered or egocentric.
         i. Children begin to use symbols, usually words.
         ii. They do not understand how to manipulate these symbols.
      c. In the concrete operations stage (7 to 12 years), children begin to develop many concepts and show that they can manipulate those concepts.
         i. Conservation involves the cognitive awareness that changing the form or appearance of something does not necessarily change what it really is.
         ii. At this stage, children begin to operate on (use and manipulate) concepts and ideas.
      d. In the formal operations stage (over 12 years), abstract, symbolic reasoning and the ability to deal with hypothetical problems develop at this stage.

C. Some research has challenged Piaget's basic ideas.
   1. The borderlines between his proposed stages are much less clear-cut than his theory suggests.
   2. Piaget significantly underestimated the cognitive talents of preschoolers.
      a. Young children have some appreciation of other points of view.
      b. His theory gives little attention to the impact of language development.

D. Erik Erikson proposed a psychosocial, stage theory of development.
   1. Erikson lists 8 stages of development covering the entire life span.
   2. Each stage consists of a series of conflicts or crises that must be resolved.
   3. A major strength is that it covers the entire life span.
      a. In the stage of autonomy vs. shame and doubt, the sense of self-esteem emerges as the child strives for independence.
      b. In the period of initiative vs. guilt, the challenge for the child (age 3 to 6) is to develop as a functioning, contributing member of a social group.
      c. The period of industry vs. inferiority (age 6 to puberty) challenges the child to move beyond the safety and comfort of the immediate family unit and operate successfully in the neighborhood and school.

E. Lawrence Kohlberg developed a stage theory of moral development.
   1. His theory consists of 6 stages of development.
   2. Not all people develop the higher stages of moral reasoning.
   3. All of his original data, which came from the responses of young boys, has been challenged by Harvard psychologist, Carol Gilligan.
      a. Gilligan argues that the moral reasoning of females is different from that of males.
      b. Males are concerned with rules, justice, and individual rights.

c. Females are concerned with caring, personal responsibility, and interpersonal relationships.

VI. Adolescence
  A. Adolescence is a developmental period of transition.
    1. Biologically, adolescence begins with the onset of puberty and ends with the end of physical growth.
    2. Psychologically, adolescence is characterized by the development of problem-solving skills and an increased reliance on the use of symbols, logic, and abstract thinking.
    3. Socially, adolescence is between childhood and adulthood.
    4. There is debate over whether to characterize adolescence in a general sense as a time of turmoil, stress, and rebellion.
      a. This view was initiated by G. Stanley Hall.
      b. It was also supported by Anna Freud.
      c. Over the past 25 years, adolescence has been seen more as a time requiring changes and adjustments that are usually accomplished in psychologically healthy ways.
  B. The onset of adolescence is generally marked by two biological changes.
    1. There is a marked increase in height and weight, known as the growth spurt.
      a. The growth spurt occurs earlier in girls than in boys, usually beginning at age 9 or 10 and slowing down about age 15.
      b. Boys generally experience increased growth between ages 12 and 17.
    2. The second biological change is sexual maturation, accompanied by an increase in the production of sex hormones.
      a. Biologically, puberty is marked by the appearance of live sperm in the testes and ejaculate of males.
      b. In females, puberty is marked by the first menstrual period, called menarche.
    3. There are advantages and disadvantages to early maturation for girls.
      a. Early-maturing girls will be larger and more athletic.
      b. They will be asked for dates, have more early sexual encounters, and marry earlier than their peers.
      c. They may have problems with self-image.
    4. Early-maturing boys are at a greater advantage than early-maturing girls.
      a. They will have more dating and sexual experiences than their peers.
      b. They will have higher status among their peers and higher self-esteem.
    5. Late bloomers of both sexes are at more of a disadvantage at the time.
      a. Late-maturing boys carry a sense of inadequacy and poor self-esteem into adulthood.
      b. Late-maturing girls seem to have fewer long-term negative effects.
  C. Cognitive and social development in adolescence is often challenging.
    1. The identity crisis is the struggle to define and integrate the sense of who one is, what one is to do in life, and what one's attitudes, beliefs, and values should be.
      a. The concept of identity formation is associated with the personality theorist Erik Erikson.
      b. Role confusion may result from perceived societal pressures on adolescents to decide what they want to be when they grow up.
    2. In adolescent egocentrism, not only do individuals engage in self-centered thinking, but they also come to believe that virtually everyone else is thinking about them too.
      a. Adolescents believe they have an imaginary audience, that everyone is watching them.
      b. They tend to overemphasize their own importance.
      c. They develop unrealistic cognitions about themselves called personal fables.
    3. Many adolescents experiment with using drugs, many use drugs on a regular basis, and many abuse drugs.
      a. The use of illicit drugs is on the decline.
      b. Attitudes about the use of drugs are also becoming more negative among teenagers.
      c. Jonathan Shedler and Jack Block, researchers at the University of California, Berkeley, recently reported on a study of adolescent drug use.
        i. Based on reports of their drug use, subjects were divided into three groups.
        ii. The major findings of this study had to do with personality characteristics of the 18-year-olds in each group.

iii. Frequent users were found to be generally maladjusted, alienated, deficient in impulse control, and "manifestly" distressed.
iv. Abstainers were found to be overly anxious, "emotionally constricted," and lacking in social skills.
v. Experimenters were found to be better adjusted and psychologically "healthier" than either of the other two groups.
vi. These data should not be misinterpreted to indicate that drug use might somehow improve an adolescent's psychological health.

4. For the adolescent, puberty is an intensely personal, private, and potentially confusing process.
   a. Collecting quality data on the sexual behaviors of adolescents is not easy.
   b. Sorenson reported that by the age of 19, 57% of females and 72% of males reported having sexual intercourse.
      i. A report from the Center for Disease Control (CDC) shows premarital activity among adolescent females has almost doubled during the last two decades from 28.6% in 1970 to 51.5% in 1991.
      ii. The largest relative increase occurred among 15-year-old girls.
      iii. Sexual activity is also increasing slightly among boys.
      iv. Many teens are not happy about their first sexual experience and report that it was not planned; it "just happened."
   c. Teenage pregnancy has surfaced as a major social problem.
      i. The physical, psychological, and financial costs of teenage pregnancy are very high.
      ii. Most adolescents do not plan to become pregnant.
      iii. Teenage pregnancy may reflect a poor understanding of sexuality.

VII. Adulthood
   A. The beginning of adulthood has two psychological markers.
      1. One is independence, in the sense of taking responsibility for one's actions and no longer being dependent on one's parents.
      2. The second is interdependence, in the sense of building new commitments and intimacies in interpersonal relationships.
   B. Early adulthood marks the transition from adolescence to adulthood.
      1. The achievement of a strong sense of self is an important predictor of the success of intimate relationships later in adulthood.
      2. Levinson described early adulthood as the era of greatest energy and abundance and of greatest contradiction and stress.
      3. Erikson described the conflict of early adulthood as intimacy vs. isolation.
         a. Marriage is one way that the need for intimacy is met.
         b. Ninety-five percent of people marry at least once.
      4. Choosing to have children is another important decision of early adulthood.
         a. Having children is becoming less popular.
         b. There is little evidence that remaining childless leads to a decline in well-being or later life satisfaction.
      5. According to Turner and Helms, career choice (another important challenge of early adulthood) is driven by such factors as family influence and earning potential, and involves seven stages.
         a. Exploration
         b. Crystallization
         c. Choice
         d. Career clarification
         e. Induction
         f. Reformation
         g. Integrative
   C. In middle adulthood, many aspects of life become settled.
      1. Middle age is generally a time of great satisfaction and true opportunity.
      2. Middle adulthood is also a time of transition and reexamination.
         a. One is forced to contemplate one's own mortality.

b. Sensory capacities begin to diminish about age 40, and the signs of decline, such as gray hair and middle-age spread, are usually apparent.
c. For some people, the notion that time is running out produces a mid-life crisis, but this is mostly a myth.

3. Havighurst (1972) delineates seven major tasks of middle adulthood:
   a. Accepting and adjusting to the physiological changes of middle age.
   b. Reaching and maintaining satisfactory performance in one's occupation.
   c. Adjusting to aging parents.
   d. Assisting teenage children to become happy and responsible adults.
   e. Achieving adult social and civic responsibility.
   f. Relating to one's spouse as a person.
   g. Developing leisure-time activities.

D. Late adulthood occurs in the early to mid-60s.
   1. More than 30.4 million Americans were in this age bracket in 1988.
   2. Ageism refers to the discrimination or negative stereotypes that are formed on the basis of age.
      a. Sensory capacities and memory may have declined, but this decline can be compensated for by wisdom and experience.
      b. Only about 5 percent of Americans over the age of 65 live in nursing homes.
      c. Many people 65 and older are active and enjoying retirement.
      d. A 1981 Harris poll found that only 31 percent of respondents over 65 claimed poor health to be a serious problem.
      e. Poor health among the elderly is very much related to income and educational levels.
      f. Psychologists divide the elderly into groups of young-old and old-old on the basis of psychological, social, and health characteristics.
   3. Age-related declines can be explained in terms of life style, habits, diet, and an array of psychosocial factors extrinsic to the aging process.
   4. The major contributors to decline in old age are as follows:
      a. Improper nutrition
      b. Smoking
      c. Alcohol consumption
      d. Inadequate calcium intake
      e. Failure to maintain a sense of autonomy and control over one's life
      f. Lack of social support
   5. These factors all have in common the fact that they can be controlled.
   6. Kübler-Ross has described five stages in facing one's own death.
      a. Denial
      b. Anger
      c. Bargaining
      d. Depression
      e. Acceptance
   7. Many dying patients do not seem to fit this pattern at all.
   8. Elderly people express the least fear about death and are generally less morbid about dying than are adolescents.

**Learning Chapter 3 Vocabulary**

Write the definition for each of the following key terms on the lines provided at the right. Then fold the paper vertically so you can see only the term and try to say the definition. Practice like this until you can say them all correctly.

CONCEPTION

ZYGOTE

PRENATAL PERIOD

STAGE OF THE EMBRYO

STAGE OF THE FETUS

VIABILITY

FETAL ALCOHOL SYNDROME

NEONATE

CHILDHOOD

SCHEMA

ASSIMILATION

ACCOMMODATION

SENSORIMOTOR STAGE

OBJECT PERMANENCE

EGOCENTRIC

PREOPERATIONAL STAGE

CONCRETE OPERATIONS STAGE

CONSERVATION ______________________

FORMAL OPERATIONS STAGE ______________________

ADOLESCENCE ______________________

ADOLESCENT EGOCENTRISM ______________________

GROWTH SPURT ______________________

PUBERTY ______________________

MENARCHE ______________________

IDENTITY CRISIS ______________________

AGEISM ______________________

**Idioms and Difficult Phrases**

**willing to hazard a guess** (p. 81) willingto take a chance by guessing

**e.g., birth defects** (p. 82) Physical or mental defects present in a child when it is born. They are rarely a result of the birth process. Congenital (meaning at birth) defects is the term doctors use to describe birth defects.

**By the same token** (p. 83) for the same reason or as a result of the same cause

**Mothers who smoke a pack a day** *(p.* 83) In America, cigarettes are sold by the pack. There are usually 20 cigarettes in a pack. People who smoke often measure their habit by the number of packs they smoke in a day.

**including crack** (p. 84) the street name for a very concentrated form of the illegal stimulant drug cocaine (see page 185).

**Mothers using illegal drugs often fail to get adequate medical care out of fear of discovery.** (p. 84) out of fear of means because of their fear. These women are afraid that doctors will report their illegal drug use to authorities.

**I think I'll paint the sky a kinda purple** (p. 91) The words *kind of* often sound like *kinda* in informal speech. It means similar to or almost the same as. *Sort of* (or sorta) is another common phrase with the same meaning.

**like throwing a clock out of a window in order to see time fly**-. p. 92) Time seems to pass quickly when one is enjoying oneself.

**even if she throws in a side trip or two** (p. 92) Throws in means to add something. This phrase is very common in advertising. Buy shoes from us today and we'll throw in a pair of socks for free.

**Piagets observations and assumptions have come under attack** (p. 94) have been criticized.

**Many boys and girls are referred to as early or late bloomers**.-p. 100) a late bloomer is a person who matures later than normal.

**Not all drug use is bad and will fry one's brain (as the commercials imply)** (p. 103) A television commercial popular a few years ago warned against drug use by showing an egg (to represent a person's brain) being dropped into a hot frying pan (that represented drugs). Thus the idea that drugs will fry your brain. *His head is fried* is an expression sometimes used to describe a person who, is under the influence of drugs or who may have actually caused permanent brain damage by using drugs.

**more likely to drop out of school** (p. 106) Drop out means to quit or withdraw from. Someone who leaves school because of failing grades is said to have flunked out. (p. 167).

**Ones middle-age spread** (p. 110) As people grow older they often gain weight, especially around their waistline. This new weight is often jokingly referred to as middle-age spread (as if the person's body were spreading).

**the notion of a midlife crisis** (p 110) It was believed that many people especially men, often experienced a midlife crisis when they reached their forties. This crisis often led men to try to rediscover their youth by doing things like trying new sports, buying a sports car, or even having an extramarital affair.

**Because of the coming of age of the baby boom generation** (p .112) *Coming of age* simply means reaching a certain important age. The baby boom generation refers to people born during the period that proceeded World War II, from about 1945-1960. Periods of high birth rates such as this are sometimes referred to as population explosions. Thus the term *baby boom.* People born during this time are sometimes called boomers.

**Children have long since left the nest** (p. 112) The phrase *left the nest* means that these children have moved from their parents' home. *Empty nest syndrome* is a term that is often used to describe the feelings of sadness and loneliness parents sometimes experience when all of their children have left home.

**Matching**

Match the following key terms from your text with the appropriate definition.

| | | | |
|---|---|---|---|
| ______ | 1. zygote | ______ | 2. neonate |
| ______ | 3. conception | ______ | 4. viability |
| ______ | 5. fetal alcohol syndrome | ______ | 6. concrete operations stage |
| ______ | 7. assimilation | ______ | 8. accommodation |
| ______ | 9. schema | ______ | 10. prenatal period |
| ______ | 11. stage of the embryo | ______ | 12. stage of the fetus |
| ______ | 13. ageism | ______ | 14. growth spurt |
| ______ | 15. menarche | ______ | 16. formal operations stage |
| ______ | 17. adolescence | ______ | 18. identity status |
| ______ | 19. puberty | ______ | 20. conservation |
| ______ | 21. egocentric | ______ | 22. object permanence |
| ______ | 23. sensorimotor | ______ | 24. preoperational stage |

a. The moment when the father's sperm cell unites with the mother's ovum to produce the zygote.
b. That period of development from conception to birth.
c. The one-cell product of the union of sperm and ovum at conception.
d. A cluster of symptoms (e.g., low birth weight, poor muscle tone, intellectual retardation) associated with a child born to a mother who was a heavy drinker of alcohol during pregnancy.
e. The developmental period from 2 to 8 weeks.
f. The developmental period from week 8 until birth.
g. The ability to survive without interference or intervention.
h. The newborn, from birth to age 2 weeks.

i. A system of organized, general knowledge, stored in long-term memory that guides the encoding and retrieval of information.
j. The developmental period between childhood and adulthood, often begun at puberty and ending with full physical growth—generally between the ages of 12 and 20.
k. A marked increase in both height and weight that accompanies the onset of adolescence.
l. The stage of physical development at which one becomes capable of sexual reproduction.
m. A female's first menstrual period, often taken as a sure sign of the beginning of adolescence.
n. The struggle to define and integrate one's sense of self and what one's attitudes, beliefs, and values should be.
o. Discrimination or negative stereotypes about someone formed solely on the basis of age.
p. In Piaget's theory, from age 7 years to age 12 years, when concepts can be manipulated, but not in an abstract fashion.
q. In Piaget's theory, an appreciation that changing the physical properties of an object does not necessarily change its essence.
r. In Piaget's theory, ages older than 12 years, when one can generate and test abstract hypotheses, and think as an adult, where thinking follows rules.
s. The process of adding new material or information to an existing schema.
t The appreciation that an object no longer in view can still exist and reappear later.
u. In Piaget's theory, the process of altering or revising an existing schema in the light of new information.
v. In Piaget's theory, from birth to age 2 years , when a child learns by sensing and doing.
w. To be characterized by self; by "me" and "mine" and "my point of view."
x. In Piaget's theory, from age 2 years to age 6 years, when a child begins to develop symbolic representations, but cannot manipulate them; also characterized by egocentricity.

**True-False Practice Test**

___ 1. Growth and development mean essentially the same thing.
___ 2. The embryonic stage typically lasts from week 2 to week 8 of the prenatal period.
___ 3. During the embryonic stage, both the number and type of cells increases.
___ 4. The central nervous system is the one part of the body that is at risk during the entire period of prenatal development.
___ 5. The fetus is generally unaffected by the nutrition of the mother.
___ 6. When a nutritional deficiency exists in a pregnant woman, she may suffer because the available nutrients go first to the fetus.
___ 7. Although research clearly establishes the harmful effects of smoking on the smoker, there is no evidence that smoking affects a fetus.
___ 8. Babies born to mothers who abused psychoactive drugs during pregnancy are likely to experience withdrawal after birth.
___ 9. The best advice to pregnant women concerning the use of drugs is to consult a doctor and use extreme caution.
___ 10. Reflexive behaviors can often be used to diagnose the quality of a neonate's development.
___ 11. A pregnant woman under stress may be unknowingly depriving her baby of oxygen.
___ 12. Relatively little of a neonate's behavior is reflexive.
___ 13. In general, the rate of development of motor skills in infancy predicts adult characteristics, such as intelligence and coordination.
___ 14. Although the rate of development may vary, the sequence of motor development is usually the same.
___ 15. There is no significant sex difference with regard to motor development.
___ 16. The biological definition for adolescence suggests that it begins with the onset of puberty and ends with the end of physical growth.
___ 17. Over the past 25 years, the view of adolescence has changed from a picture of turmoil to a view of adjustments that are generally made in healthy ways.
___ 18. Boys usually begin the growth spurt earlier than girls and end it with greater strength and size.
___ 19. Some changes during adolescence, such as the change in voice pitch, are more noticeable in boys.
___ 20. Whereas girls are very much aware of the onset of puberty, boys may not know when it occurs.

___ 21. In general, late maturation is preferable to early maturation.
___ 22. In general, both drug use and positive attitudes about drugs are on the decline.
___ 23. Drug use among adolescents is greater than for any other segment of the population.
___ 24. In general, sexual activity is increasing among males but not among females.
___ 25. Teenage pregnancy is less of a problem in the United States than in other developed countries.
___ 26. Adult development may not follow orderly transitions and may be significantly different for men and women.
___ 27. The decision not to have children is being made more often even though it results in a decline in satisfaction later in life.
___ 28. The notion of a mid-life crisis is mostly myth.
___ 29. One misconception about the elderly is that they live in misery.
___ 30. The theory of Kübler-Ross that describes stages of grief in terminally ill patients is generally accepted without question or criticism.

**Fill-in Practice Test**

1. The union of the sperm and egg cell is referred to as ________________.
2. The single-cell organism created by the union of the sperm cell and the ovum is called a/an __________.
3. The time from conception to birth is called the ______________ period.
4. The stage of the zygote ends when ______________ occurs.
5. The developing organism is at greatest risk during the ___________ stage.
6. The bodily organs actually begin to function during the stage of the __________.
7. The time when the fetus is capable of sustaining life outside the uterus is referred to as the point of ____________.
8. Consuming 3 ounces or more of alcohol per day during pregnancy results in __________ __________ ____________.
9. During the first two weeks after birth, the infant is referred to as a ____________.
10. Although all senses are functioning to some degree at birth, the last sense to develop is ___________.
11. The apparatus used to test depth perception in children is called a _________ _________.
12. An organized mental representation of the world is called a/an ___________.
13. When children take new information and fit it into an existing schema, they are practicing _________________.
14. When children change or revise existing schema, they are practicing __________________.
15. When a child understands that changing the form or the appearance of something does not really change what the thing is, he/she has mastered ______________.
16. The two physical signs of adolescence are sexual maturation and the _________ _________.
17. The onset of _________ marks a significant increase in the production of sex hormones.
18. An adolescent is in Piaget's stage of ____________ ______________ in terms of cognitive development.
19. When one struggles to define and integrate the sense of who one is, what one is to do in life, and what one's attitudes, beliefs, and values should be, one is having a/an __________ ________.
20. A pattern of self-centered thinking in which the individual believes that everyone else is thinking about him/her too is _____________ ____________.
21. Stories that teenagers generate about themselves on the basis of irrational beliefs are called __________ ________.
22. According to Turner and Helms, one is in the __________________ stage of career development when one gives up part of the self to the job.
23. In the career stage of ____________, the career decision is actually implemented.
24. The period of ______________________ is marked by transition.
25. According to Erikson, one who does not experience generativity in middle adulthood will experience _____________.
26. The psychologist who described seven tasks that must be accomplished in middle adulthood was _______________.
27. Discrimination on the basis of age is referred to as ________.

28. The elderly are sometimes categorized according to health and social factors as young-old and ____________.
29. The first stage of grief according to Kübler-Ross's theory is ____________.
30. The final stage of grief according to Kübler-Ross's theory is ____________.

**Chapter 3 Multiple Choice Practice Test**

1. Birth defects are most likely to develop during the stage of the
   a. zygote
   b. embryo
   c. fetus
   d. birth process
2. Which of the following is NOT true of smoking mothers?
   a. They have more miscarriages than nonsmoking mothers.
   b. They experience more stillbirths than nonsmoking mothers.
   c. Their babies have increased risk of dying soon after birth.
   d. Their babies are only affected if they smoke two packs of cigarettes per day.
3. The fact that one of the first motor skills an infant masters is control over his head is evidence for
   a. the cephalocaudal sequence of motor development
   b. the proximodistal sequence of motor development
   c. the presence of reflexive responses
   d. a regular rate of development
4. During which of the Piagetian stages does object permanence develop?
   a. sensorimotor
   b. preoperational
   c. concrete operational
   d. formal operations
5. Your eight-year-old brother is upset because you have two pieces of gum and he has only one. You break his piece in half and say, "There, now you have as many as I do." Your brother would probably
   a. be satisfied that he too now has two pieces of gum
   b. still be upset because he knows that you still have more gum than he does
   c. forget about the whole incident and act as though it never happened
   d. not understand any of your efforts
6. A major strength of Erikson's theory is that it
   a. gives an opposing view of cognitive development
   b. offers a better explanation of childhood cognitive processes
   c. deals with social development instead of cognition
   d. covers the entire lifespan, dealing with issues of adult development
7. Which of the following statements about Kohlberg's theory of moral development is NOT true?
   a. Research supports the basic theory and suggests that it has crosscultural applications.
   b. There is little evidence that many people operate at the higher levels.
   c. Children may be capable of operating at much higher levels than Kohlberg suggested.
   d. A child's answers to the Kohlberg dilemmas can predict criminal behavior later in life.
8. Carol Gilligan (1982) has argued that the moral reasoning of females is ____________ when compared to that of males.
   a. slower to develop
   b. faster to develop
   c. less complex
   d. different in nature

9. Which of the following is NOT a characteristic of fetal alcohol syndrome?
   a. retarded physical growth
   b. poor coordination and muscle tone
   c. heart defects
   d. intellectual retardation

10. Which of the following statements most accurately describes the development of depth perception in children?
   a. Neonates appear to have no sense of depth perception.
   b. Depth perception develops as a product of increased visual acuity and experience.
   c. Depth perception develops after the fear of heights.
   d. Few children can make an appropriate response to depth perception before they can walk.

11. The abilities to manipulate concepts and to organize things into categories appear during the _____________ stage of cognitive development.
   a. sensorimotor
   b. preoperational
   c. concrete operational
   d. formal operational

12. The ability to reason about hypothetical situations appears during the __________ stage.
   a. sensorimotor
   b. preoperational
   c. concrete operational
   d. formal operational

13. Marco is considering taking a cookie even though his father has told him not to. He thinks to himself, "I better not, because if I do, I'll be punished." This child is showing thinking characteristic of _________________ morality.
   a. utilitarian
   b. preconventional
   c. conventional
   d. postconventional

14. Which of the following is NOT true of early-maturing girls?
   a. They are likely to approached more for dates and have more sexual encounters.
   b. They may have problems with self-image.
   c. They may fall behind in intellectual functioning.
   d. They are rated below average in leadership skills and popularity.

15. The concept of the identity crisis faced by adolescents is part of the social development theory of
   a. Anna Freud
   b. G. Stanley Hall
   c. Lawrence Kohlberg
   d. Erik Erikson

16. According to a major study of adolescent drug use, the group who were better adjusted and more psychologically healthy individuals were the
   a. abstainers
   b. experimenters
   c. frequent users
   d. ones who could not be categorized

17. The period of development in which individuals turn their attention to social concerns and civic responsibilities is
   a. adolescence
   b. early adulthood
   c. middle adulthood
   d. late adulthood

18. In the stages of death and dying, the final stage is marked by
    a. resentment and envy of others
    b. dealing with God
    c. a sense of hopelessness
    d. a rather quiet acceptance, facing the final reality of death

**Check Your Knowledge of the Learning Objectives**

The following questions are examples of what you should know when you have finished studying this chapter. Write the answers to these questions. Use your book to verify the answers. Page references are provided.

1. List the three stages of prenatal development. p. 81-82

2. Discuss the impact of diet, drugs, and stress on prenatal development. p .83-84

3. List the reflexes that neonates possess and discuss their importance. p. 85

4. Describe the landmarks of early motor development. p. 86, figure 3.3

5. Describe the basic sensory capacities of the neonate. p. 87-88

6. Describe the cognitive skills that develop during each of Piaget's cognitive stages. 89-93

7. Discuss the criticisms of Piaget's theory. p. 93-94

8. Describe Erikson's eight crisis stages of development. p. 95 figure 3.8

9. Explain Kohlberg's theory of moral development. p. 96 figure 3.9

10. Describe the physical changes that accompany adolescence. p. 99-100

11. Discuss drug use and abuse in adolescence. p. 102-103

12. Describe sexuality in adolescence and the associated problem of teenage pregnancy. p. 104-106

13. Describe the characteristic developments of early adulthood. p. 107-108

14. Discuss the issues that are typically faced during middle adulthood. p. 109-111

15. Describe the elderly population in the United States and the problems associated with ageism. p. 112-113

16. Discuss Kübler-Ross's theory of death and dying. p. 113-114

## Dr. G's Best Study Tips #3

**Be A Star in Class**

Prepare for class by reading assignments ahead of time. As you read, make notes about topics that are particularly interesting to you. Also note any material you do not understand. Becoming familiar with the text information will invariably help you in taking notes as you will more readily understand the lecture material. You will not be struggling for spelling of key terms.

Pose potential questions that you can ask in class. Write them down. If there is something you don't understand, you can be sure there are others who are also finding the information puzzling. Asking a question is a very good way to get involved and turn yourself on to a class that might otherwise be of less interest (although with the subject matter of psychology, I cannot imagine such a situation).

# CHAPTER 4—SENSORY PROCESSES

**Learning Objectives**

1. Define sensation, psychophysics, absolute threshold, difference threshold, and signal detection theory.
2. Discuss the affect of subliminal perception on behavior.
3. Understand how the amplitude, length, and purity of light waves affect psychological experience.
4. Discuss the major eye structures and their functions.
5. Discuss rods and cones and differentiate between the visual experiences attributed to each.
6. Compare and contrast the trichromatic and opponent-process theories.
7. Discuss the three major physical characteristics of sound and the psychological experiences they produce.
8. Explain how sound passes through the ear.
9. Describe the stimulus, receptor, and primary qualities of the chemical senses.
10. List the cutaneous senses and explain how sensory adaptation is demonstrated.
11. Explain the position senses and how they operate.
12. Explain how the sensation of pain is produced.
13. Discuss gate control theory.

**Chapter 4 Outline**

I. Preview
   - A. Sensation is the first stage in processing information about the world.
   - B. Sensation is defined as a process that converts physical energy into neural energy.

II. Some Basic Concepts About Information Processing
   - A. Sensory thresholds are measured by psychophysical methods.
     1. Psychophysics is the study of the relationship between the physical attributes of stimuli and the psychological experiences they produce.
     2. Absolute threshold is the physical intensity of a stimulus that a subject reports detecting 50 percent of the time.
        - a. Absolute thresholds can be used to discover if one's senses are operating properly.
        - b. Products can be developed that utilize absolute thresholds, such as speakers, warning lights, flavors in food, etc.
     3. Difference threshold is the minimal difference between stimulus attributes that can be detected.
        - a. The difference threshold may vary from moment to moment.
        - b. The difference threshold is the difference in some stimulus attribute that can be detected 50 percent of the time.
        - c. Just noticeable difference, or j.n.d., is the amount of change in a stimulus attribute that makes it just noticeably different from what it was.
        - d. The j.n.d. is essentially the same as a difference threshold.
     4. Signal detection theory proposes that stimulus detection involves a decision-making process of separating a signal from background noise.
   - B. Sensory adaptation is a condition in which sensory experience tends to decrease with the continued exposure to a stimulus.
     1. Sense receptors respond to changes in stimulation.
     2. Constant stimulation of a receptor leads to adaptation.
     3. Dark adaptation refers to the eye's ability to become more sensitive to light after a prolonged time in the dark.

III. The Stimulus for Vision: Light
   - A. Light is radiant energy that can be represented in wave forms called light waves.
   - B. Differences in light intensity correspond to differences in the wave amplitude of light.
     1. The amplitude of a wave is represented by its height.
     2. The amplitude is the representation of a light's physical intensity.
     3. Our psychological experience of intensity is what we call brightness.
   - C. Wavelength is the distance between any point in a wave and the corresponding point on the next cycle.

1. The nanometer (nm) is the unit of measurement that is one billionth of a meter or one millionth of a millimeter.
2. Wavelengths visible to the human eye are roughly between 380 and 760 nanometers.
    a. X-rays and ultraviolet rays are too short (less than 380 nm) to stimulate eye receptors.
    b. Other forms of energy with wavelengths longer than 760 nm (i.e., microwaves and radar) do not stimulate eye receptors.
3. Hue is determined by wavelength. As wavelengths shorten or lengthen, we perceive different colors.
4. Brightness is an interaction between wavelength and wave amplitude.

D. Wave purity occurs when many light waves are one length or hue.
1. Such light is called monochromatic.
2. Saturation is the psychological characteristic determined by the physical purity of light.
3. White light contains all wavelengths and is the most impure of lights.

IV. The Eye

A. Vision involves changing light-wave energy into neural energy.

B. Structures that focus visual images ensure that the light waves entering the eye are well focused.
1. The cornea is the transparent outer shell of the eye.
    a. The cornea protects the delicate structures behind it.
    b. It bends entering light waves to focus an image in the back of the eye.
2. The pupil is the opening in the iris.
3. The iris is the pigmented portion of the eye.
    a. The iris contracts or expands in response to light and emotion.
    b. It is largely a reflexive action.
4. The function of the lens is to focus a visual image.
    a. The lens becomes flatter for far distance.
    b. It becomes rounder when objects are closer.
5. Ciliary muscles change the shape of the lens by a process called accommodation.
6. The aqueous humor is between the cornea and lens.
    a. It consists of fluid that nourishes the cornea and the structures at the front of the eye.
    b. If this fluid cannot pass out of this space, pressure builds and glaucoma may result.
7. The vitreous humor keeps the eyeball rounded by filling the space behind the lens.

C. At the retina, light energy is changed to neural energy.
1. Photoreceptors at the very back of the retina called rods and cones are light-sensitive cells.
    a. Rods are most active in low levels of illumination and do not respond differentially to different wavelengths of light.
    b. Cones operate best at high levels of illumination and are responsible for color vision.
2. The optic nerve is a fiber composed of neurons that leave the eye and carry impulses to the occipital lobe.
3. The fovea, the region at the center of the retina, is filled with cones.
    a. There are no rods in the fovea.
    b. Visual acuity is best at the fovea.
4. At the blindspot there are no rods or cones, only the optic nerve.

V. Rods and Cones

A. The two types of photoreceptors differ in number and distribution.
1. There are 120 million rods and 6 million cones.
2. Cones tend to be concentrated at the fovea.
3. Rods are concentrated toward the periphery.

B. Rods and cones have different functions.
1. Cones function best with medium to high levels of illumination.
2. Cones are responsible for color vision.
3. Rods operate best with reduced illumination.
4. Rods are more sensitive to light.

C. Everyday experiences demonstrate the functions of rods and cones.

D. With dark adaptation, rod sensitivity to light increases for 20 to 30 minutes, but cone sensitivity plateaus after 6 or 7 minutes.

VI. Color Vision and Color Blindness
   A. Theories of color vision try to explain how the eye codes different wavelengths of light to produce different experiences of color.
   B. The trichromatic theory, devised by Thomas Young and revised by von Helmholtz, proposes that the eye contains three separate color receptors.
      1. Each type responds best to one of three primary colors of light: red, green, or blue.
      2. Such receptors (cones) do exist in the retina.
   C. The opponent-process theory, devised by Ewald Hering, proposes three pairs of visual receptors that respond to different light wave characteristics.
      1. The pairs are sensitive to blue-yellow, red-green, and black-white.
      2. Each mechanism is capable of responding to either characteristic but not to both at the same time.
      3. The pairs work to oppose or inhibit one another.
      4. There is also evidence to support this theory.
         a. Excitatory-inhibitory mechanisms have been found in the ganglion cells.
         b. Color blindness usually occurs in pairs of either red-green or yellow-blue.
         c. Negative afterimages can be explained by fatigue of half of the opponent pair.
         d. Defective color vision occurs in 8 percent of males and .5 percent of females.
         e. Most color vision defects are caused by lack of a particular cone.

VII. Hearing
   A. The stimulus for hearing is sound
      1. Sound occurs when air pressure beats against our ears.
      2. Wave amplitude is the physical intensity with which the air strikes our ears.
         a. Wave amplitude is responsible for our psychological experience of loudness.
         b. The decibel scale of sound intensity reflects perceived loudness in humans.
      3. Wave frequency is a measure of the number of times a wave repeats itself within a given period of time.
         a. The unit of sound frequency is the Hertz (Hz).
         b. The psychological experience corresponding to sound wave frequency is pitch.
         c. The normal human ear responds to sound-wave frequencies between 20 and 20,000 Hz.
         d. Sound wave intensities and frequencies interact to produce our sensation of loudness.
      4. Wave purity is a pure sound in which all waves vibrate at exactly the same frequency.
         a. Timbre is the psychological quality of sound, reflecting its degree of purity.
         b. Different instruments have different timbre.
         c. The opposite of pure sound is white noise, a random mixture of sound frequencies.
   B. The ear is the organ in which sound waves are changed into neural impulses.
      1. The pinna is the outer ear, which collects and funnels sound waves.
      2. The eardrum vibrates at the rate of the sound source.
      3. The ossicles are composed of three bones called the malleus, incus, and stapes.
         a. The ossicles transmit vibrations to the oval window.
         b. The ossicles amplify sound vibrations.
      4. The oval window is a membrane similar to but smaller than the eardrum.
      5. The main organ of the inner ear, just beyond the oval window, is the cochlea.
         a. It contains the actual receptor cells for hearing.
         b. The basilar membrane runs the full length of the cochlea.
         c. Fluid in the cochlea is set in motion by the vibrations of the oval window.
         d. Hair cells within the cochlea are set in motion with the fluid.
         e. Movement of the hair cells stimulates a neural impulse that travels along the auditory nerve to the temporal lobe.
      6. The frequency theory of hearing suggests that the whole length of the basilar membrane vibrates so as to stimulate hair cells and send impulses to the brain that match the frequency of the sound entering the ear.
      7. The place theory argues that some places on the basilar membrane are more sensitive to particular frequencies of sound than are other places, and thus different hair cells are stimulated as different pitches reach our ears.

VIII. The Chemical Senses
  A. Taste and smell are stimulated by chemical molecules.
  B. Taste and smell are interrelated.
  C. Taste (gustation) seems to have four basic psychological qualities.
    1. The primary taste qualities are sweet, salty, sour, and bitter.
    2. Many foods derive their unique tastes from a combination of these four qualities.
    3. Taste receptors are located in the taste buds.
      a. Different taste buds respond primarily to chemicals that produce one of the basic taste qualities.
      b. Sweet taste receptors are at the tip of the tongue.
      c. Salty taste receptors are toward the front.
      d. Sour receptors are on the sides.
      e. Bitter receptors are at the back.
  D. Smell (olfaction) is poorly understood.
    1. Receptor cells are located high in the nasal cavity, close to the brain itself.
    2. How these receptors are stimulated by molecules suspended in air is not understood.
    3. Many lower animals have very well developed senses of smell.
    4. Many organisms emit pheromones or chemicals that produce an odor used as a method of communication between organisms.
      a. Pheromones are secreted by cells in the skin, in urine, or from special glands.
      b. The purpose of pheromones is to mark or delineate one's territory.
      c. Most common pheromones carry sexually related messages to the other sex of the same species.

IX. The Skin (Cutaneous) Senses
  A. The skin contains a large number of receptors.
    1. There are 20 million cells per square inch.
    2. Some receptors have free nerve endings.
    3. Others are encapsulated (covered) nerve endings.
  B. Cutaneous sensation is probably due to the unique combination of responses that receptor cells have to different types of stimulation.
  C. Warm and cold stimulate different locations on the skin.

X. The Position Senses
  A. These senses give us the capacity to know how and where our bodies are positioned in space.
    1. We are aware of the pull of gravity.
    2. We also get sensory information about where different parts of our bodies are in relation to each other.
    3. We can sense if we are moving or standing still.
  B. Position is sensed by the vestibular sense.
    1. It tells us about balance, gravity, acceleration, or deceleration.
    2. Receptors are located near the inner ears.
    3. There are five fluid-filled chambers in the inner ear.
      a. Changes in the fluid of the three semicircular canals are sensed as motion.
      b. The two vestibular sacs have small particles suspended in fluid that bump together when moved, stimulating neural firings.
  C. Position is also sensed by the kinesthetic sense.
    1. It tells us about the movement or position of our muscles and joints.
    2. Receptors are located primarily in our joints and, to a lesser extent, in muscles and tendons.
    3. These receptors act reflexively through the spinal cord.

XI. Pain: A Special Sense
  A. Pain, or the fear of it, is a very strong motivator.
  B. Feeling pain creates an awareness of problems occurring somewhere in our bodies.
  C. Very intense stimulation of virtually any sense receptor can produce pain.
  D. Pain receptors are found both on the skin and within the body.
  E. The gate-control theory suggests that pain happens not at the receptor site, but within the central nervous system.

1. The theory proposes that pain centers in the brain are responsive to particular nerve fiber stimulation.
2. It also proposes that other nerve fibers offset pain, or close the gate.
   a. Additional support for the theory comes from the study of endorphins, or natural painkillers.
   b. The belief that pain will go away can help to close the gate.
   c. Pain near the surface of the skin can be lessened by forceful stimulation.
3. There is also evidence that placebos (substances a person believes will be effective) can be effective in treating pain.

**Learning Chapter 4 Vocabulary**

Write the definition for each of the following key terms on the lines provided at the right. Then fold the paper vertically so you can see only the term and try to say the definition.

LOUDNESS ______________________________

DECIBEL SCALE ______________________________

HERTZ ______________________________

PITCH ______________________________

TIMBRE ______________________________

WHITE NOISE ______________________________

PINNA ______________________________

EARDRUM ______________________________

MALLEUS, INCUS, STAPES ______________________________

COCHLEA ______________________________

BASILAR MEMBRANE ______________________________

HAIR CELLS ______________________________

TASTE BUDS ______________________________

PHEROMONES ______________________________

VESTIBULAR SENSE ______________________________

KINESTHETIC SENSE

GATE-CONTROL THEORY

PLACEBO

SENSATION

PSYCHOPHYSICS

ABSOLUTE THRESHOLD

SUBLIMINAL PERCEPTION

DIFFERENCE THRESHOLD

JUST NOTICEABLE DIFFERENCE (J.N.D.)

SIGNAL DETECTION THEORY

SENSORY ADAPTATION

DARK ADAPTATION

LIGHT

WAVE AMPLITUDE

BRIGHTNESS

WAVELENGTH

NANOMETER (NM)

HUE

MONOCHROMATIC

SATURATION

WHITE LIGHT

CORNEA

PUPIL

IRIS

LENS

CILIARY MUSCLES

ACCOMMODATION

AQUEOUS HUMOR

VITREOUS HUMOR

RETINA

PHOTORECEPTORS

RODS

CONES

OPTIC NERVE

FOVEA

BLINDSPOT

OPTIC CHIASMA

PRIMARY HUES

**IDIOMS AND DIFFICULT PHRASES**

**Such as many varieties of owl** (p. 134) The large bird in the picture on the left side of page 134 is an owl. (In the United States owls are often associated with wisdom)

**this is my turf** (p. 144) The word *turf* actually means grass although in more informal language it is often used to mean territory or property. Street gangs often refer to their neighborhoods as their turf.

**as when our leg falls asleep** (p. 149) When you hold your leg in a cramped position for a long time without moving, the blood circulation is blocked. Then your leg feels numb and heavy and difficult to move. *Falling asleep* is an informal phrase that describes this. It can also happen to a hand, arm, or foot. When the blood flow begins again, you may feel a tingling sensation that is sometimes painful.

**Matching A**

Match the following key terms from your text with the appropriate definition.

| | |
|---|---|
| ______ 1. hertz | ______ 2. malleus, incus, and stapes |
| ______ 3. placebo | ______ 4. taste buds |
| ______ 5. loudness | ______ 6. white noise |
| ______ 7. basilar membrane | ______ 8. pitch |
| ______ 9. pheromones | ______ 10. gate-control theory |
| ______ 11. decibel scale | ______ 12. pinna |
| ______ 13. timbre | ______ 14. cochlea |
| ______ 15. eardrum | ______ 16. hair cells |
| ______ 17. kinesthetic sense | ______ 18. vestibular sense |

a. The psychological experience correlated with the intensity, or amplitude, of a sound wave.
b. A scale of our experience of loudness in which 0 represents the absolute threshold and 140 is sensed as pain.
c. The standard measure of sound wave frequency that is the number of wave cycles per second.
d. The psychological experience that corresponds to sound wave frequency and gives rise to high (treble) or low (bass) sounds.
e. The psychological experience related to wave purity by which we differentiate the sharpness, clearness, or quality of a tone.
f. A sound composed of a random assortment of all wave frequencies from the audible spectrum.
g. The outer ear that collects and funnels sound waves into the auditory canal toward the eardrum.
h. The outermost membrane of the ear that is set in motion by the vibrations of a sound; and transmits vibrations to the ossicles.
i. (Collectively known as ossicles) Three small bones that transmit and intensify sound vibrations from the eardrum to the oval window.
j. Part of the inner ear where sound waves become neural impulses.
k. A structure within the cochlea that vibrates and thus stimulates the hair cells of the inner ear.
l. The receptor cells for hearing, located in the cochlea, stimulated by the vibrating basilar membrane; and send neural impulses to the temporal lobe.
m. The receptors for taste located on the tongue.
n. Chemicals that produce an odor that is used as a method of communication between organisms.
o. The position sense that tells us about balance, where we are in relation to gravity, and acceleration, or deceleration.
p. The position sense that tells us the position of different parts of our bodies and what our muscles and joints are doing.
q. The theory of pain sensation that argues that there are brain centers that regulate the passage of pain messages from different parts of the body to the brain.
r. An inactive substance that has its effect because a person has come to believe that it will be effective.

**Matching B**

Match the following key terms from your text with the appropriate definition.

| | |
|---|---|
| ______ 1. wavelength | ______ 2. light |
| ______ 3. iris | ______ 4. saturation |
| ______ 5. rods | ______ 6. pupil |
| ______ 7. brightness | ______ 8. white light |
| ______ 9. subliminal perception | ______ 10. dark adaptation |
| ______ 11. J.N.D. | ______ 12. retina |
| ______ 13. ciliary muscles | ______ 14. lens |
| ______ 15. blind spot | ______ 16. nanometer |
| ______ 17. hue | ______ 18. cornea |
| ______ 19. sensation | ______ 20. signal detection theory |
| ______ 21. difference threshold | ______ 22. fovea |
| ______ 23. monochromatic | ______ 24. photoreceptors |
| ______ 25. cones | ______ 26. accommodation |
| ______ 27. aqueous humor | ______ 28. vitreous humor |
| ______ 29. optic nerve | ______ 30. psychophysics |
| ______ 31. sensory adaptation | ______ 32. absolute threshold |
| ______ 33. wave amplitude | |

a. The process of receiving information from the environment and changing that input into nervous system activity.
b. A mechanism that converts energy from one form to another..
c. The study of the relationship between physical attributes of stimuli and the psychological experiences they produce.
d. The physical intensity of a stimulus that one can detect 50 percent of the time.
e. The process of responding to, or perceiving, stimuli that are presented at levels below one's absolute threshold.
f. The minimal difference in some stimulus attribute, such as intensity that one can detect 50 percent of the time.
g. The minimal change in some stimulus attribute, such as intensity, that can be detected.
h. The view that stimulus detection is a matter of decision-making, of separating a signal from background noise.
i. (In most cases) the process in which our sensory experience tends to decrease or diminish with continued exposure to a stimulus.
j. The process by which our eyes become more sensitive to light as we spend time in the dark.
k. A radiant energy that can be represented in wave form with wave lengths between 380 and 760 nanometers.
l. A characteristic of waveforms (the height of the wave) that indicates intensity.
m. The psychological experience associated with a light's intensity or wave amplitude.
n. A characteristic of wave forms that indicates the distance between any point on a wave and the corresponding point on the next cycle of the wave.
o. One millionth of a millimeter—the unit of measurement for the wavelength of light.
p. The psychological experience associated with a light's wavelength.
q. Literally, one-colored; a pure light made up of light waves all of the same wavelength.
r. The psychological experience associated with the purity of a light wave, where the most saturated lights are monochromatic and the least saturated are white light.
s. A light of the lowest possible saturation, containing a mixture of all visible wavelengths.
t The outermost structure of the eye that protects the eye and begins to focus light waves.
u. The opening in the iris that changes size in relation to the amount of light available and emotional factors.
v. The colored structure of the eye that reflexively opens or constricts the pupils.
w. The structure behind the iris that changes shape to focus visual images in the eye.
x. Small muscles attached to the lens that control its shape and focusing capability.
y. The process in which the ciliary muscles change the shape of the lens in order to focus.
z. Watery fluid found in the space between the cornea and the lens that nourishes the front of the eye.
aa. The thick fluid behind the lens of the eye that helps keep the eyeball spherical.

bb. Layers of cells at the back of the eye that contain the photosensitive rod and cone cells.
cc. Light-sensitive cells of the retina that convert light energy into neural energy (cones and rods).
dd. Photosensitive cells of the retina that are most active in low levels of illumination and do not respond differentially to different wavelengths of light.
ee. Photosensitive cells of the retina that operate best at high levels of illumination and are responsible for color vision.
ff. The fiber composed of many neurons that leaves the eye and carries impulses to the occipital lobe of the brain.
gg. The region at the center of the retina, comprised solely of cones, where acuity is best in daylight.
hh. The small region of the retina, containing no photoreceptors, where the optic nerve leaves the eye.

**True-False Practice Test**

___ 1. Sensory adaptation is a process by which sensory experiences increase with continued exposure to a stimulus.
___ 2. Absolute threshold is absolute, and is not affected by such things as motivation or attention.
___ 3. Subliminal stimuli can produce dangerous and harmful behaviors after repeated exposures.
___ 4. To reach a threshold, stimuli must be detected at least fifty percent of the time.
___ 5. A just noticeable difference and a difference threshold are essentially the same.
___ 6. According to what we know about sensation of light, it would be better to paint firetrucks yellow-green instead of red.
___ 7. Vision actually takes place in the brain, not in the eyes.
___ 8. The blindspot and the fovea are the same.
___ 9. Glaucoma is a disorder of the eye related to problems with the vitreous humor.
___ 10. Nocturnal animals rely heavily on their cones for good night vision.
___ 11. The three primary colors of light are red, blue, and green.
___ 12. The trichromatic theory appears to be the most widely accepted theory of color vision.
___ 13. Rods and cones serve the same function in terms of vision.
___ 14. Damage to the rods will produce color blindness.
___ 15. The lowest possible saturation of light is white light.
___ 16. Vision is considered to be the dominant sense.
___ 17. The absolute threshold for sound is zero decibels.
___ 18. Sound that is of greater intensity than 100 decibels is experienced more as pain than as audition.
___ 19. One similarity between sight and hearing is that in both cases the stimulus energy is represented as waves.
___ 20. One unique thing about taste buds is that they reproduce or replace themselves when they die.
___ 21. Pheromones are chemicals that produce very distinctive tastes and warn us about potentially poisonous plants.
___ 22. In general, there is agreement on seven primary odors that can be detected by humans.
___ 23. In order to produce a sensation of pain, any kind of stimulus must be very intense.
___ 24. There is really no such thing as the placebo effect.
___ 25. The experience of pain is related to both psychological and physical factors.
___ 26. The gate-control theory suggests that the experience of pain happens not at the receptor sites, but in the nervous system.
___ 27. Pain is usually considered to be a vestibular sense.

**Fill-in Practice Test**

1. _______________ is the distance between any point in a wave and the corresponding point in the next cycle.
2. _______________ is the study of the relationships that exist between the physical attributes of stimuli and the psychological experiences that they produce.
3. When a stimulus registers at a level beyond our conscious awareness, this is known as ___________ ___________.
4. The smallest difference between stimulus attributes that can be detected is called ___________ ___________.

5. ________ __________ is a condition in which our sensory experience tends to decrease with the continued exposure to a stimulus.
6. The fact that our visual receptors become more sensitive to light if we spend time in the dark is referred to as __________ ______________.
7. When sensory sensitivity increases, threshold ____________.
8. The unit of measure for a wavelength of light is a __________.
9. The colored part of the eye is called the _________.
10. The part of the eye where vision actually begins to take place is the __________.
11. Color vision relies heavily on the __________.
12. Red, blue, and yellow are primary colors for pigment; but red, blue, and green are primary colors for __________.
13. According to the concept of negative afterimages, if you stare at a blue figure for a long time and then look away you will see a _________ colored figure.
14. The outermost structure of the eye that protects the eye is the __________.
15. A light made up of light waves that are all the same length is described as ____________.
16. The ___________ of a sound wave depicts its intensity or loudness.
17. Sound intensity is measured in units called _________.
18. The purity of sound is referred to as _______.
19. A random mixture of sound frequencies produces ______ ______.
20. The outer ear is called the ______.
21. The malleus, incus, and stapes are all _________.
22. Our senses of smell, texture, and temperature contribute heavily to our sense of ______.
23. The sense with the shortest, most direct pathway from the receptor site to the brain is the sense of _______.
24. Chemicals that produce distinctive odors are called ____________.
25. Another term for the senses of temperature and pressure is __________ senses.
26. The ___________ sense tells us about balance, where we are in relation to gravity.
27. The ____________ sense tells us about the movement or position of our joints and muscles.
28. A substance that a person believes will be effective in treating a symptom such as pain is called a/an ___________.
29. The neurotransmitters that help reduce pain are the ___________.
30. The sense that is partially explained by gate-control theory is our sense of ______.

**Chapter 4 Multiple Choice Practice Test**

1. Which of the following would a researcher in psychophysics be most likely to study?
   a. perceptual development in adolescents
   b. cognitive aspects of perceptions
   c. variables in artistic ability
   d. sensory thresholds in color-blind subjects
2. Ronda hears the so-called "silent" alarm that is present in many institutional buildings. Most people do not hear this high-frequency pitch. It would be most accurate to say that in regard to hearing, Ronda's absolute threshold is
   a. lower than that of most people
   b. higher than that of most people
   c. about the same as that of most people, except for certain frequencies
   d. not functioning appropriately
3. Charlie and Sharon live near an airport. However, they are no longer awakened by the sound of planes flying low overhead. The best explanation for this is
   a. subliminal perception
   b. signal detection theory
   c. sensory adaptation
   d. difference threshold
4. The characteristic of a stimulus that our sense receptors will most likely respond to is
   a. intensity
   b. quality
   c. change
   d. constancy

5. The theory of color vision based on the idea that we possess three distinct receptor areas for the three primary colors of light is the
   a. primary color theory
   b. signal detection theory
   c. opponent process theory
   d. trichromatic theory

6. The fovea and the blindspot are both features of the
   a. cornea
   b. lens
   c. retina
   d. pupil

7. Which of the following statements best describes the rods and cones?
   a. rods outnumber cones twenty to one
   b. they are represented in equal numbers in the eyes
   c. they function similarly
   d. they are found in different parts of the eye

8. Joe asks Tess if the tie he has selected matches the new suit he is buying. He is concerned with a/an
   a. absolute threshold
   b. just noticeable difference
   c. difference threshold
   d. detected signal

9. Applying the principles related to sensory adaptation, the best way to get attention from an audience to whom you are speaking is to
   a. speak louder
   b. whisper
   c. speak faster
   d. all of the above

10. Problems such as nearsightedness and farsightedness are the result of
   a. problems with the shape of the lens
   b. disease in the cornea
   c. glaucoma
   d. over-accommodation

11. The part of the eye where vision is most acute is the
   a. fovea
   b. iris
   c. cornea
   d. retina

12. Ramone dropped a quarter in the movie theater. Since it is quite dark in there, the part of his eye that will help him most in finding the lost coin is his
   a. cones
   b. rods
   c. lens
   d. cornea

13. The psychological experience associated with a light's wavelength is
   a. hue
   b. brightness
   c. amplitude
   d. intensity

14. The most accurate statement about vision is that it occurs in the
   a. cornea
   b. lens
   c. rods and cones
   d. brain

15. The amplitude of sound is measured in units called
    a. frequencies
    b. hertz
    c. wavelengths
    d. decibels

16. Pheromones carry messages that are related to
    a. sexual availability
    b. sexual preference
    c. repelling members of the opposite sex
    d. identifying women with PMS

17. Motion sickness is the result of a disturbance of the _________ sense.
    a. kinesthetic
    b. vestibular
    c. visual
    d. cutaneous

18. The gate-control theory of pain proposes that pain actually occurs
    a. at the receptor cite
    b. only in the external receptors
    c. in the central nervous system
    d. only under intense stimulus levels

19. Neurotransmitters that reduce the sense of pain are called
    a. enkaphalins
    b. endorphins
    c. pheromones
    d. hormones

20. The psychological experience of the purity of sound is referred to as
    a. frequency
    b. hertz
    c. timbre
    d. decibels

21. The part of the ear that marks the transition from the middle ear to the inner ear is the
    a. oval window
    b. incus
    c. cochlea
    d. eardrum

22. Which of the following taste-receptor site pairs is INCORRECT?
    a. sweet--tip of tongue
    b. salty--center of the tongue
    c. sour--sides of the tongue
    d. bitter--back of the tongue

23. The receptors for the kinesthetic sense are located primarily in the
    a. inner ear
    b. skin cells
    c. pheromones
    d. joints

24. Sharon's three-year-old son, Jess, is worried about going to the doctor to get a shot. To help him deal with the pain, Sharon should
    a. give him some apple juice and tell him it has magic power against pain
    b. rub his arm vigorously near the area where he will get the injection
    c. have him repeat the phrase "It really won't hurt very much."
    d. all of the above

**Check Your Knowledge of the Learning Objectives**

The following questions are examples of what you should know when you have finished studying this chapter. Write the answers to these questions. Use your book to verify the answers. Page references are provided.

1. Discuss theefect of subliminal perception on behavior. p. 146-147

2. Explain how the amplitude, length, and purity of light waves affect psychological experience. p. 127-129

3. List the major eye structures and their functions. p. 130-133

4. Discuss rods and cones and differentiate between the visual experiences attributed to each. p. 134-135

5. Compare and contrast the trichromatic and opponent-process theories. p. 136-137 (compare means tell how they are alike and contrast means tell how they are different)

6. List the three major physical characteristics of sound and the psychological experiences they produce. p. 139-141

7. Explain how sound passes through the ear. p. 142

8. Describe the stimulus, receptor, and primary qualities of the chemical senses. p. 143-144

9. List the cutaneous senses and explain how sensory adaptation is demonstrated. p. 145-148

10. Explain the position senses and how they operate. p. 148-149

11. Explain how the sensation of pain is produced. p. 149

12. Discuss gate control theory. p. 150

## Dr. G's Best Study Tips #4

**Get to know your textbook.**

1. **Learn about the author**. Do this by reading the preface in the text. Also, look for any information about the author. Does the author specialize in a specific area of psychology? Is the author a faculty member at a college or university? Where? Where was the author educated? Has the author published other texts or scholarly writing?
2. **Learn about the publisher.** What company published the text? Where is the company located? Have you used other texts by this publisher? What did you like or not like about them?
3. **Learn about the book itself.** Read the table of contents to get an overview as to how the book is organized. Find out from your professor if the course organization will follow the structure of the book. Determine from your course calendar about how much of the text you will need to read on a weekly basis. What edition is the text? What does this mean? Look for the date of publication. How current is the text? Scan a few chapters. Look at the figures, tables, charts, graphs, cartoons, and any other illustrations. Note special features such as the running glossary, appendices, and reference sections.
4. **See Dr. G's Best Study Tips** at the end of Chapter 5 for more information on reading your textbook.

# CHAPTER 5—PERCEPTION AND CONSCIOUSNESS

**Learning objectives**

1. Explain how and why stimulus factors determine our selection of perceptions.
2. Describe how personal factors are involved in perceptual activity.
3. Discuss how stimulus factors and personal factors determine how we organize stimuli in perception.
4. List the cues that provide us with information about depth and distance.
5. Describe how the two illusions of motion are produced.
6. Explain how the types of perceptual constancy operate.
7. Define an altered state of consciousness.
8. Distinguish between the EEG and EMG.
9. Describe the four stages of sleep.
10. Explain how REM sleep differs from NREM sleep.
11. Define hypnosis, and describe how it affects consciousness.
12. Define dependence, tolerance, withdrawal, drug abuse, and addiction.
13. Discuss the effects of stimulant drugs, depressant drugs, hallucinogenic drugs, and marijuana.

**Chapter 5 Outline**

I. Preview
  A. Perception is a process that involves the selection, organization, and interpretation of stimuli.
  B. Consciousness refers to our awareness of the environment and our own mental processes.

II. The Nature of Perception and Consciousness
  A. Consciousness is always changing.
  B. Consciousness is a personal experience.
  C. Consciousness is continuous.
  D. Consciousness is selective.

III. Perception
  A. Variables that influence our perceptual selectivity can be divided into two types.
    1. Perceptual selectivity, or attention, is the process of determining which stimuli attract and hold our attention.
      a. Stimulus factors are characteristics of stimuli that make them compelling or attention-grabbing.
      b. Personal factors are the characteristics of the perceiver that influence which stimuli attract attention.
    2. Stimulus factors in selectivity
      a. Contrast and repetition are stimulus factors that determine attention.
      b. Contrast is the extent to which a given stimulus differs from other stimuli around it in terms of:intensity, size, motion, novelty.
      c. With repetition, the more often a stimulus is presented, the more likely it will be attended to.
    3. Personal factors in selectivity
      a. Personal factors that may influence attention are motivation, expectation, and/or past experience.
      b. Motivation may lead to differing perceptions of the same stimuli by various individuals.
      c. Expectation is psychological readiness or preparedness to perceive something.
        i. Mental set is the development of an expectation about certain stimuli.
        ii. A mental set may interfere with finding solutions to problems.
      d. Past experience is an important personal factor in perceptual selectivity and includes both motivation and mental set.
  B. Perceptual Organization
    1. Perceptual organization involves organizing the bits and pieces of experience that are presented to our senses into meaningful, organized wholes.
      a. Gestalt is a German word roughly meaning whole, configuration, or totality.
      b. Gestalt psychologists studied ways that we group together and organize stimuli to form meaningful gestalts, or patterns.

2. Stimulus factors are characteristics of stimuli that promote their organization into meaningful units.
   a. Figure-ground relationship is the Gestalt principle that stimuli are selected and perceived as figures against a background.
   b. Proximity is the Gestalt principle of organization claiming that stimuli will be perceived as belonging together if they occur together in space or time.
      i. Another term for this is contiguity.
      ii. Proximity operates on more than just visual stimuli.
   c. Similarity is the Gestalt principle that states that stimulus events that are alike in some way tend to be grouped together perceptually.
   d. Continuity is the Gestalt principle of organization claiming that a stimulus or a movement will be perceived as continuing in the same direction as first established.
   e. Common fate is the Gestalt principle of organization claiming that we group together into the same figure elements of a scene that move together in the same direction at the same speed.
   f. Closure is the Gestalt principle of organization claiming that we tend to perceive incomplete figures as whole and complete.
3. Personal factors that influence perceptual organization are motivation, expectation, and past experiences.
   a. We perceive stimuli as going together, as part of the same gestalt or figure, because we want to, because we expect to, and/or because we have perceived them together in the past.
   b. How we perceive a stimulus is also influenced by the context, or the other stimuli presented at about the same time.

C. The Perception of Depth and Distance
1. Depth and distance in our environment are not sensed directly; they are perceived.
2. Ocular cues are feedback based on the ways the eyes work.
   a. Binocular cues involve both eyes.
      i. Retinal disparity provides cues based on the slightly different images provided by each eye.
      ii. Convergence is the action of the eyes turning inward as we focus on nearby objects.
   b. Monocular cues are those that only require one eye.
      i. Accommodation is the changing of the shape of the lens by ciliary muscles to focus images on the retina.
      ii. Accommodation probably only functions as an effective cue for distances of less than an arm's length.
3. Physical cues to depth and distance are those received from the structure of the environment.
   a. Linear perspective is the appearance of two parallel lines converging in the distance.
   b. Interposition reflects our knowledge that objects in the foreground tend to hide or overlap objects in the background.
   c. Relative size cues us that objects with larger retinal images tend to be closer to us.
   d. Texture gradient means that a gradual change in texture will be interpreted as a gradual change in distance.
   e. Patterns of shading tell us about shape and solidity based on patterns of light and shade created by objects.
   f. Motion parallax is the phenomenon in which, as we move, nearby objects appear to move quickly and faraway objects appear to move slowly.

D. Perceptual Constancies and Illusions
1. Perceptual constancies help us organize and interpret stimuli provided by our senses.
   a. Size constancy is our tendency to view objects as remaining the same size regardless of the size of the retinal image.
   b. Shape constancy refers to our perception of objects as maintaining their shapes even though their retinal images may change.
   c. Brightness constancy is the tendency to see objects as being the same brightness or color regardless of the actual intensity of light reflected from them.

2. Geometric illusions and impossible figures are experiences in which our perceptions are at odds with what we know as physical reality.
   a. Illusions do not depend on our ignorance of the situation.
   b. Illusions do not occur at the retina.
   c. The effects of illusions do not depend on eye movement.
   d. The phi phenomenon is the illusionary movement in a series of lights that flash sequentially.
   e. The autokinetic effect is the apparent movement of a pinpoint of light in an otherwise darkened environment.

IV. "Altered States" of Perceptions and Consciousness

A. Sleep and Dreams

1. Sleep is a normal process that alters consciousness by gradually reducing our alertness, awareness, and perception of events around us.
2. Stages of sleep can be measured by an electroencephalogram (EEG), which measures the brain's electrical activity, and by an electromyogram (EMG), which measures muscle activity, tone, or state of relaxation.
   a. In a relaxed, presleep stage, the brain produces alpha wave activity.
   b. Stage 1, which lasts about 10 minutes, is very light sleep characterized by theta waves.
   c. Stage 2 sleep is similar to stage 1, with the addition of sleep spindles in the EEG record.
   d. Stage 3 is deep sleep, with a reduction of general brain-wave activity, and consists of 20 to 50 percent delta waves.
   e. Stage 4 is dominated by delta waves.
3. Sleep is divided between REM and NREM stages.
   a. Dreams occur during REM (rapid eye movement) sleep.
   b. During NREM sleep (no rapid eye movement), dreams are greatly reduced and their content more fragmented.
   c. Eye movements are unrelated to dream content.
   d. REM sleep occurs throughout the night in segments lasting a few minutes to half an hour.
   e. Everyone dreams.
   f. Three hypotheses about the causes of dreams have been proposed.
      i. Sigmund Freud theorized that dreams provided an opportunity for fantasy and wish fulfillment.
      ii. Dreams may help the brain consolidate memories of the day's events.
      iii. Dreams may represent random firings of brain neurons.
   g. Internal changes during REM are paradoxical, or conflicting.
      i. Sleepers experience atonia, or total muscle relaxation.
      ii. Some people experience REM sleep disorder and thrash about wildly during REM sleep.
      iii. Excitement of the sex organs can also occur during REM sleep.
      iv. At the same time, breathing becomes more rapid, and blood pressure and heart rate increase.

B. Hypnosis

1. Hypnosis is a voluntary altered state of consciousness characterized by the following:
   a. A marked increase in suggestibility
   b. Focused attention
   c. Exaggerated use of imagination
   d. Inability/unwillingness to act independently
   e. Acceptance of reality distortion
2. Hypnosis and sleep have little in common.
3. Not everyone can be hypnotized.
4. The ability to fantasize and daydream is an important indicator of who can be hypnotized.
5. It is unlikely that hypnotized people can be made to do things they wouldn't do ordinarily.

6. Whether hypnosis is a special state of consciousness or just a state of heightened suggestibility is still debatable.
7. Perceived pain can be reduced via hypnosis.
8. Hypnotized subjects are aware of what is going on.
9. Memory (information retrieval) is probably not improved with hypnosis nor is one's ability to learn new material.

C. Altering Consciousness with Drugs
1. The following definitions are necessary to discuss psychoactive drugs.
    a. Dependence: use of the drug is required to maintain functions; may be either physical or psychological
    b. Tolerance: more and more of the drug is needed to produce the same effect
    c. Withdrawal: a negative reaction, physical or psychological, that occurs when one stops taking the drug
    d. Addiction: extreme physical or psychological dependency with tolerance and withdrawal usually present.
    e. Drug abuse: a lack of control, a disruption of interpersonal relationships and/or difficulties at work, and maladaptive use that lasts at least one month.
2. Stimulants activate the nervous system.
    a. Caffeine is the most widely used stimulant.
        i. It is found in many foods, drinks, and over-the-counter and prescription painkillers.
        ii. It does not appear to be dangerous.
        iii. It increases cellular metabolism.
        iv. It seems to block the effects of inhibitory neurotransmitters.
    b. Nicotine is also a popular stimulant.
        i. It activates excitatory synapses in both the central and peripheral nervous systems.
        ii. Users typically become dependent on and addicted to nicotine.
    c. Cocaine is a naturally occurring stimulant.
        i. It produces a rush of pleasure and energy when it enters the bloodstream.
        ii. It blocks the reuptake of norepinephrine and dopamine.
        iii. Users feel depressed after using cocaine, leading to more use.
    d. Amphetamines are synthetically manufactured chemical stimulants.
        i. They block the reuptake of and cause the release of dopamine and norepinephrine.
        ii. The drugs do not create alertness but, instead, mask fatigue.
        iii. The drugs cause irregular heartbeat and increase blood pressure.
        iv. Tolerance and dependency build quickly.
3. Depressants reduce one's awareness of external stimuli, slow normal body functions, and decrease overt behavior.
    a. Alcohol is the most commonly used depressant.
        i. Two-thirds of all Americans drink on a regular basis.
        ii. Alcohol increases urination, leading to a loss of fluids.
        iii. Alcohol raises visual thresholds, making it difficult to detect dim lights.
        iv. Alcohol alters mood.
        v. In most states, a person with one-tenth of 1 percent alcohol in the bloodstream is considered legally drunk.
    b. Opiates, such as morphine and codeine, are called analgesics because they can reduce or eliminate sensations of pain.
        i. In small doses, they create feelings of well-being, relaxation, and trancelike states.
        ii. Heroin is derived from morphine and is highly addictive.
        iii. Methadone has many of the chemical properties of heroin but does not create a rush.
    c. Barbiturates are synthetically produced sedatives.
        i. These drugs slow nervous system activity.
        ii. They work by either blocking the receptor sites or by enhancing the effects of inhibitory neurotransmitters.

iii. Some barbiturates are addictive, and all produce dependency.

4. Hallucinogens have very unpredictable effects on consciousness.
   a. LSD raises levels of emotionality and alters perception.
      i. It produces vivid hallucinations.
      ii. LSD has a chemical composition like serotonin.
      iii. It increases serotonin levels in the brain.
      iv. LSD appears to act like a neurotransmitter at receptor sites.
      v. LSD sometimes produces synesthesia, a stimulus of one modality perceived in another modality.
5. Marijuana does not fit into any of the previous three categories.
   a. In small doses it acts like a depressant.
   b. In higher doses it may act like a hallucinogen.
   c. The active ingredient is THC (tetrahydrocannabinol), also found in hashish.
   d. There is evidence that marijuana tolerance may develop, but virtually none that it is addictive.
   e. Marijuana has a number of negative effects.
      i. Like alcohol, excessive use leads to impaired judgment and reflexes, unrealistic moods, and poor physical coordination.
      ii. Marijuana is associated with bronchitis and other lung ailments.
      iii. It may produce some chromosomal abnormalities.
      iv. It may depress the immune system.
      v. It may impair memory function.
      vi. It has been associated with negative consequences during pregnancy, such as smaller babies and miscarriages.

**Learning Chapter 5 Vocabulary**

Write the definition for each of the following key terms on the lines provided at the right. Then fold the paper vertically so you can see only the term and try to say the definition. Practice this until you can say them all correctly.

PERCEPTION ______________________________

CONTRAST ______________________________

MENTAL SET ______________________________

GESTALT ______________________________

FIGURE-GROUND RELATIONSHIP ______________________________

PROXIMITY ______________________________

SIMILARITY ______________________________

CONTINUITY ______________________________

COMMON FATE ______________________________

CLOSURE

SUBJECTIVE CONTOURS

RETINAL DISPARITY

CONVERGENCE

ACCOMMODATION

ILLUSION

PHI PHENOMENON

AUTOKINETIC EFFECT

ELECTROENCEPHALOGRAM (EEG)

CONSCIOUSNESS

INSOMNIA

ALPHA ACTIVITY

REM SLEEP

ATONIA

HYPNOSIS

ELECTROMYOGRAM (EMG)

HALLUCINOGENS

PSYCHOACTIVE DRUG

DEPENDENCE

TOLERANCE ____________________

WITHDRAWAL ____________________

ADDICTION ____________________

DRUG ABUSE ____________________

STIMULANTS ____________________

DEPRESSANTS ____________________

**IDIOMS AND DIFFICULT PHRASES**

**birds of a feather are perceived together** (p. 166) A common saying in America is -*Birds of a feather flock together*.- It simply means that birds (and people) tend to associate with other birds (or people) who are like themselves.

**he or she didn't sleep a wink last night** (p. 176) The phrase *didn't sleep a wink* means that you did not sleep at all not even the short period of time it takes to wink your eye. It is probably an exaggeration referring to a restless night of little sleep rather than no sleep at all.

**then Surgeon General C. Everett Koop** (p. 185) The Surgeon General is a medical doctor who serves as a government official advising the president on important national health issues. C. Everett Koop became very famous as Surgeon General because of his outspokenness on issues such as cigarette smoking and AIDS.

**speed (yet another name for amphetamines) does kill**. (p. 186) As explained here, speed is a street name for amphetamines. The phrase -*speed kills*- is a common one but has its origins in traffic safety instruction (driving too fast can be deadly), not drug abuse prevention. However, it is true that the use of amphetamines can be deadly as is implied here.

**heroin's predictable rush** (p. 187) *Rush* refers to the physical sensation created by heroin. Although you hopefully will never use heroin it is still easy to get a rush. It is the same kind of feeling of excitement or exhilaration you get when you ride a roller coaster or ski down a steep mountainside.

**it was an important crop in the American Colonies** (p. 188) The 13 American colonies were the areas on the Eastern Coast of the U.S., first settled by Europeans who came to the United States beginning in 1620.

**Matching A**

Match the following key terms from your text with the appropriate definition.

| | | | |
|---|---|---|---|
| ______ | 1. gestalt | ______ | 2. figure-ground |
| ______ | 3. subjective contours | ______ | 4. size constancy |
| ______ | 5. convergence | ______ | 6. autokinetic effect |
| ______ | 7. perception | ______ | 8. similarity |
| ______ | 9. accommodation | ______ | 10. illusion |
| ______ | 11. phi phenomenon | ______ | 12. closure |
| ______ | 13. contrast | ______ | 14. continuity |
| ______ | 15. retinal disparity | ______ | 16. mental set |
| ______ | 17. proximity | | |

a. The cognitive process of selecting, organizing, and interpreting stimuli.
b. The extent to which a stimulus is in some physical way different from other surrounding stimuli.
c. A predisposed (set) way to perceive something; an expectation.
d. Whole, totality, configuration; the whole being perceived as more than the sum of its parts.
e. The Gestalt psychology principle that stimuli are selected and perceived as figures against a ground or background.
f. The Gestalt principle of organization claiming that stimuli will be perceived as belonging together if they occur together in space or time.
g. The Gestalt principle of organization claiming that stimuli will be perceived together if they share some common characteristics.
h. The Gestalt principle of organization claiming that a stimulus or a movement will be perceived as continuing in the same smooth direction as first established.
i. The tendency to see objects as being of constant size regardless of the size of the retinal image.
j. The Gestalt principle of organization claiming that we tend to perceive incomplete figures as whole and complete.
k. The perception of a contour (a line or plane) that is not there, but is suggested by other aspects of a scene.
l. The phenomenon in which each retina receives a different (disparate) view of the same three-dimensional object.
m. The tendency of the eyes to move toward each other as we focus on objects up close.
n. The process in which the ciliary muscles change the shape of the lens in order to focus a visual image.
o. A perception that is at odds with (different from) what we know as physical reality.
p. The visual illusion of the apparent motion of stationary lights flashing on and off in sequence.
q. The visual illusion of apparent motion in which a stationary pinpoint of light in an otherwise dark environment appears to move.

**Matching B**

Match the following key terms from your text with the appropriate definition.

| | | | |
|---|---|---|---|
| ______ | 1. hallucinogens | ______ | 2. depressants |
| ______ | 3. withdrawal | ______ | 4. electroencephalogram |
| ______ | 5. psychoactive drug | ______ | 6. REM sleep |
| ______ | 7. tolerance | ______ | 8. drug abuse |
| ______ | 9. dependence | ______ | 10. stimulants |
| ______ | 11. consciousness | ______ | 12. alpha activity |
| ______ | 13. atonia | ______ | 14. addiction |
| ______ | 15. insomnia | ______ | 16. hypnosis |
| ______ | 17. electromyogram | | |

a. Our awareness or perception of the environment and of our own mental processes.
b. The chronic inability to get to sleep and to get an adequate amount of sleep.
c. An instrument used to measure and record the electrical activity of the brain.
d. An instrument used to measure and record muscle tension/relaxation.

e. An EEG pattern associated with quiet relaxation and characterized by slow wave cycles of 8 to 12 per second.
f. Rapid eye movement sleep during which vivid dreaming occurs, as do heightened levels of physiological functioning.
g. Muscular immobility—associated with REM sleep—caused by the total relaxation of the muscles.
h. Drugs (such as alcohol, opiates, heroin, and barbiturates) that slow or reduce nervous system activity.
i. An altered state of consciousness characterized by an increase in suggestibility, attention, and imagination.
j. A chemical that has an effect on psychological processes and consciousness.
k. Drugs (such as LSD) whose major effect is the alteration of perceptual experience and mood.
l. A state in which drug use is either necessary or believed to be necessary to maintain functioning at some desired level.
m. In using a drug, a state in which more and more of the drug is required to produce the same level of effect.
n. A negative, painful reaction that may occur when one stops taking a drug.
o. An extreme dependency, usually accompanied by symptoms of tolerance and painful withdrawal.
p. Lack of control, a disruption of interpersonal relationships or difficulties at work, and a history of maladaptive use for at least one month.
q. Drugs (such as caffeine, cocaine, and amphetamines) that increase nervous system activity.

**True-False Practice Test**

___ 1. Sensation is more influenced than perception by such things as motivation and experience.
___ 2. Psychological preparedness for perception is referred to as having a mental set.
___ 3. Proximity is a perceptual stimulus factor that applies only to visual stimuli.
___ 4. Similarity, closure, continuity, and proximity are all examples of gestalt principles.
___ 5. The personal factors that influence perception are the same as the ones that influence stimulus selection.
___ 6. Retinal disparity is a monocular depth cue.
___ 7. Stereoscopes and 3-D movies illustrate convergence.
___ 8. We tend to see small objects as moving faster than large objects, even if their speed is the same.
___ 9. Objects seen against a plain background will be perceived as moving faster than when seen against a patterned background.
___ 10. Our perception of motion is not influenced by personal factors such as experience and expectation.
___ 11. When a woman looks in a small lipstick mirror, her lips will appear to be their normal size.
___ 12. Size constancy depends a great deal on the quality of depth perception cues available and familiarity with the stimulus.
___ 13. Human perception consists of three different constancies; size, shape, and color.
___ 14. EEGs measure brain activity and muscle activity.
___ 15. Dreams occur in "real" time.
___ 16. Everybody experiences REM sleep and dreams every night.
___ 17. Anyone can be hypnotized, even against his/her will.
___ 18. Tolerance and withdrawal are both associated with addiction.
___ 19. Stopping the intake of caffeine can result in a rebound effect.
___ 20. Nicotine and caffeine are the most commonly used stimulants.
___ 21. The effects of a depressant drug is about the same regardless of whether a large or small dose is taken.
___ 22. Alcohol is the most deadly of all drugs.

**Fill-in Practice Test**

1. The selection, organization, and interpretation of stimuli is known as ____________.
2. A powerful stimulus factor in determining visual attention is ________.
3. The ____________ psychologists studied factors that influence perception.
4. Our tendency to fill in gaps in our perception is known as ___________.

5. Cues about depth and distance that require both eyes are called ______________ cues.
6. The difference between what the right eye sees and what the left eye sees is called __________ __________.
7. When our perceptions seem to be at odds with what we know as reality, we are experiencing a/an ____________.
8. A roller coaster is outlined with lights that flash on and off in a sequential pattern. This will produce the ______ ____________.
9. The apparent movement of a pinpoint source of light in an otherwise darkened environment defines the ________________ effect.
10. __________ ____________ refers to our perception of objects maintaining their shape even though the retinal image they cast may change.
11. Looking at a car in the rearview mirror would provide an example of ________ constancy.
12. The Muller-Lyer is a well-known __________.
13. ________________ is the process in which the shape of the lens is changed by the ciliary muscles to focus an image on the retina.
14. ___________ is the chronic inability to get to sleep and to get an adequate amount of sleep.
15. __________ waves occur mainly during sleep stages 3 and 4 .
16. ________ sleep is the period during which dreaming occurs.
17. _________ sleep consists mostly of stages 2, 3, and 4 .
18. ________ believed that dreaming provides the opportunity for fantasy and wish fulfillment.
19. During dreams, the muscles are inactive or immobilized. This is called ________.
20. Drugs that create changes in perception, mood, and behavior are referred to as ______________ drugs.
21. A condition in which the use of a drug leads to a state where more and more of it is needed to produce the same effect is referred to as ____________.
22. ____________ is a negative reaction that results when one stops taking a drug.
23. Dependence on drugs can be either physical or ________________.
24. Drugs that stimulate or activate the nervous system are called _____________.
25. ____________ is the most commonly used depressant drug.

**Chapter 5 Multiple Choice Practice Test**

1. Events that occur close together in space or time are generally perceived as belonging together. Gestalt psychologists refer to this as
   a. proximity
   b. closure
   c. similarity
   d. continuity

2. While hunting, Charlie unknowingly approaches a well-camouflaged snake. He is surprised when the snake slithers away through the grass. His perception of the snake is best explained by the gestalt principle of
   a. proximity
   b. common fate
   c. similarity
   d. figure-ground

3. We are able to experience 3-D movies because of the perceptual phenomenon of
   a. convergence
   b. accommodation
   c. similarity
   d. retinal disparity

4. The distance cue that is limited to "arm's length" is
   a. convergence
   b. retinal disparity
   c. accommodation
   d. linear perspective

5. Jorge is standing in the middle of a railroad track. As he looks far ahead, the tracks seem to come together in the distance. This illustrates
   a. linear perspective
   b. interposition
   c. similarity
   d. convergence

6. As you drive by a construction site at night, you notice that a number of stationary, flashing warning lights appear to be moving back and forth. You are experiencing
   a. a primitive, sensory delusion
   b. the autokinetic effect
   c. motion parallax
   d. the phi phenomenon

7. You walk into a dark movie theater wearing a white shirt, and notice that the shirt now looks gray. However, you know that the shirt is still white because of
   a. size constancy
   b. brightness constancy
   c. linear perspective
   d. texture gradient

8. Which of the following is NOT an example of perceptual constancy?
   a. size
   b. shape
   c. color
   d. dimension

9. Which of the following perceptual cues could not be experienced by a Cyclops (one-eyed monster)?
   a. size constancy
   b. accommodation
   c. convergence
   d. linear perspective

10. As Dorothy traveled down the "yellow brick road," if she looked down at her feet, the bricks appeared their normal size. However, if she looked ahead down the road, the bricks appeared to be smaller. This can be explained by the perceptual phenomenon of
   a. linear perspective
   b. texture gradient
   c. interposition
   d. relative size

11. Pick and Jo are on a cross-country train ride. As night falls and a full moon appears, they notice that the moon seems to follow the train. This can be explained by
   a. convergence
   b. linear perspective
   c. accommodation
   d. motion parallax

12. Early one night, you notice a single star in the sky and at first cannot decide if it is stationary or moving. This is probably an example of the
   a. moon illusion
   b. Purkinje effect
   c. effect of imagination on perception
   d. autokinetic effect

13. Assuming that a cat's visual perception is similar to human perception, a kitten raised in the dark for research purposes would likely be lacking in the perceptual ability of
   a. lightness constancy
   b. shape constancy
   c. size constancy
   d. all of the above

14. Subjects deprived of REM sleep for a few nights and then left alone will spend long periods in REM sleep. This is referred to as
   a. microsleep
   b. REM rebound
   c. atonia
   d. REM exaggeration

15. Which of the following is NOT true of hypnosis?
   a. Avid readers and runners do not make good hypnotic subjects.
   b. People do not do anything under hypnosis that they would not do otherwise.
   c. Hypnosis can be used to alleviate pain.
   d. Hypnosis cannot improve memory or learning ability.

16. The feeling of relaxation that smokers seem to enjoy can be attributed to
   a. the psychological effects of having something to do with their hands
   b. the effect of nicotine on the brain
   c. the ritual of smoking after meals and at other times when people are normally relaxed
   d. the effects of nicotine on the central nervous system that causes muscle tone to relax

17. Being legally drunk is defined as having a blood alcohol level of
   a. 5 percent
   b. 3 percent
   c. 1 percent
   d. 1/10 percent

18. Which of the following drugs is most likely to produce hallucinations?
   a. heroin
   b. nicotine
   c. LSD
   d. alcohol

19. Which of the following is NOT associated with long-term marijuana use?
   a. bronchitis and other lung ailments
   b. chromosomal abnormalities in offspring
   c. hallucinations
   d. adverse effects on the immune system

20. An instrument that measures and records the electrical activity of the brain is called a/an
   a. electromyogram
   b. electrocardiogram
   c. electroencephalogram
   d. polygraph

21. Sexual arousal or excitement usually occurs during ________ sleep.
   a. stage 2
   b. REM
   c. NREM
   d. stage 4

22. Which of the following is NOT true of depressants?
   a. Depressants reduce a person's awareness of external stimuli.
   b. Depressants slow bodily functions.
   c. Depressants cause the user to feel emotions of sorrow and sadness.
   d. Depressants decrease levels of overt behavior.

23. In many ways, the most dangerous of all drugs is
   a. alcohol
   b. LSD
   c. cocaine
   d. nicotine

24. Death from heroin use is often associated with
   a. long-term damage to the nervous system
   b. impaired function of the internal organs
   c. increased dosages, causing breathing to stop
   d. weakening of the body's immune system

25. The drugs that have the most unpredictable effect on consciousness are
   a. hallucinogens
   b. barbiturates
   c. stimulants
   d. depressants

**Check Your Knowledge of the Learning Objectives**

The following questions are examples of what you should know when you have finished studying this chapter. Write the answers to these questions. Use your book to verify the answers. Page references are provided.

1. Explain how and why stimulus factors determine our selection of perceptions. p. 162-163

2. Describe how personal factors are involved in perceptual activity. p. 163-164

3. Discuss how stimulus factors and personal factors determine how we organize stimuli in perception. p. 165-167

4. List the cues that provide us with information about depth and distance. p. 169-170

5. Describe how the two illusions of motion are produced. p. 174-175

6. Explain how the types of perceptual constancy operate. p. 171-172

7. Define an altered state of consciousness. p. 176

8. Distinguish between the EEG and EMG. p. 176

9. Describe the four stages of sleep. p. 176-177

10. Explain how REM sleep differs from NREM sleep. p. 178-180

11. Define hypnosis, and describe how it affects consciousness. p. 180-183

12. Discuss the effects of stimulant drugs. p. 184

13. Discuss the effects of depressant drugs. p. 186-187

14. Discuss the effects of hallucinogenic drugs. p. 187-188

15. Discuss the effects of marijuana. p. 188-189

## Dr. G's Best Study Tips #5

**How to Read Your Textbook**

If you followed Study Tips #4, you should be familiar with your text by now. In this segment, I want to help you develop a system for chapter-by-chapter reading.

1. **Preread the chapter.**
   a. First read the outline at the beginning. This will give you an idea as to the structure and organization of the chapter. What topics are being covered? Are there issues with which you are already familiar?
   b. Then skip to the end of the chapter and read the summary. This will fill in a little more fully the ideas that will be presented in detail in the chapter. By reading this summary, you are preparing yourself to learn the more detailed information.
   c. Now skim through the chapter, examining the charts, graphs, tables, figures, and any other illustrations. Students are tempted to ignore anything that isn't print. This is a big mistake. The author has carefully chosen these illustrative materials to emphasize and explain important points. See what you can learn from them. Think of them as sign posts indicating important material.
   d. Finally, read through the chapter, taking only one section at a time. When you have finished a section, you need to check your comprehension in some way. Try to say out loud the major points or write them down. This generativity was mentioned in the first study tips. You must turn the passive process of reading into an active one.
2. **Plan to read the chapter only once.** For most people, rereading an entire chapter is a very inefficient study method. It is far better to do one thorough and comprehensive reading.
3. **Keep a pencil and a highlighter handy.** Use the highlighter to underline important points that you want to return to or emphasize. Use the pencil to make notes to yourself in the form of questions or your own interpretations of what you have read. When you are ready to review, you should be able to review what you have underlined and the notes you have read. Reserve rereading only for the most difficult concepts or ideas that seem unfamiliar or unclear.
4. **Sit at the keyboard.** I often use a strategy of sitting at a typewriter or word processor and typing notes in the form of a summary or outline as I read. Then I study my notes as I review, going back to the text only for clarification. Typing the notes is at least twice as fast as handwriting, even if you are a poor typist.

# CHAPTER 6—LEARNING

**Learning Objectives**

1. Define learning and conditioning.
2. Describe the essential features of classical conditioning.
3. Define acquisition, extinction, spontaneous recovery, generalization and discrimination.
4. Describe the sorts of responses that are most readily influenced by classical conditioning.
5. Describe the "Little Albert" experimental demonstration.
6. Understand what makes an effective CS.
7. Explain the principles of operant conditioning.
8. Discuss shaping, acquisition, extinction, and spontaneous recovery in operant conditioning.
9. Understand the operational definition of reinforcer.
10. Define a negative reinforcer and explain how it is used in escape and avoidance conditioning.
11. Distinguish between primary and secondary reinforcers.
12. Explain intermittent schedules of reinforcement and the advantages of using each of them.
13. Discuss the notions of cognitive maps and latent learning.
14. Relate the basic concepts of social learning theory and modeling.
15. Explain the role of vicarious reinforcement and vicarious punishment in learning.

**Chapter 6 Outline**

I. Preview

II. A Definition of Learning
   A. Learning is demonstrated by a relatively permanent change in behavior that occurs as a result of practice or experience.
      1. Learning is a process that cannot be observed directly.
      2. Learning is relatively permanent, not fleeting or cyclical.
      3. The need for practice and experience in order for learning to occur sets it apart from changes in behavior due to automatic physiological reactions.
      4. Bad, ineffective habits can be learned as readily as good, adaptive ones.
   B. The most basic, fundamental types of learning are called conditioning.

III. Classical Conditioning
   A. Ivan Pavlov, a Russian physiologist, received the 1904 Nobel Prize for his study of digestion.
      1. He studied the salivary reflex in dogs.
      2. A reflex is an unlearned, automatic response that occurs in the presence of a specific response.
   B. Pavlov's observation that dogs would salivate at the sight of food or the sight of the lab assistant led him to study classical conditioning.
      1. Classical conditioning is a type of learning in which an originally neutral stimulus comes to evoke a new response after having been paired with another stimulus that reflexively evokes that same response.
      2. The unconditioned stimulus (UCS) is any stimulus that reflexively elicits a response without the need for prior learning.
      3. The response evoked by the UCS is called the unconditioned response (UCR).
      4. The conditioned stimulus (CS) is any neutral stimulus that does not initially elicit the UCR.
      5. The orienting reflex is the unlearned response toward a new or unusual stimulus.
      6. Habituation is a simple form of learning in which an organism comes to ignore a stimulus of no consequence.
   C. The classical conditioning paradigm consists of the presentation of the CS and the UCS, which then elicits the UCR.
      1. Each pairing of the CS and UCS represents one conditioning trial.
      2. After a number of trials, the CS will elicit the same response as the UCS.
      3. The response elicited by the CS is called the conditioned response (CR).
      4. The CR seldom reaches the strength of the UCR, regardless of the number of pairings.
      5. Presentation of the CS with the UCS seems to work best.
   D. Classical Conditioning Phenomena

1. Acquisition is the stage of classical conditioning during which the strength of the CR increases.
2. Extinction occurs after a series of trials in which the CS is presented without the UCS.
   a. The strength of the CR will weaken and eventually cease.
   b. After rest, the CR may reappear after presentation of the CS, which is called spontaneous recovery.
3. Spontaneous recovery indicates the following two things:
   a. One series of extinction trials may not be sufficient to eliminate a conditioned response.
   b. Extinction may constitute suppression of the CR rather than forgetting.
4. Generalization occurs when a CR is elicited by stimuli different from, but similar to, the CS.
   a. The more the stimulus varies from the original CS, the weaker the CR will be.
   b. Generalization means it is not necessary to pair the UCS with all possible CSs.
5. Discrimination, the opposite of generalization, occurs when the organism is taught to respond only to one specific CS.

E. The Significance of Classical Conditioning: What About People?
   1. Classical conditioning has special significance because of its role in affecting our emotional responses to stimuli in the environment.
      a. Experiences with stimuli in the environment are able to classically condition emotional reactions.
      b. Examples are presented of how a CS and UCS are paired to create emotional responses.
   2. Watson and Raynor's experiments with Little Albert are classic examples of conditioned fear.
      a. Albert was conditioned to be fearful of a white rat by pairing its presentation with a loud, unexpected noise.
      b. Watson and Raynor demonstrated that Albert's fear generalized to other stimuli.
      c. These experiments raise the issue of unethical treatment of human subjects.
      d. Other researchers were not totally successful in replicating Watson and Raynor's experimental results.

F. Rethinking What Happens in Classical Conditioning
   1. Psychologists today are interested in understanding the factors that influence the effectiveness of classical conditioning.
   2. Pavlov argued that any stimulus paired with a UCS could effectively serve as a conditioned stimulus.
   3. Conditioning is the learning of relationships that exist among events in the world.
   4. At least two lines of research suggest that one cannot just present any stimulus with an unconditioned stimulus and expect conditioning to result.
      a. Blocking is a phenomenon where a second stimulus remains a neutral stimulus and is not paired with another UCS.
      b. Later experiments found that a stimulus will act as a CS to the extent to which that stimulus provides useful information or predicts the occurrence of another stimulus.

IV. The Basics of Operant Conditioning

A. B. F. Skinner, who did much of the early research, used the term operant to refer to a behavior that operates on the environment.
   1. Operants are controlled by their consequences.
   2. Operant conditioning changes the probability or rate of responses on the basis of the consequences that result from those responses.

B. E. L. Thorndike's law of effect states that responses are learned when they are followed by a satisfying state of affairs.

C. The procedures of operant conditioning can be demonstrated with an operant chamber (or Skinner box).
   1. The base rate of the subject is taken by observing how often it emits the bar-pressing response.
   2. The reinforcer is then instituted.
   3. Bar pressing increases and learning has occurred.

D. Operant conditioning involves several procedures.

1. Shaping involves reinforcing successive approximations of the response.
   a. A reinforcement is delivered each time an approximation of the response is made.
   b. The reinforcer should come soon after the behavior it reinforces if it is to be effective.
2. Acquisition is the stage of conditioning in which the response rate that follows reinforcement becomes more and more rapid.
3. Extinction occurs when reinforcement is withheld.
4. Spontaneous recovery is the return of an extinguished response following a rest period.

E. Reinforcement and Punishment
1. Reinforcement is a process that increases the rate or probability of the response that it follows.
2. A reinforcer is something that increases the rate of the response it follows.
3. Positive and negative reinforcers are used to bring about desired responses.
   a. A positive reinforcer is a stimulus presented to an organism that increases (or maintains above baseline) the rate of a response that precedes it.
      i. Positive reinforcers are sometimes like rewards.
      ii. Positive reinforcers do not always appear to be pleasant.
   b. A negative reinforcer is a stimulus that increases the rate of a response that precedes its removal.
      i. Negative reinforcers are things that an organism will work to avoid or escape.
      ii. Examples of negative reinforcers are shocks, enforced isolation, or low grades.
4. Reinforcers can be classified as primary or secondary.
   a. Primary reinforcers are those that do not require any previous experience to be effective.
      i. They are usually biological or physiological in nature.
      ii. Attention may also qualify as an unlearned, primary reinforcer for children.
   b. Secondary reinforcers are often referred to as learned or conditioned reinforcers.
      i. They acquire their reinforcing properties by having been paired with primary reinforcers or because of prior learning experiences.
      ii. The distinction between primary and secondary reinforcers applies to negative reinforcers as well as positive.
      iii. Contingency contracting is the setting up of a system that provides secondary reinforcers for appropriate behaviors.
      iv. The established system is referred to as a token economy.
5. There are a number of ways to deliver reinforcements, called schedules of reinforcement.
   a. A continuous reinforcement schedule (CRF) consists of reinforcing every response and may reduce the effectiveness of the reinforcer.
   b. With intermittent (or partial) reinforcement schedules, a behavior is reinforced less frequently than every time it occurs.
      i. A fixed ratio (FR) schedule establishes a ratio of reinforcers to responses.
      ii. A fixed interval (FI) schedule reinforces after the first response that occurs once a fixed interval of time has passed.
      iii. Both FR and FI schedules are very resistant to extinction.
      iv. In a variable ratio (VR) schedule, the ratio of reinforcer to responses varies.
      v. An average ratio number is used to establish this schedule.
      vi. Gambling devices are programmed to pay off (reinforce) on a VR schedule.
      vii. Time intervals are established in a random fashion in a variable interval (VI) schedule.
      viii. These schedules are set around an average time interval.
      ix. Pop quizzes may be set on a VI schedule.

F. Punishment
1. Punishment occurs when a stimulus decreases the rate or probability of occurrence of the response that preceded it.
   a. It is a painful, unpleasant, aversive stimulus.
   b. Punishers may be difficult to determine for people.
2. In order for punishment to be effective, it must be used correctly.
   a. Punishment should be delivered immediately after the response.

b. It needs to be administered consistently.
c. Punishment may decrease (suppress) overall behavior.
d. When responses are punished, alternatives should be introduced.

G. Generalization and Discrimination
1. Generalization occurs when reinforced responses that have been conditioned to a specific stimulus may appear in response to other, similar stimuli.
2. Discrimination learning means that responses made to appropriate stimuli will be reinforced, while responses made to inappropriate stimuli will be ignored or extinguished.
a. Discrimination learning is basically a matter of differential reinforcement.
b. Withholding reinforcers for inappropriate responses is not the same as punishing the response.

V. Cognitive Approaches to Learning
A. Cognitive approaches to learning emphasize changes that occur within an organism's system of cognitions.
1. Cognitions are mental representations that include ideas, beliefs, understanding, and knowledge.
2. Cognitive learning involves the acquisition of knowledge or understanding and may not be directly reflected in behavior.
B. Edward Tolman proposed that reinforcement only rewards a change in performance.
1. He argued that actual learning may have already taken place but not have been demonstrated.
2. He called this latent learning.
3. Tolman used the term cognitive map to refer to the mental picture, or representation, of the learning situation or physical environment.
4. Tolman emphasized the cognitions of the organisms by drawing a distinction between performance and what is actually learned.
5. There are examples of humans displaying cognitive maps.
C. Albert Bandura's approach to learning is known as social learning theory.
1. The central idea is that learning often takes place through observation and imitation of models.
2. It is social because we often learn from others.
3. It is cognitive because it is learned through observation or modeling, usually involving changes in cognitions that may never be expressed as behavior or directly reinforced.
4. His classic demonstration involved 96 children randomly assigned to one of four experimental conditions.
a. One group observed an adult model act aggressively toward a "Bobo" doll.
b. The second group viewed a filmed model also attack the "Bobo" doll.
c. Group three viewed a cartoon version with a cartoon cat attacking the "Bobo" doll.
d. The fourth group was a control group.
e. Children in all three experimental groups acted aggressively in their play with the "Bobo" doll after they viewed either the live, filmed, or cartoon version.
5. According to social learning theory, all three groups learned by observing the behavior of others.
6. A later study that replicated Bandura's work added reward or punishment to the aggressive episode.
a. Children who saw aggression rewarded were more likely to engage in aggression.
b. Those who viewed punishment were significantly less likely to engage in similar aggression.
7. These studies have several applications.
a. Children can and do learn behaviors by watching TV.
b. Reinforced behaviors of valued models are more likely to be imitated than punished behaviors of less valued models.
8. Learning about the consequences of one's behaviors by observing the consequences of someone else's behavior is called vicarious reinforcement or vicarious punishment.

**Learning Chapter 6 Vocabulary**

Write the definition for each of the following key terms on the lines provided at the right. Then fold the paper vertically so you can see only the term and try to say the definition. Practice like this until you can say them all correctly.

LEARNING

REFLEX

CLASSICAL CONDITIONING

UNCONDITIONED STIMULUS (UCS)

UNCONDITIONED RESPONSE (UCR)

ORIENTING REFLEX

HABITUATION

CONDITIONED STIMULUS (CS)

CONDITIONED RESPONSE (CR)

ACQUISITION

EXTINCTION

SPONTANEOUS RECOVERY

GENERALIZATION

DISCRIMINATION

OPERANT

OPERANT CONDITIONING

LAW OF EFFECT

SHAPING

ACQUISITION ______________________________

EXTINCTION ______________________________

SPONTANEOUS RECOVERY ______________________________

REINFORCEMENT ______________________________

REINFORCERS ______________________________

POSITIVE REINFORCER ______________________________

NEGATIVE REINFORCER ______________________________

PRIMARY REINFORCER ______________________________

SECONDARY REINFORCER ______________________________

CONTINUOUS REINFORCEMENT SCHEDULE ______________________________

INTERMITTENT REINFORCEMENT SCHEDULE ______________________________

PUNISHMENT ______________________________

GENERALIZATION ______________________________

DISCRIMINATION ______________________________

LATENT LEARNING ______________________________

COGNITIVE MAP ______________________________

SOCIAL LEARNING THEORY ______________________________

VICARIOUS REINFORCEMENT/PUNISHMENT ______________________________

**IDIOMS AND DIFFICULT PHRASES**

**and catch the flu** (p. 196) Catching the flu is an informal way to say that someone has contracted influenza (the flu). People often say that they catch the flu or a cold.

**what is called warm up** (p. 197) The phrase getting warmed up or warming up refers to practicing or getting ready for an event. Thus, in this example if the secretary has been typing for a few hours she has had the opportunity to practice or warm up.

**I know that the pain is just in my head** (p. 202) To say that something is all in your head means that you are imagining it.

**experiences a satisfying state of affairs** (p. 203) The phrase state of affairs means situation.

**I wanna candy bar** (p. 207) In informal speech the words *want a* or *want to* often sound like wanna. Chocolate and other candies are often packaged in bars. Another product you might use in a bar is body soap (a bar of soap).

**I'll pay you .25 for every 12 gizmos you assemble** (p. 214) Gizmo is a slang word that can be used to refer to any unnamed or imaginary object (or perhaps something you have forgotten the name of). If you are taking an economics class you may encounter a similar word widget.

**you may hold off studying** (p. 215) In informal speech, to hold off doing something means to postpone or delay doing it. It is not a good idea to hold off studying.

**if you watch a PBS station** (p. 223) PBS (Public Broadcasting System) television (and radio) stations are noncommercial stations that often feature educational "how to do it"and documentary programs.

**Matching A**

Match the following key terms from your text with the appropriate definition.

| | | | |
|---|---|---|---|
| ______ | 1. acquisition | ______ | 2. unconditioned response |
| ______ | 3. unconditioned stimulus | ______ | 4. conditioned stimulus |
| ______ | 5. reflex | ______ | 6. orienting reflex |
| ______ | 7. extinction | ______ | 8. discrimination |
| ______ | 9. learning | ______ | 10. conditioned response |
| ______ | 11. classical conditioning | ______ | 12. generalization |
| ______ | 13. habituation | ______ | 14. spontaneous recovery |

a. Demonstration of a relatively permanent change in behavior that occurs as the result of practice or experience.
b. An unlearned, automatic response that occurs in the presence of specific stimuli.
c. Learning in which an originally neutral stimulus comes to elicit a new response after having been paired with a stimulus that reflexively elicits that same response.
d. In classical conditioning, a stimulus that reliably and reflexively evokes a response.
e. In classical conditioning, a response reliably and reflexively evoked by a stimulus.
f. The simple, unlearned response of orienting toward, or attending to a new or unusual stimulus.
g. In classical conditioning, a simple form of learning in which an organism comes to ignore a stimulus of no consequence.
h. In classical conditioning, an originally neutral stimulus that, when paired with a UCS, comes to evoke a new response.
i. In classical conditioning, the learned response evoked by the CS after conditioning.
j. The process in classical conditioning in which the strength of the CR increases with repeated pairings of the CS and the UCS.
k. The process in classical conditioning in which the strength of the CR decreases with repeated presentations of the CS alone.

l. The phenomenon in classical conditioning in which a previously extinguished CR returns after a rest interval.
m. The phenomenon in classical conditioning in which a CR is elicited by stimuli different from, but similar to, the CS.
n. The phenomenon in classical conditioning in which an organism learns to make a CR in response to only one CS, but not to other stimuli.

**Matching B**

Match the following key terms from your text with the appropriate definition.

| | | | |
|---|---|---|---|
| ______ | 1.vicarious reinforcement | ______ | 2. discrimination |
| ______ | 3. negative reinforcer | ______ | 4. latent learning |
| ______ | 5. secondary reinforcer | ______ | 6. cognitive map |
| ______ | 7. extinction | ______ | 8. positive reinforcer |
| ______ | 9. operant | ______ | 0. reinforcement |
| ______ | 11. law of effect | ______ | 12. reinforcers |
| ______ | 13. social learning theory | ______ | 14. shaping |
| ______ | 15. intermittent reinforcement | ______ | 16. continuous reinforcement |
| ______ | 17. primary reinforcers | ______ | 18. operant conditioning |
| ______ | 19. generalization | ______ | 20. acquisition |
| ______ | 21. punishment | ______ | 22. spontaneous recovery |

a. Referring to behavior(s) used by an organism to operate on its environment.
b. Changing the rate of a response on the basis of the consequences that result from that response.
c. The observation that responses that lead to satisfying states of affairs tend to be repeated, while those that do not, are not.
d. A procedure of reinforcing successive approximations of a desired response until that desired response is made.
e. The process in operant conditioning in which the rate of a reinforced response increases.
f. The process in operant conditioning in which the rate of a response decreases as reinforcers are withheld.
g. The phenomenon in operant conditioning in which a previously extinguished response returns after a rest interval.
h. A process that increases the rate or probability of the response that it follows.
i. Stimuli that increase the rate or probability of the responses they follow.
j. A stimulus that increases the rate of a response when that stimulus is presented after the response is made.
k. A stimulus that increases the rate of a response when that stimulus is removed after the response is made.
l. Stimuli that increase the rate of a response with no previous experience required.
m. Stimuli that increase the rate of a response because of their having been associated with other reinforcers; also called conditioned, or learned, reinforcers.
n. A reinforcement schedule in which each and every response is followed by a reinforcer.
o. Reinforcement schedules in which responses are not reinforced every time they occur.
p. The administration of a punisher, which is a stimulus that decreases the rate or probability of a response that precedes it.
q. The process by which a response that was reinforced in the presence of one stimulus appears in response to other, similar stimuli.
r. The process of differential reinforcement wherein one stimulus is reinforced while another stimulus is not.
s. Hidden learning that is not demonstrated in performance until that performance is reinforced.
t A mental representation of the learning situation or physical environment.
u. The theory that learning takes place through observation and imitation of others.
v. Increasing the rate (with reinforcement) or decreasing the rate (with punishment) of responses due to observing the consequences of someone else's behaviors.

**True-False Practice Test**

___ 1. Learning results in a relatively permanent change in behavior.
___ 2. The disappearance of an orienting reflex is caused by habituation.

___ 3. A conditioned stimulus and an unconditioned stimulus can produce responses with equal strength.
___ 4. The more trials that are presented during the acquisition stage, the greater the strength of the conditioned response to the conditioned stimulus.
___ 5. When a CS is repeatedly presented without being paired with the UCS, spontaneous recovery will occur.
___ 6. In classical conditioning, the CR and the UCR are actually the same behavior.
___ 7. One series of extinction trials is usually sufficient to eliminate a response permanently.
___ 8. Extinction in classical conditioning can be considered a type of forgetting.
___ 9. Conditioning trials do not have to be applied over and over again in order for the organism to respond to separate stimuli.
___ 10. Recent research on classical conditioning indicates that any stimulus can become a conditioned stimulus.
___ 11. There really are limited applications of classical conditioning where human behavior is concerned.
___ 12. In operant conditioning, learning is a matter of increasing responses that produce positive consequences and decreasing responses that produce negative consequences.
___ 13. Classical conditioning applies to animal behavior, whereas operant conditioning applies to human behavior.
___ 14. Thorndike's work on operant conditioning preceded Skinner's research.
___ 15. In some cases, operant conditioning does not result in the learning of a new response, but rather it results in a change in the rate of the response.
___ 16. A positive reinforcer always increases the rate of the response it follows.
___ 17. A negative reinforcer decreases the rate of the response it follows.
___ 18. One cannot be sure that a particular stimulus will be a reinforcer until it is actually presented to the organism.
___ 19. Positive reinforcement is effective in changing behaviors, but negative reinforcement is not.
___ 20. Primary reinforcers are preferred over secondary reinforcers.
___ 21. Most of the reinforcers that humans work for are secondary reinforcers.
___ 22. Secondary reinforcers tend to be biological or physiological in nature and related to the survival of the organism.
___ 23. To decrease the rate of the response, use negative reinforcement.
___ 24. Intermittent reinforcement schedules are more effective than continuous reinforcement schedules.
___ 25. Learning that remains hidden until it is useful is called latent learning.

**Fill-in Practice Test**

1. The most basic fundamental types of learning are called __________.
2. A ________ is an unlearned, automatic response that occurs in the presence of a specific stimulus.
3. The stage of classical conditioning during which the strength of the conditioned response increases is called ______________.
4. The repeated presentation of the CS without the UCS will result in ____________.
5. In Pavlov's conditioning research, the conditioned response was ______________.
6. When an extinguished response reappears automatically after a rest period, this is called ________________ ___________.
7. In classical conditioning, an extinguished response is not forgotten, rather it is ______________.
8. The process in which an organism learns to make a conditioned response to only one conditioned stimulus, but not to other stimuli is called _________________.
9. The psychologist who conducted the famous classical conditioning experiment with Little Albert was __________.
10. A simple form of learning in which an organism comes to ignore a stimulus is called ______________.
11. Approaches that focus more on the mental processes of the learner are referred to as ____________.
12. A behavior that an organism uses to operate on its environment is called a/an _____________.
13. Operant behaviors are controlled by _____________.

14. The psychologist who studied operant conditioning before Skinner was ____________.
15. Another name for an operant chamber is __________ _____.
16. The number of times a response is made when it is not being reinforced is referred to as ______ ______.
17. Reinforcing successive approximations of the response that you want to condition is referred to as _________.
18. In operant conditioning the rate of response increases during _______.
19. The return of an extinguished response following a rest period is called ______________ _________.
20. The process that increases the rate or the probability of the response it follows is _______________.
21. ___________ reinforcers do not require previous experience in order to be effective.
22. Learned or acquired reinforcers are called ____________.
23. A reinforcement schedule that does not reinforce every response is called a/an ______________ reinforcement schedule.

**Chapter 6 Multiple Choice Practice Test**

1. In Pavlovian conditioning, the relationship between the unconditioned response and the unconditioned stimulus is
   a. learned
   b. reflexive
   c. hereditary
   d. conditioned
2. If a conditioned stimulus is repeatedly presented without being paired with the unconditioned stimulus, the behavior will eventually fail to occur. This is known as
   a. conditioning failure
   b. stimulus rejection
   c. extinction
   d. habituation
3. As a child, Carmelita was attacked by a large black dog. She was only scratched and knocked down, but terribly frightened. Now, as an adult she is afraid of all large dogs. This is an example of
   a. stimulus generalization
   b. stimulus discrimination
   c. spontaneous recovery
   d. reflexive relationships
4. John Watson's conditioning of Little Albert to fear a white rat was based on
   a. Little Albert's natural fear of the rat
   b. the reflexive relationship between fear and loud noises
   c. the child's natural anxiety in the presence of strangers
   d. Little Albert's ability to generalize fear to many different stimuli
5. If a person blinks when a puff of air hits his/her eyes, a/an _________ is being exhibited.
   a. conditioned response
   b. generalized response
   c. discriminatory response
   d unconditioned response
6. Which of the following is the correct order of stimuli and responses during the acquisition stage?
   a. UCS-CS-CR
   b. UR-UCS-US
   c. CS-UCS-UCR
   d. CS-UCR-UCS

7. If spontaneous recovery of a classically conditioned response occurs, it will occur immediately following
   a. the presentation of the UCS
   b. acquisition
   c. a rest period
   d. extinction

8. Rescorla's recent classical conditioning research demonstrated that
   a. rats do not fear electric shock
   b. every stimulus cannot become a conditioned stimulus
   c. lights will not become conditioned stimuli for rats
   d. a tone will not serve as a UCS for fear responses in rats

9. One problem with John Watson's research involving Little Albert is that
   a. the conclusions were misinterpreted
   b. Little Albert was an atypical subject
   c. the research was interrupted and never completed
   d. by today's standards, the research was unethical

10. In classical conditioning, the first response made to the neutral stimulus is called
   a. orienting reflex
   b. learned response
   c. reflexive response
   d. unconditioned reflex

11. Which of the following reinforcement schedules produces responses that are resistant to extinction?
   a. fixed ratio
   b. fixed interval
   c. variable ratio
   d. all of the above

12. Which of the following is NOT true of punishment?
   a. It is most effective if administered immediately.
   b. It should be administered consistently.
   c. It decreased only the punished response.
   d. It does not give the organism any information about appropriate behavior.

13. A major implication of Albert Bandura's classic study with the BoBo doll is that
   a. children can and do learn all sorts of behaviors from watching television
   b. children will do behaviors that they see others doing even when the others are punished
   c. children will only do behaviors that are modeled by live models
   d. children are most influenced by adult models viewed on television

14. In regard to observational learning, the role of reinforcement and punishment is
   a. still undetermined
   b. demonstrated to be significant
   c. of little importance
   d. only related to positive behaviors

15. Skinner is to operant conditioning as ______________ is to ______________.
   a. Wolpe; Little Albert
   b. Watson; classical conditioning
   c. Raynor; instrumental conditioning
   d. Pavlov; classical conditioning

16. The primary purpose of an operant chamber is to
   a. provide reinforcement
   b. control the environment
   c. serve as punishment
   d. all of the above

17. A rat is bar pressing at a very high response rate. Then reinforcement is withheld. The predictable outcome is
    a. acquisition
    b. extinction
    c. generalization
    d. spontaneous recovery

18. What is the difference between positive reinforcement and negative reinforcement?
    a. Positive reinforcement is classically conditioned and negative reinforcement is operantly conditioned.
    b. Positive reinforcement increases the probability of a response and negative reinforcement decreases the probability of a response.
    c. Positive reinforcement uses primary reinforcers and negative reinforcement uses secondary reinforcers.
    d. A stimulus is presented after a response in positive reinforcement and a stimulus is removed in negative reinforcement.

19. Juan got a speeding ticket. However, he took a defensive driving class and did not have to pay the ticket. Having the fine removed is an example of
    a. positive reinforcement
    b. negative reinforcement
    c. secondary reinforcement
    d. primary reinforcement

20. In a token economy, the tokens serve as
    a. secondary reinforcers
    b. primary reinforcers
    c. stimuli
    d. bribes

21. A psychology professor gives ten points of extra credit for each lab project students turn in. This represents a ___________ schedule of reinforcement.
    a. variable interval
    b. fixed interval
    c. variable ratio
    d. fixed ratio

22. Learning about the consequences of one's behaviors by observing the consequences of someone else's behaviors is called
    a. vicarious reinforcement
    b. modeling
    c. role playing
    d. variable learning

23. The learning that a college student does is best described by the _________ approach.
    a. cognitive
    b. behavioristic
    c. classical conditioning
    d. operant conditioning

24. You take an aspirin to relieve a headache. It works and you feel better. Your aspirin taking response has been
    a. generalized
    b. extinguished
    c. negatively reinforced
    d. positively reinforced

25. Some people are disturbed by the idea of using token economies to manage the behavior of children and compare it to
    a. child abuse
    b. communism
    c. mental cruelty
    d. bribery

**Check Your Knowledge of the Learning Objectives**

The following questions are examples of what you should know when you have finished studying this chapter. Write the answers to these questions. Use your book to verify the answers. Page references are provided.

1. Describe the essential features of classical conditioning. p. 198-199

2. Describe the sorts of responses that are most readily influenced by classical conditioning. p. 202-203

3. Describe the "Little Albert" experimental demonstration. p. 203-204

4. Describe an effective CS. p. 206

5. Explain the principles of operant conditioning. p. 207-209

6. Discuss shaping, acquisition, extinction, and spontaneous recovery in operant conditioning. p. 210-211

7. What is the operational definition of reinforcer? p. 212

8. Define a negative reinforcer and give an example. p. 212

9. Distinguish between primary and secondary reinforcers. p. 213

10. Explain intermittent schedules of reinforcement and the advantages of using each of them. p. 214-215

11. Discuss the notions of cognitive maps and latent learning. p. 219-221

12. What are the basic concepts of social learning theory and modeling? p. 221-223

13. Explain the role of vicarious reinforcement and vicarious punishment in learning. p. 222

## Dr. G's Best Study Tips #6

**Using the Premack Principle**

Now that you are studying learning theory, let's apply what you have learned to your own studying behavior. The Premack principle tells us that we can use a high frequency behavior to reinforce a low frequency one. For many students, studying is a low frequency behavior. They simply do not do it often enough or for sufficient periods of time.

Select a behavior that you really like to do and do often (a high frequency response). You might choose making a phone call to a friend, going out, working out, eating out, or even watching TV. Now comes the difficult part. You must withhold this high frequency response and only do this behavior after you study. Then making the call or getting the pizza becomes a reward for studying. Using the Premack principle in this way is a good idea because we have learned that for reinforcement to be effective, it should be immediate. The other reinforcers for studying, getting good grades, graduation, and so forth are usually delayed for long periods after we have studied very hard. You may feel as if your study behavior is not reinforced at all if you don't take the reinforcement into your own hands and use the Premack principle to reward yourself.

# CHAPTER 7—MEMORY

**Learning Objectives**

1. Define memory and repression.
2. Discuss sensory memory, including its capacity and duration.
3. Describe how material is put into short-term memory and how long it is kept there.
4. Know how much information is held in short-term memory and how chunking effects that amount.
5. Discuss the issues of acoustic coding in short-term memory.
6. Discuss the issue of permanence in long-term memory.
7. Explain how elaborative rehearsal and maintenance rehearsal encode information into long-term memory.
8. Describe three possible types of long term memory.
9. List the ways that information may be represented in long-term memory.
10. Explain how measures of recall, recognition, and relearning affect assessment of retrieval.
11. Explain implicit tests of retention and what they tell us about long-term memory.
12. Describe how the situation in which encoding is done affects retrieval.
13. Define meaningfulness and explain how it relates to retrieval.
14. Define mnemonic devices and describe four examples.
15. Define schemas and explain how they affect retrieval.
16. Define overlearning, massed practice, and distributed practice and explain how they affect retrieval.
17. Distinguish between retroactive and proactive interference and explain how each affects retrieval.

**Chapter 7 Outline**

I. Preview
   A. Memory stores the information that makes us individuals.
   B. There have been striking changes in the way memory is viewed in psychology.
      1. Memory may not be one unified structure or process.
      2. Memory is no longer viewed as a passive receptacle but as an active, creative process.

II. Memory: Some Basic Terms
   A. According to the information processing view, memory is a cognitive activity that involves three processes.
      1. Encoding is putting information into memory.
      2. Storage involves keeping it in memory.
      3. Retrieval involves getting information back out of memory.
   B. Memory is now seen as the last step in information processing.

III. Sensory Memory
   A. Sensory memory involves the storage of large amounts of sensory information for very short periods of time.
      1. The capacity of sensory memory is very large.
      2. Memories remain in sensory memory briefly.
         a. Visual information remains for about 0.5 seconds.
         b. Auditory information seems to remain for about 3 to 10 seconds.
   B. Sensory memory is viewed as being rather physical or mechanical.
      1. Sensory memory can be described as reverberant.
      2. Our senses hold on to information as it reverberates or echoes within our nervous system.

IV. Short-term Memory (STM)
   A. STM has a limited capacity and, without tehearsal, a brief duration.
      1. To encode information into STM requires that we pay attention to it.
      2. It is referred to as working memory.
      3. It acts like a bottleneck in processing information.
   B. Recall from STM depends on the length of the retention interval.
      1. Duration can be stretched with maintenance rehearsal or rote rehearsal.
      2. Unrehearsed material will stay in STM for about 15 to 20 seconds.

C. The capacity of STM was described by George Miller as being limited to 5 to 9 bits of information.
   1. Chunking information into meaningful clusters increases the capacity of STM.
   2. A chunk is a somewhat imprecise concept referring to a meaningful unit of information.

D. Conrad argued that information is represented in STM by an acoustic code.
   1. Material tends to be processed in terms of what it sounds like.
   2. Acoustic similarity causes confusion within STM.
   3. Some material may be represented visually or semantically.

V. Long-term Memory (LTM)

A. LTM consists of holding large amounts of information for long periods of time.

B. Many psychologists believe that information is permanently stored.
   1. Forgetting is a failure of retrieval.
   2. The bulk of evidence for this view is neither experimental nor reliable.

C. Distant memories may be a reconstruction of a reasonable facsimile of the original information.
   1. This applies to the reliability of eyewitness testimony.
   2. Memories can be distorted or replaced by information processed later.

D. Encoding in LTM may consist of rote repetition (maintenance rehearsal) and elaborative rehearsal.
   1. We must repeat it.
   2. We must also reorganize it and make it meaningful.

E. Endel Tulving suggested that three types of information are stored in LTM.
   1. Procedural memory is the lowest level.
      a. Recollections of learned responses to particular stimuli are stored here.
      b. Well-learned, patterned responses are stored here.
   2. Semantic memory stores vocabulary, simple concepts, and rules for language use.
   3. Episodic memory stores life events and experiences.
      a. It is time-related memory.
      b. It is autobiographical.

VI. How to Improve Memory: Factors Affecting Retrieval

A. Four factors influence our ability to retrieve information from long-term memory.
   1. How memory is measured.
   2. How encoding strategies influence later retrieval.
   3. How encoding or practice is scheduled.
   4. How interference and repression can adversely affect retrieval.

B. Retrieval can be measured by direct, explicit methods.
   1. Recall is a difficult retrieval task that provides the fewest number of cues.
      a. Fill-in-the-blank tests require recall.
      b. Essay tests are also recall tasks.
   2. Recognition requires the subject to simply identify material learned previously.
      a. Retrieval by recognition will be superior to retrieval by recall in virtually all cases.
      b. Maximum cues for retrieval are provided in a recognition task.
      c. Multiple-choice tests are recognition tasks.

C. Tests that do not require that a subject retrieve any information from memory are referred to as indirect, or implicit, tests of memory.
   1. Relearning almost always takes less effort than did original learning.
   2. Most current tests of retention focus on procedural memories.
      a. These include the storage of "knowing how to go about doing things."
      b. These procedures reflect prior learning, but seem to resist conscious remembering.

D. How we encode information
   1. Information needs to be encoded appropriately in order to be retrieved effectively.
      a. Retrieval tends to be best when the context in which retrieval takes place matches the context that was present at encoding.
         i. This is called the encoding specificity principle.
         ii. This principle states that we can only retrieve what has been stored and how we retrieve information depends on how it was encoded.

b. State-dependent memory means that to some degree, retrieval depends on the extent to which a person's state of mind at retrieval matches the person's state of mind at encoding.
    i. Research by Gordon Bower supports this idea.
    ii. He found that retrieval was best when mood at retrieval matched mood at learning.
    iii. Flashbulb memories are particularly vivid memories associated with emotional arousal.

2. Strategies that guide encoding will meaningfully encode information into our long-term memories so that we can easily retrieve them.
    a. Meaningfulness is the extent to which information evokes existing associations in one's memory.
    b. Mnemonic devices are strategies for improving retrieval that take advantage of existing memories.
        i. Organizing materials into a meaningful story is known as narrative chaining.
        ii. Forming meaningful mental images or pictures in our minds aids in remembering.
        iii. Atkinson suggests, in studying a foreign language, visually tying the foreign and English word together (key word method of study).
        iv. The peg word method consists of associating common nouns (peg words) that rhyme with the numbers from 1 to 10.
        v. The second step is to form an interactive image of the word to be memorized and the appropriate peg word.
        vi. The method of loci consists of visualizing a familiar location and placing each word to be memorized somewhere within the location.
    c. A schema is an organized, general knowledge structure that we have stored in long-term memory.
        i. Schemas provide a general framework to use in encoding or retrieving information.
        ii. Schemas seem to help retrieval only if the same schemas were available at encoding.

3. Amount and distribution of encoding practice affects ability to retrieve information.
    a. Overlearning is the process of practicing or rehearsing material over and above what is needed to just barely learn it.
        i. Measurement of retrieval shows that forgetting is rather significant and quite sudden.
        ii. Overlearning improves retrieval and has its greatest effects with longer retention intervals.
        iii. There is a diminishing returns phenomenon.
    b. Retrieval can be improved if practice is spread out over time with rest intervals spaced in between.
        i. Massed practice (no rest) produces the poorest performance.
        ii. Distributed practice is superior to massed practice.
        iii. Do not break up practice in such a way as to disrupt the meaningfulness of the material you are studying.

4. How we overcome Interference or repression.
    a. Retroactive interference involves interfering activities that come after the learning of material to be remembered.
    b. Proactive interference occurs when previously learned material interferes with the retrieval of material learned later.
        i. Proactive interference is generally not as detrimental as retroactive interference.
        ii. Meaningful, well-organized material is less susceptible to interference than is less meaningful material.
        iii. The more similar the interfering material is to material being retrieved, the greater will be the interference.
    c. Repression is the process of forcing anxiety-producing events into our unconscious.
        i. Forgetting a dreaded dentist appointment is an example of repression.

**Learning Chapter 7 Vocabulary**

Write the definition for each of the following key terms on the lines provided at the right. Then fold the paper vertically so you can see only the term and try to say the definition. Practice like this until you can say them all correctly.

MEMORY

ENCODING

STORAGE

RETRIEVAL

SENSORY MEMORY

SHORT-TERM MEMORY

MAINTENANCE REHEARSAL

CHUNK

LONG-TERM MEMORY

ELABORATIVE REHEARSAL

PROCEDURAL MEMORY

SEMANTIC MEMORY

EPISODIC MEMORY

RECALL

RELEARNING

ENCODING SPECIFICITY PRINCIPLE

STATE-DEPENDENT MEMORY

FLASHBULB MEMORIES

MEANINGFULNESS ____________________

MNEMONIC DEVICES ____________________

NARRATIVE CHAINING ____________________

PEG WORD METHOD ____________________

METHOD OF LOCI ____________________

SCHEMA ____________________

OVERLEARNING ____________________

RETROACTIVE INTERFERENCE ____________________

PROACTIVE INTERFERENCE ____________________

RECOGNITION ____________________

REPRESSION ____________________

**IDIOMS AND DIFFICULT PHRASES**

**so you turn to the yellow pages** (p. 228) The yellow pages is a kind of business telephone directory usually printed on yellow paper. Businesses are listed according to the type of service they provide (you would find the number for Pizza City under the restaurants listing).

**you cannot for the life of you remember their phone number** (p. 228) This phrase I cannot for the life of me remember is one used in informal speech by someone who is having great difficulty trying to remember something. It literally means you could not remember even if remembering would save your life.

**if you've never smelled them in the first place** (p. 230) To say that something was not done in the first place means that it has not been done before.

**As a rule of thumb** (p. 235) Rules of thumb are basic rules or guidelines, they have nothing to do with your fingers.

**material we have stashed away in LTM** (p. 237) To stash away something means that we have stored it carefully or hidden it.

**When we hear that soandso doesn't have** (p. 257) If you cannot remember someone's name you might refer to them as soandso. More often this phrase is used by someone who wants to call a person a bad name but so as not to offend others will refer to that person as a soandso. For example, "Can you believe that no good soandso stole my bicycle?"

**Matching A**

Match the following key terms from your text with the appropriate definition.

_______ 1. episodic memory
_______ 2. short-term memory
_______ 3. retrieval
_______ 4. chunk
_______ 5. sensory memory
_______ 6. long-term memory
_______ 7. memory
_______ 8. elaborative rehearsal
_______ 9. semantic memory
_______ 10. procedural memory
_______ 11. storage
_______ 12. maintenance rehearsal
_______ 13. encoding

a. The cognitive ability to encode, store, and retrieve information.
b. The active process of representing, or putting of information into memory.
c. The process of holding encoded information in memory.
d. The process of locating, removing, and using information that is stored in memory.
e. The type of memory that holds large amounts of information registered at the senses for very brief periods of time.
f. A type of memory with limited capacity (7 plus or minus 2 bits of information) and limited duration (15-20 seconds).
g. A process of rote repetition (reattending) to keep information in short-term memory.
h. A somewhat imprecise concept, referring to a meaningful unit of information as represented in memory.
i. A type of memory with virtually unlimited capacity and very long, if not limitless, duration.
j. A mechanism for processing information into long-term memory that involves the meaningful manipulation of the information to be remembered.
k. In long-term memory, where learned stimulus-response associations and skilled patterns of responses are stored.
l. In long-term memory, where vocabulary, facts, simple concepts, rules, and the like are stored.
m. In long-term memory, where life events and experiences are stored.

**Matching B**

Match the following key terms from your text with the appropriate definition.

| | | | |
|---|---|---|---|
| _____ 1. | peg word method | _____ 2. | proactive interference |
| _____ 3. | state-dependent memory | _____ 4. | mnemonic devices |
| _____ 5. | narrative chaining | _____ 6. | overlearning |
| _____ 7. | encoding specificity principle | _____ 8. | recall |
| _____ 9. | retroactive interference | _____ 10. | recognition |
| _____ 11. | meaningfulness | _____ 12. | schema |
| _____ 13. | flashbulb memories | _____ 14. | relearning |
| _____ 15. | method of loci | _____ 16. | metamemory |

a. A measure of retrieval in which an individual is given the fewest possible cues to aid retrieval.
b. A measure of retrieval in which an individual is required to identify material previously learned as being familiar.
c. A measure of memory in which one notes the improvement in performance when learning material for a second time.
d. The hypothesis that we can only retrieve what we have stored and that retrieval is enhanced to the extent that retrieval cues match encoding cues.
e. The hypothesis that retrieval can be enhanced by the extent to which one's state of mind at retrieval matches one's state of mind at encoding.
f. Particularly clear, and vivid memories that are easily retrieved, but not necessarily accurate in all detail.
g. The extent to which information evokes associations with information already in memory.
h. Strategies for improving retrieval that take advantage of existing memories in order to make new material more meaningful.
i. The mnemonic device of relating words together in a story, organizing them in a meaningful way.
j. The mnemonic device of forming interactive visual images of materials to be learned and items previously associated with numbers.
k. The mnemonic device that mentally places information to be retrieved in a series of familiar locations (loci).
l. A system of organized, general knowledge, stored in long-term memory, that guide the encoding and retrieval of information.
m. The practice or rehearsal of material over and above what is needed to learn it.
n. The inhibition of retrieval of previously learned material caused by material learned later.
o. The inhibition of retrieval of recently learned material caused by material learned earlier.
p. In long-term memory, our stored knowledge of how our own memory systems work.

**True-False Practice Test**

___ 1. The information processing view of memory comes from an ancient theory held by the Greeks.
___ 2. All the information in our memories first passes through sensory memory.
___ 3. There is evidence of sensory memory for all five senses.
___ 4. Information can be stored in short-term memory for several minutes.
___ 5. Based on the idea of chunking, our memory can hold between 5 and 9 meaningful bits of information.
___ 6. Information in our sensory memory is held in the same form in which it was initially presented.
___ 7. Information is always represented in short-term memory acoustically.
___ 8. The capacity for long-term memory can be described as virtually limitless.
___ 9. Eliminating the effects of injury or illness, one could assume that certain information in long-term memory would never be forgotten.
___ 10. The majority of psychologists agree that once information is transferred to long-term memory, it stays there till we die.
___ 11. Retrieval failure suggests that information is no longer in long-term memory.
___ 12. Asking subjects to remember a word list in the order it was presented is an example of serial recall.

___ 13. Retrieval by recognition is always superior to retrieval by recall.
___ 14. A multiple choice test item and an essay item would both measure retrieval by recall.
___ 15. Relearning generally takes as many trials or presentations of the material as the first learning.
___ 16. Recognition memory tasks require fewer cues than recall memory tasks.
___ 17. In tests of implicit memory, amnesia victims have performed as well as non-amnesia subjects.
___ 18. The encoding specificity principle applies only to humans.
___ 19. According to the encoding specificity principle, when cues that were present at encoding are also present at retrieval, retrieval is enhanced.
___ 20. According to research by Gordon Bower, even the mood a person is in when material is encoded can be an important factor for retrieval.
___ 21. There is evidence that memories of emotionally arousing events are easier to recall than memories of emotionally neutral events.
___ 22. Meaningfulness of material to be learned is determined by the nature of the material.
___ 23. The greatest effect of overlearning appears with longer retention intervals.
___ 24. Research results clearly indicate that massed practice is superior to distributed practice.
___ 25. As a general study strategy, cramming is very inefficient.

**Fill-in Practice Test**

1. The process of putting information into memory is called __________.
2. The type of memory with the shortest duration is called ____________ memory.
3. Short-term memory is also called __________ memory.
4. In regard to memory, a meaningful unit of information is called a/an _________.
5. The type of rehearsal used to keep material active in short-term memory is called _______________ rehearsal.
6. In order to get information into long-term memory, one should use _______________ rehearsal.
7. According to Tulving, organisms retain learned connections between stimuli and responses through _____________ memory.
8. Vocabulary, rules, and simple concepts are stored in ___________ memory.
9. Life events and experiences are stored in ___________ memory.
10. A memory task where the fewest possible cues are provided to aid retrieval is called ________.
11. A memory task requiring a subject to identify previously learned material is called _____________.
12. A fill-in item such as this one measures retrieval by _________.
13. Relearning is referred to as a/an ____________ test of memory.
14. Recall is an example of a/an ____________ test of memory.
15. Knowing how to swim is an example of ______________ knowledge.
16. Although amnesia victims seem to have forgotten everything, their ______________ memories are actually still in tact.
17. Memories of important events that are especially clear and vivid are called ____________ memories.
18. Complex cognitive representations of general knowledge are referred to as __________.
19. Aids to retrieval that help organize material and make it meaningful are called ____________________.
20. ___________ __________ is a technique by which information is organized into a meaningful story.
21. An organized general knowledge structure that is stored in long-term memory is a/an ________.
22. The process of practicing or rehearsing material over and above what is needed to learn it is called _______________.
23. When interfering activities follow the material to be learned, the interference is called _______________.

**Chapter 7 Multiple Choice Practice Test**

1. Which of the following represents the correct sequence of events for the process of memory?
   a. encoding-retrieving-storing
   b. storing-retrieving-encoding
   c. retrieving-storing-encoding
   d. encoding-storing-retrieving
2. The practical problem with sensory memory is that
   a. the capacity is limited
   b. the duration is limited
   c. so much information is not easily categorized
   d. both capacity and duration are limited
3. Which type of memory is also referred to as working memory?
   a. sensory memory
   b. short-term memory
   c. long-term memory
   d. metamemory
4. Repeating a phone number over and over while waiting to use a pay phone is an example of
   a. chunking
   b. elaboration
   c. metamemory
   d. maintenance rehearsal
5. When information is stored or represented by sound, it is in our _________ memory.
   a. short-term
   b. long-term
   c. sensory
   d. metamemory
6. In regard to long-term memory, Elizabeth and Geoffrey Loftus believe that
   a. all information in long-term memory can be retrieved at any time
   b. long term memories are largely reconstructions from the original information
   c. people don't remember anything that happened before age three
   d. memory failure involves permanent forgetting, not just retrieval failure
7. To get information into long-term memory, one should use
   a. attention
   b. maintenance rehearsal
   c. elaborative rehearsal
   d. repetition
8. Your memory of how to swim is recorded in
   a. episodic memory
   b. metamemory
   c. semantic memory
   d. procedural memory
9. One significant change in the way we think about memory today as opposed to 30 years ago is that we now see memory as
   a. processing much less information than we once believed
   b. a much more active processor of information
   c. being much less likely to fail us
   d. a remarkably accurate recorder of everyday experiences
10. What type of memory is employed when you are computing the answer to a multiplication problem in your head, without the use of pencil and paper?
    a. sensory memory and long-term memory
    b. sensory memory, short-term memory, and long term memory
    c. short-term memory and long-term memory
    d. long-term memory, metamemory, and short-term memory

11. The capacity of short-term memory can be increased through
  a. chunking
  b. attention
  c. rehearsal
  d. selective encoding
12. A person's memory of their first kiss would be stored in ________ memory.
  a. semantic
  b. episodic
  c. metamemory
  d. procedural
13. Which of the following is NOT a correct match?
  a. fill-in test item - recall
  b. multiple choice test item - recognition
  c. essay test item - recognition
  d. true-false test item - recognition
14. All of the following factors may have some influence on our ability to retrieve information from our memory. Which of these is probably the MOST important, or influential?
  a. where in memory the information is stored (i.e. short-term, sensory, or long-term)
  b. the relationship between how (or if) it was encoded and how we are searching for it
  c. the manner in which the information is stored in memory (i.e. the code used: acoustic, semantic, etc.)
  d. the extent to which we are able to overcome the inhibitory influence of repression
15. According to the encoding specificity principle, the best place to study for an exam in this course is
  a. at home where you are in familiar surroundings
  b. in the library where it is quiet
  c. at a friend's house where you can get help
  d. in the classroom where the test will be administered
16. Words like angel, redwood, and vehicle are easier to retrieve than words like political, religious, and betrayal because
  a. they are shorter words
  b. they are more meaningful words
  c. they lend themselves better to the use of mental images
  d. they don't require elaborative rehearsal techniques to transfer to long-term memory
17. Geraldine reported that she wasn't nervous on her first night to teach a creative writing class even though she had never taught before. She explained that she knew what a teacher should do because she had taken so many classes herself. Her knowledge of appropriate behavior for a teacher can best be explained by
  a. a schema
  b. rote practice
  c. elaborative rehearsal
  d. mnemonics
18. If you prepare for your next psychology exam by studying for several short periods separated by rest periods or breaks, you are using
  a. massed practice
  b. distributed practice
  c. cramming
  d. elaborative rehearsal
19. Research indicates that in order to protect recently learned information from interference, the best thing to do right after studying would be
  a. get something to eat
  b. reread your notes
  c. go to sleep
  d. watch TV or listen to the radio

20. Which of the following factors influences the impact of interference on learning?
    a. the nature of the material being learned
    b. the organization and meaningfulness of the information learned
    c. the type of activity that follows studying
    d. all of the above

**Check Your Knowledge of the Learning Objectives**

The following questions are examples of what you should know when you have finished studying this chapter. Write the answers to these questions. Use your book to verify the answers. Page references are provided.

1. Discuss sensory memory, including its capacity and duration. p. 231

2. Describe how material is put into short-term memory and how long it is kept there. p. 232-235

3. Explain how much information is held in short-term memory and how chunking effects that amount. p. 235-236

4. What is the importance of acoustic coding in short-term memory? p. 236

5. How permanent is long-term memory? p. 238

6 Explain how elaborative rehearsal encodes information into long-term memory. p. 239

7. Describe three possible types of long term memory. p. 239-240

8. Explain how measures of recall, recognition, and relearning affect assessment of retrieval. p. 240-244

9. Explain implicit tests of retention and what they tell us about long-term memory. p. 242-244

10. Describe how the situation in which encoding is done affects retrieval. p. 245-246

11. Define meaningfulness and explain how it relates to retrieval. p. 246

12. Define mnemonic devices and describe four examples. p. 247-250

13. Define schemas and explain how they affect retrieval. p. 250

14. Define overlearning, massed practice, and distributed practice and explain how they affect retrieval. p. 251-252

15. Distinguish between retroactive and proactive interference and explain how each affects retrieval. p. 254-255

## Dr. G's Best Study Tips #7

**Using Mnemonic Strategies as Study Methods**

Some of the concepts presented in Chapter 7 can be directly applied to study methods. For example, the serial position effect tells us that when we study a series, the natural tendency is that the items at the beginning and end of the series will be easiest to learn. Our application should be to study the information in the middle of a chapter or in the middle of our notes a little more thoroughly to offset the serial position effect.

The concepts of state-dependent and context-dependent recall have some application to studying. State-dependent recall tells us that for optimum recall, we should take the test in the same state we were in when we learned the material. Context-dependent recall tells us that the setting actually serves as a cue. I sometimes suggest that my students return to their classroom in the afternoons when they are usually empty, and spend time studying psychology there. After all, it is the context in which they will take their exams.

We can also use other ideas such as the concept of chunking. Many mnemonic strategies employ this technique to create greater memory capacity. For instance, you may have learned this mnemonic to help you remember the order of operations in algebra: "Please excuse my dear Aunt Sally," or PEMDAS. This chunk forms a cue to help us remember to solve algebraic equations by attending to P = parenthesis, E = exponents, M = multiply, D = divide, A = add, and S = subtract in that order. Many of these mnemonics already exist, FACE tells us the notes on the spaces of the music scale and HOMES reminds us of the names of the great lakes, Huron, Ontario, Michigan, Erie, and Superior.

You may use other mnemonics that you have learned, but you can also create your own. If the letters do not conveniently spell a word, such as HOMES or FACE, simply form a chunk by creating a sentence that uses words beginning with the appropriate letters. For example, rehearsal, elaboration, and chunking are ways of extending the length of time that information stays in short-term memory. The first letters of these words are r, e, and c. You might put these into a sentence such as "Rats eat cheese."

You may remember that meaningfulness is an important aspect of long-term memory. Since words and sentences have meaning to us, they are easily stored and retrieved, making great cues. Mnemonic devices work even better when you create your own because you are processing the information while making the mnemonic. Try creating your own using some information from your text.

If you are intrigued by the idea of improving your memory and would like to know more, I recommend a small paperback book by Harry Lorraine and Jerry Lucas called, The Memory Book. I am confident that you can find other excellent sources of information on memory in the library.

# CHAPTER 8—HIGHER COGNITIVE PROCESSES

**Learning Objectives**

1. List three components of a problem and explain how to distinguish problems that are well-defined or ill-defined.
2. Describe problem representation.
3. Discuss how algorithmic and heuristic strategies are used to solve problems.
4. Define mental set and explain how it affects problem-solving.
5. Define functional fixedness and describe its effects on problem-solving.
6. Contrast divergent thinking and convergent thinking.
7. List the defining characteristics of language.
8. Describe the landmark events that occur during language acquisition.
9. Explain the learning-oriented and biology-oriented theories of language acquisition.
10. Understand the operational definition of intelligence.
11. Define psychological test.
12. Understand test-retest reliability.
13. Differentiate between concurrent validity, predictive validity, and content validity.
14. Define norms and understand their use in psychological testing.
15. Describe the 1986 revision of the Stanford-Binet Intelligence Test.
16. Describe the Wechsler Intelligence Scales.
17. Discuss the advantages and disadvantages of group and individual intelligence tests.
18. Describe Terman's study of gifted individuals, including selection, problems, and results.
19. List six ways in which individuals can be considered to be gifted.
20. Define mental retardation.
21. Discuss the causes, treatment, and prevention of mental retardation.
22. Describe Down's syndrome and phenylketonuria.

**Chapter 8 Outline**

I. Preview
   A. Cognitions include one's ideas, beliefs, thoughts, and images.
   B. Cognitive processes are mental activities that involve formation, manipulation, and the use of cognitions.
   C. Three complex cognitive processes include problem solving, language use, and intelligence.

II. Problem Solving
   A. A problem exists when there is a discrepancy between one's present state and one's perceived goal state, and there is no clear way of getting from one to the other.
   B. A problem-solving situation has three components:
      1. The initial state is the situation as it exists or is perceived to exist.
      2. The goal state is the situation as the problem solver would like it to be.
      3. Possible routes or strategies are ways of getting from the initial state to the goal state.
   C. Well-defined problems are those in which both the initial state and the goal state are clearly defined.
      1. It is easy to know when the goal has been reached.
      2. Reaching the goal may require undertaking a new or different way of doing things.
   D. Most everyday problems tend to be ill-defined.
      1. The initial state and goal state are not known.
      2. These problems involve many variables that are difficult to define or control.
   E. Problem representation
      1. The problem must first be represented in our minds in order to make it meaningful.
      2. Problem representation often involves sorting out what matters and what doesn't.
      3. Problem representation is often the stumbling block to problem solution.
         a. Represent the probem in a variety of ways.
         b. Eliminate unessential information.
         c. Relate the problem to other problems of a similar type that you have solved before.
   F. Problem-solving strategies
      1. A strategy is a systematic plan for generating possible solutions that can be tested to see if they are correct.

a. Strategies permit the learner or problem solver to exercise some degree of control over the task at hand.
b. Strategies allow learners to choose the skills and knowledge that they will bring to bear on any particular problem at any time.

2. An algorithm is a problem-solving strategy that guarantees that one will eventually arrive at a solution if the strategy is correctly applied.
   a. Algorithms are sometimes called a generate-test strategy.
   b. One generates hypotheses about potential solutions and then tests each one in turn.
   c. In concept formation, each attribute of a concept is examined and tested separately for its relevance to the concept's definition.
   d. Using an algorithm guarantees a solution but can be extremely time-consuming.
3. A heuristic strategy is a more economical technique for generating possible solutions to a problem.
   a. There is no guarantee of success.
   b. Heuristic strategies are less time-consuming.

G. Barriers to Effective Problem Solving
1. A mental set is a tendency to perceive or respond to something in a given (set) way.
   a. Expectations or set tendencies about problem solving may interfere with finding the problem's solution.
   b. Assumptions may also interfere.
2. Functional fixedness is an inability to discover an appropriate new use for an object because of experience using the object in some other function.
   a. The problem solver may fail to see the solution because he or she has fixed some function to an object that would be useful in the solution if it were used in a new and different way.
   b. Some subtle changes in the way in which materials are presented have an effect on solving problems.

H. Overcoming barriers with creative problem solving.
1. Divergent thinking involves starting with one idea and generating from it a large number of alternative possibilities.
2. Convergent thinking takes many different ideas and tries to focus and reduce them to just one possible solution.
3. Generally, divergent thinking is more useful than convergent thinking, in creative problem solving.

III. Language

A. Language is defined as a large collection of arbitrary symbols that have significance for a language-using community and that follow certain rules of combination.
1. Symbols are words that are used as arbitrary labels assigned to concepts.
2. Language is a social enterprise.
3. Symbols need to have significance for a language-using community.
4. Language is structured, or rule-governed.
5. Language use is a creative, generative process.
6. Language and speech are not synonymous terms.

B. Language acquisition is one of the most significant achievements of childhood.
1. The acquisition of language is the process of developing each facet of language.
   a. Infants create speech sounds spontaneously.
   b. At about 6 months, random cries are replaced by babblings.
   c. Comprehension or understanding comes before production.
   d. The first use of vocalization as language is called holophrasic speech.
   e. At about 2 years, we can note the appearance of two-word utterances.
   f. Following the two-word-utterance stage there is a period that is typified by telegraphic speech, comprised of nouns, verbs, and adjectives.
   g. At about age 5, children demonstrate both the understanding and the production of virtually every type of acceptable sentence structure in language.
2. Theories of acquisition suggest that language development is a function of learning, while other theories suggest a biological basis.
   a. Acquisition involves a variety of learning.
   b. The learning theory has some problems.

3. Overregularization is the continued application of an acquired language rule in a situation where it is not appropriate.
   a. Most adults are able to teach language even though they do not know the rules for its use.

IV. Intelligence
   A. Intelligence can be defined as the capacity to understand the world and the resourcefulness to cope with its challenges.
      1. There are some ambiguities in this definition.
      2. Intelligence can be defined operationally as "that which intelligence tests measure."
   B. The nature of psychological tests
      1. A working definition of a psychological test is that it is an objective, standardized measure of a sample of behavior.
         a. A psychological test measures behavior.
         b. A psychological test can only measure a sample of behavior.
            i. There is no way to assess feelings directly.
            ii. One must make inferences based on a sample of behavior.
         c. If a psychological test is to have value, its administration must be standardized and its scoring must be objective.
            i. Everyone taking a test should take it under the same standard conditions, follow the same instructions, and have the same time limits.
            ii. Objective test scoring refers to the evaluation of the responses that exam-takers make to test items.
   C. A test must meet several criteria to be a good test.
      1. Reliability refers to consistency or dependability.
         a. Test-retest reliability is a check of a test's consistency found by correlating the results of a test taken by the same group of subjects at two different times.
         b. Reliability can also be tested by devising alternate forms of the test, administering both forms to the same subjects, and comparing the scores statistically.
      2. In testing, validity is the extent to which a test measures what it claims to be measuring.
         a. Predictive validity is the extent to which a test can be used to predict future behaviors.
         b. Concurrent validity is the extent to which the scores on a test are correlated with the scores on other tests claiming to measure the same characteristic.
         c. Content validity is the extent to which a test provides an adequate and fair sample of the behaviors being measured.
            i. It should measure what it claims to measure.
            ii. Content validity is usually determined by the judgment of content area experts.
      3. Norms consist of results of a test taken by a large group of subjects whose scores can be used to make comparisons or give meaning to new scores.
   D. Tests of Intelligence
      1. The Stanford-Binet Intelligence Scale was initially the result of the work of Alfred Binet (1857-1911).
      2. Binet was the leading psychologist in France at the turn of the century.
         a. Binet set out to construct a test to assess the intelligence of children in the Paris school system who seemed unable to profit from the education offered them.
      3. The first test appeared in 1905 and was revised in 1908.
      4. Lewis Terman, at Stanford, translated it into English and supervised a revision of the test in 1916.
         a. The test has undergone a number of revisions.
         b. The most recent revision was published in 1986.
      5. The test follows what its authors call a three-level hierarchical model of cognitive abilities.
         a. The current edition yields an overall test score that reflects *g*, or general intellectual ability; underlying the g-factor are three second-level factors.
            i. *Crystallized abilities* represent those skills required for acquiring and using information about verbal and quantitative concepts to solve problems.
            ii. *Fluid-analytic abilities* are typified by skills needed to solve problems that involve figural or nonverbal types of information.

    iii. *Short-term memory*, the third factor, which tests one's ability to hold information in memory for relatively short periods of time.
  b. Consult Figure 8.8 in the text for a review of the 15 subtests of the Stanford-Binet.
6. In earlier versions of the Stanford-Binet test, the examiner's job was to determine the subject's mental age (or *MA*), the age level at which the subject was functioning in terms of intellectual abilities.
7. David Wechsler published his first intelligence scale in 1939 for use with adult populations and to reduce the heavy reliance on verbal skills found in the old versions of the Stanford-Binet test.
  a. The WAIS-R is for subjects between the ages of 16 and 74.
  b. It is the most commonly used of all tests in clinical practice.
  c. The Wechsler Scale for Children (WISC-R) is for ages 6 to 17.
  d. The Wechsler Preschool and Primary Scale of Intelligence (WPPSI) is for ages 4 to 6 1/2.
  e. The WAIS-R is made up of 11 subtests.
    i. Six subtests define the verbal scale.
    ii. Five subtests define the performance scale.
    iii. Refer to Figure 8.10 in the text for a description of the WAIS-R subtests.
  f. With each of the Wechsler tests, three scores can be computed: Verbal, Performance, and Total (or Full Scale) scores.
  g. Administration consists of giving all 11 subtests.
    i. You alternate between verbal and performance tests.
    ii. Each item on each subtest is scored.
    iii. How a subject's score compares to the scores earned by subjects of the same age in the norm group determines your subject's standard score.
  h. There has been controversy and debate about the use and quality of individually administered intelligence tests.
    i. Such tests may be culturally biased.
    ii. They may measure academic success rather than intelligence.
    iii. Test results can be used as a basis for discrimination.
    iv. A survey of more than 600 experts in psychological testing indicates considerable agreement about the basic value of intelligence tests.
8. Group IQ tests are generally paper-and-pencil tests that can be administered to many individuals at one time.
  a. At the beginning of World War I, a committee was asked to create a group test to assess army recruits.
    i. The Army Alpha Test was developed.
    ii. The Army Beta Test was designed for illiterates who could not read the Alpha Test.
  b. The military continues to be a major publisher and consumer of group intelligence tests.
    i. World War II provided the opportunity for a major revision of the Army Alpha and Beta tests.
    ii. The resultingtest was called the Army General Classification Test (AGCT).
    iii. It consisted of subscores for verbal ability, arithmetic computation, arithmetic reasoning, and spatial relations.
    iv. The AGCT has now been replaced by the Armed Forces Qualification Test (AFQT).
  c. The educational establishment is the other large-scale consumer of group intelligence tests.
    i. Arthur Otis has developed many group IQ tests.
    ii. The Otis-Lennon School Ability Test (OLSAT) is designed for children in kindergarten through high school.
  d. Aptitude tests are used to make predictions about future behaviors.
    i. The SAT (Scholastic Aptitude Test) and ACT (American College Testing Program) are used to predict future academic success in college.
    ii. The PSAT (Preliminary Scholastic Aptitude Test) is for high school juniors for scholarships or SAT practice.

iii. Each type of professional school has its own type of exam.
iv. The Graduate Record Exam (GRE) is like an advanced form of the SAT.

E. The Mentally Gifted
1. There are many ways in which a person can be mentally gifted.
   a. Psychomotor ability includes outstanding abilities in skills that require agility, strength, speed, quickness, and coordination.
   b. Visual and performing arts include talent for arts, music, drama, and writing.
   c. Leadership ability often emerges in even very young children..
   d. Creative or productive thinking includes the ability to generate unique and different solutions to problems.
   e. Specific academic aptitude includes a flair for a particular subject or two.
   f. The intellectually gifted are those with an IQ above 130, less than 3 percent of the population.
2. A lot of information about the mentally gifted comes from a classic longitudinal study begun by L. M. Terman in the early 1920s.
   a. It focused on 1,500 children who scored above 135 on IQ tests.
   b. Terman died in 1956, but the study continues.
   c. The study has drawbacks.
      i. He used only IQ scores as his definition of giftedness.
      ii. There was no control for socioeconomic level or parents' educational level.
   d. What does this study tell us?
      i. It does not support the negative stereotype of bright people.
      ii. Gifted children experienced advantages in virtually everything.
      iii. They received more education; found better, higher-paying jobs; and had more intelligent children.
      iv. Not all their lives were successes, but many were.

F. Mental retardation is a condition indicated by an IQ below 70 that begins during the developmental period and is associated with impairment in adaptive functioning.
1. The AAMD categorizes retardation in 5 categories.
2. These categories are suggested limits.
3. Diagnosis is not made on the basis of IQ alone.
4. The term "developmentally delayed" is coming to replace the narrower term "mentally retarded."
5. Being mentally retarded does not necessarily mean being totally helpless.
6. Standard estimates indicate that approximately 3 percent of the population falls within the IQ range for retardation.

G. The number of causes of retardation exceeds 200.
1. About one-quarter of all cases of retardation reflect a problem that developed before, during, or just after birth.
   a. Between 15 and 20 percent of those referred to as retarded were born prematurely.
   b. Prenatal conditions cause developmental delays.
   c. Some cases stem from difficulties or injuries during the birth process itself.
2. Down's syndrome is a condition with many symptoms, including mental retardation, caused by an extra (47th) chromosome.
3. Fragile X syndrome is another variety of mental retardation with a genetic basis.
   a. It is found primarily in males.
   b. It creates characteristics such as long faces, big ears, and in adults, large testes.
4. Most cases of mental retardation do not have obvious causes.
5. We will probably be more successful in prevention of mental retardation than in treatment.
   a. Special education classes have helped.
   b. Impressive results can be achieved in raising the IQs of some mildly and moderately retarded children.
   c. The emphasis in education is on specific skill building.
6. There is greater hope in the area of prevention.
   a. Phenylketonuria (PKU) can now be prevented with diet.
   b. PKU is a genetically caused disorder that produces mental retardation and that is now detectable and preventable.

**Learning Chapter 8 Vocabulary**

Write the definition for each of the following key terms on the lines provided at the right. Then fold the paper vertically so you can see only the term and try to say the definition. Practice like this until you can say them all correctly.

PROBLEM ______________________

STRATEGY ______________________

ALGORITHM ______________________

HEURISTIC ______________________

MENTAL SET ______________________

FUNCTIONAL FIXEDNESS ______________________

DIVERGENT THINKING ______________________

CONVERGENT THINKING ______________________

LANGUAGE ______________________

OVERREGULARIZATION ______________________

HOLOPHRASTIC SPEECH ______________________

INTELLIGENCE ______________________

PSYCHOLOGICAL TEST ______________________

RELIABILITY ______________________

VALIDITY ______________________

TEST-RETEST RELIABILITY ______________________

PREDICTIVE VALIDITY ______________________

CONCURRENT VALIDITY ______________________

CONTENT VALIDITY ____________________

NORMS ____________________

MENTAL RETARDATION ____________________

DOWN'S SYNDROME ____________________

PHENYLKETONURIA ____________________

**IDIOMS AND DIFFICULT PHRASES**

**two eggs over easy** (p. 265) over easy is a way of cooking eggs. Eggs that are cooked over easy are gently turned over in the skillet so as not to break the yoke.

**problem representation is the stumbling block** (p. 268) a "stumbling block" can be anything that interferes with progress. For example, not having enough money may be the "stumbling block" that prevents you from going to the beach for spring break.

**we can communicate about owls and pussycats in teacups, fourdimensional, timewarped hyperspace, and a beagle that flies his doghouse into battle** (p. 273) The Owl and the Pussycat is a wellknown children's story. Four-dimensional, timewarped hyper-space describes a kind of space travel popular in science fiction. The beagle who flies his doghouse into battle is the popular cartoon character, Snoopy, from the Peanuts cartoon strip written by Charles Schultz.

**or signing (as in American Sign Language)** (p. 274) American Sign Language is a system of hand signs and signals used by deaf persons to communicate.

**gooing, cooing, babbling** (p. 275) These words describe the sounds babies make before they begin talking.

**Yuck, not milk again** (p. 275) The word yuck is used in informal speech to express strong dislike.

**Most adults (by far)** (p. 277) The phrase '"by far" is used to express degree. In this sentence, the term tells us that "most adults" is a very large majority of the adult population.

**In many circles** (p. 292) This phrase simply means in many different areas. The word circles is often used to describe in this context. The friends you associate with might be described as your circle of friends. Your professor works in academic circles, a doctor in medical circles...

**Matching**

Match the following key terms from your text with the appropriate definition.

| | | | |
|---|---|---|---|
| ______ | 1. overregularization | ______ | 2. holophrastic speech |
| ______ | 3. psycholinguistics | ______ | 4. language |
| ______ | 5. mental retardation | ______ | 6. Down's syndrome |
| ______ | 7. phenylketonuria | ______ | 8. babbling |
| ______ | 9. convergent thinking | ______ | 10. problem |
| ______ | 11. mental set | ______ | 12. divergent thinking |
| ______ | 13. strategy | ______ | 14. functional fixedness |
| ______ | 15. test-retest reliability | ______ | 16. heuristic |
| ______ | 17. reliability | ______ | 18. intelligence |
| ______ | 19. psychological test | ______ | 20. validity |
| ______ | 21. norms | ______ | 22. content validity |
| ______ | 23. predictive validity | ______ | 24. concurrent validity |
| ______ | 25. algorithm | | |

a. A situation in which there is a discrepancy between one's current state and one's desired, or goal state, with no clear way of getting from one to the other.
b. In problem solving, a systematic plan for generating possible solutions that can be tested to see if they are correct.
c. A problem-solving strategy in which all possible solutions are generated and tested and an acceptable solution is guaranteed.
d. A problem-solving strategy in which hypotheses about problem solutions are generated and tested in a time-saving and systematic way that does not guarantee an acceptable solution.
e. A predisposed (set) way to perceive something; an expectation.
f. The phenomenon in which one is unable to see a new use or function for an object because of experience using the object in some other function.
g. The creation of many ideas or potential problem solutions from one idea.
h. The reduction or focusing of many different ideas into one possible problem solution.
i. A large collection of arbitrary symbols that have significance for a language-using community, and that follow certain rules of combination.
j. Speech sounds produced in rhythmic, repetitive patterns.
k. The use of one word to communicate a number of different meanings.
l. The excessive application of an acquired language rule (e.g. ,for forming plurals or past tense) in a situation where it is not appropriate.
m. The capacity to understand the world and the resourcefulness to cope with its challenges; that which an intelligence test measures.
n. An objective, standardized measure of a sample of behavior.
o. Consistency or dependability; in testing, consistency of test scores.
p. A check of a test's consistency determined by correlating the results of a test taken by the same subjects at two different times.
q. In testing, the extent to which a test measures what it claims to be measuring.
r. The extent to which a test can be used to predict future behaviors.
s. The extent to which the scores on a test are correlated with other assessments made at about the same time.
t The extent to which a test provides an adequate and fair sample of the behaviors being measured.
u. Results of a test taken by a large group of subjects whose scores can be used to make comparisons or give meaning to new scores.
v. The science that studies the cognitive processes involved in the use and acquisition of language.
w. A condition indicated by an IQ below 70 that began during the developmental period and is associated with impairment in adaptive functioning.
x. A condition of many symptoms, including mental retardation, caused by an extra (47th) chromosome.
y. A genetically caused disorder that produces mental retardation and that is now detectable and preventable.

**True-False Practice Test**

___ 1. Effective problem-solving requires perceiving, learning, and remembering.
___ 2. Psychologists are more likely to study ill-defined problems than well-defined ones.
___ 3. Mental sets always hinder problem-solving.
___ 4. Creativity and intelligence appear to be highly correlated.
___ 4. Divergent and convergent thinking are just two different names for the same cognitive process.
___ 6. The negative effects of mental set and functional fixedness can present a problem in the preparation stage of creative problem-solving.
___ 7. In general, the American education system seems to be succeeding at teaching creative problem solving and higher-level thinking skills.
___ 8. Research indicates that little is gained by simply teaching students about problem solving.
___ 9. Problem solving is generally enhanced if the learners have a general knowledge base.
___ 10. A "knowledge-free" approach to problem solving indicates that no particular expertise is required on the part of the student.
___ 11. Speech and language are synonymous terms.
___ 12. The question of how humans acquire language remains basically unanswered.
___ 13. Babies of various nationalities have their own way of babbling, according to the phonetic structure of the language their parents speak.
___ 14. In vocabulary acquisition, comprehension precedes production.
___ 15. Virtually all babies babble, even those with hearing problems.
___ 16. Most babies speak in two-word phrases by age one.
___ 17. Defining intelligence as "that which intelligence tests measure" exemplifies an operational definition.
___ 18. A psychological test should be a standardized objective test.
___ 19. Predictive validity is one characteristic of a good psychological test that is not established by correlation.
___ 20. The usefulness of a psychological test often depends on the adequacy of the norms used to make comparisons of scores.
___ 21. A test can be reliable without being valid, but it cannot be valid without being reliable.
___ 22. Lewis Terman wrote the first intelligence test.
___ 23. The Stanford-Binet intelligence test yields a measure similar to Spearman's g-factor.
___ 24. The average standard age score on the Stanford-Binet test always equals 100.
___ 25. Unlike the Stanford-Binet, Wechsler's first intelligence test was designed primarily for adults.
___ 26. Surveys indicate that psychologists agree that intelligence tests are valuable in spite of the controversies surrounding them.
___ 27. The biggest advantage of individual intelligence tests is that they are economical and save time.
___ 28. A person who has outstanding leadership skills can be considered gifted.
___ 29. A talented gymnast would NOT be considered a gifted individual.
___ 30. Terman's study of gifted individuals destroyed most of the stereotypes about bright children.
___ 31. The IQ cutoff score for mental retardation is 70.

**Fill-in Practice Test**

1. Visualizing a problem situation in order to solve the problem is an example of ________________.
2. A systematic plan for generating possible problem solutions that can be tested is called a/an ____________.
3. A/an _________ is a problem-solving strategy that guarantees that you will eventually arrive at a solution if the strategy is correctly applied.
4. An informal, rule-of-thumb method of generating and testing problem solutions is called a/an ____________.
5. The tendency to perceive or respond to something in a specific way is called _________ _____.
6. _____________ thinking involves starting with one idea and generating from it a number of alternative possibilities.

7. ______________ thinking involves taking many different ideas and reducing them to just one possible solution.
8. The production of phonemes in rhythmic, repetitive patterns is called ____________.
9. The use of just one word to communicate a range of intentions and meanings is referred to as ________________ speech.
10. ________________________ is the continued application of an acquired language rule in situations where it is not appropriate.
11. A _________________ ________ is an objective, standardized measure of a sample of behavior.
12. Consistency or dependability in a psychological test is referred to as _______________.
13. In __________________ reliability, a test is administered to the same group on two different occasions.
14. The statistical procedure used to establish test reliability is ________________.
15. The extent to which a test actually measures what it claims to measure is called ______________.
16. If a psychological test is highly correlated with other tests or measures of the same characteristic, it is said to have _______________ validity.
17. The extent to which a test adequately samples the behaviors that it claims to be testing is called ___________ validity.
18. Results of a test taken by a large group of subjects whose scores can be used to make comparisons are called ___________.
19. The author of the first intelligence test was _________ _________.
20. In terms of content, a major difference between the Stanford-Binet test and the WAIS is that the WAIS relied less on __________ skills.
21. The most commonly used of all psychological tests is the ____________.
22. The first group intelligence test was the ________ _________.
23. Average IQ for any age is ____________.
24. People who use the term "mentally gifted" are most likely referring to people who are gifted ______________________.
25. To be considered intellectually gifted, one would have to score above ____________ on a standardized IQ test.
26. The psychologist who contributed most to our knowledge of gifted individuals was ___________________.
27. The individuals in Terman's study are sometimes referred to as _______________.
28. The term mentally retarded is being replaced with the term __________________ ___________.
29. A genetic cause of mental retardation characterized by the presence of a 47th chromosome is _____________ _________________.
30. PKU is the abbreviation for a disorder called ______________________ which can cause mental retardation if untreated.

**Chapter 8 Multiple Choice Practice Test**

1. Trying to choose a college major would be an example of a/an
   a. unsolvable problem
   b. ill-defined problem
   c. well-defined problem
   d. common problem
2. The inability to discover an appropriate new use for an object because of experience using the object in some other way defines
   a. mental set
   b. tunnel vision
   c. functional fixedness
   d. heuristic thinking

3. A motorist returning from the grocery store is stuck on an icy patch of roadway. The car will not move in any direction, as the tires spin freely on the ice. A passenger takes a bag of "kitty litter" from a grocery sack and spreads it on the ice under the tires, thus freeing the car. The driver is impressed, and claims that he never would have thought of doing that, thus demonstrating
   a. poor problem representation
   b. functional fixedness
   c. the availability heuristic
   d. divergent thinking
4. The fictional detective, Sherlock Holmes, was well-known for his ability to observe many different clues and use them to solve a difficult mystery. His ability demonstrates
   a. divergent thinking
   b. convergent thinking
   c. availability heuristic
   d. means-end analysis
5. An old saying goes, "You can't see the forest for the trees." If a person could put all the trees together to see the forest, he would be demonstrating
   a. mental set
   b. convergent thinking
   c. divergent thinking
   d. means-end analysis
6. Attempting to discover all the uses for a paper towel is an example of
   a. divergent thinking
   b. convergent thinking
   c. creativity
   d. availability heuristic
7. Working a crossword puzzle would be an example of a/an
   a. unsolvable problem
   b. ill-defined problem
   c. well-defined problem
   d. common problem
8. Vu has a problem. He is unemployed. He knows that his goal is to get a job. However, he has no idea how to begin finding employment. We might say that his problem-solving skills have broken down at the ________ stage.
   a. initial
   b. goal
   c. routes or strategies
   d. solutions
9. A psychological test can measure
   a. behavior
   b. aptitudes
   c. feelings
   d. all of the above
10. If a test is administered in such a way that all who take the test get the same instructions, the same time limits, and virtually the same testing conditions, we say that the test is
    a. objective
    b. standardized
    c. valid
    d. reliable
11. To qualify as a good psychological test, an instrument should have
    a. reliability
    b. validity
    c. adequate norms
    d. all of the above

12. The foreman of the Peter Piper Pickle Packing Plant wants to test new trainees to determine which ones will become the best pickle packers. If the company psychologist develops a test that will accurately measure this, we could say the test has
   a. validity generalizability
   b. predictive validity
   c. test-retest reliability
   d. adequate norms

13. Your psychology teacher brings in a pop quiz and as you begin taking the test, you notice that the questions are about history rather than psychology. For this class, the test lacks
   a. test-retest reliability
   b. split-half reliability
   c. concurrent validity
   d. content validity

14. A psychologist working in a rehabilitation center needs to know the IQ of a single adult client. The best test to use would be the
   a. WAIS-R
   b. AFQT
   c. Stanford-Binet
   d. OLSAT

15. Juanita is a junior in high school. She would like to prepare as much as possible for the college entrance exams she must take next year. The best test for her to take is the
   a. GRE
   b. ACT
   c. WPPSI
   d. PSAT

16. A significant difference between aptitude tests and intelligence tests is the
   a. content of the tests
   b. purpose for which each is used
   c. standardization and objectivity of the tests
   d. norms

17. Which of the following is NOT one of the problems associated with Lewis Terman's research on gifted individuals?
   a. failing to control for factors such as socioeconomic level or parent's education level
   b. using too narrow a definition for giftedness
   c. failing to include black children
   d. excluding children who had psychological problems

18. According to the AAMD, the definition of mental retardation should include
   a. only individuals whose IQ is lower than 70
   b. some measure of a person's ability to adapt to the environment
   c. only a deficiency in skills measured by IQ tests
   d. the 5 percent of the population with the lowest IQ scores

19. Perhaps the greatest hope in dealing with mental retardation is in the area of
   a. increasing the IQ of the profoundly retarded
   b. curing Down's syndrome
   c. preventing retardation by learning more about the prenatal environment
   d. redefining retardation so that fewer individuals are labeled

20. PKU is treated by
   a. drugs
   b. radiation
   c. diet
   d. physical therapy

21. Cognitive processes rely on
    a. perception
    b. learning
    c. memory
    d. all of the above

22. A baby's first words are usually produced at about age
    a. six months
    b. nine months
    c. twelve months
    d. eighteen months

23. One fact that fails to support the learning theory explanation of language is that
    a. parents correct content rather than form
    b. parents do not reinforce language learning
    c. parents do not model correct language usage
    d. all of the above

24. Intellectually gifted individuals make up only about _____ percent of the population.
    a. 3
    b. 5
    c. 10
    d. 15

**Check Your Knowledge of the Learning Objectives**

The following questions are examples of what you should know when you have finished studying this chapter. Write the answers to these questions. Use your book to verify the answers. Page references are provided.

1. List three components of a problem and explain how to distinguish problems that are well-defined or ill-defined. p. 265

______________________________________________
______________________________________________
______________________________________________
______________________________________________
______________________________________________
______________________________________________

2. Describe problem representation. p. 266-268

______________________________________________
______________________________________________
______________________________________________
______________________________________________

3. Discuss how algorithmic and heuristic strategies are used to solve problems. p. 268-269

______________________________________________
______________________________________________
______________________________________________
______________________________________________
______________________________________________

4. Define mental set and explain how it affects problem-solving. p. 270

______________________________________________
______________________________________________
______________________________________________

5. Define functional fixedness and describe its effects on problem solving. p. 270

______________________________________________
______________________________________________

6. Contrast divergent thinking and convergent thinking. p. 271

______________________________________________
______________________________________________
______________________________________________
______________________________________________

7. List the defining characteristics of language. p. 272-274

8. Describe the landmark events that occur during language acquisition. p .275-276

9. Explain the learning-oriented and biology-oriented theories of language acquisition. p. 276-278

10. What is the operational definition of intelligence? p. 278

11. Define psychological test. p. 279

12. Explain test-retest reliability. p. 280

13. Differentiate between concurrent validity, predictive validity, and content validity. p. 281

14. Define norms and explain their use in psychological testing. p. 281

15. Describe the 1986 revision of the Stanford-Binet Intelligence Test. p. 282

16. Describe the Wechsler Intelligence Scales. p. 284-286

17. Discuss the advantages and disadvantages of group and individual intelligence tests. p. 286-288

18. Describe Terman's study of gifted individuals, including selection, problems, and results. p. 289

19. List six ways in which individuals can be considered to be gifted. p. 288-289

20. Define mental retardation. p. 292

21. Discuss the causes, treatment, and prevention of mental retardation. p .293-294

22. Describe Down's syndrome and phenylketonuria. p. 294

## Dr. G's Best Study Tips #8

**Getting Along With Your Professor**

Although your grade may not depend on it, you may enjoy your class more and learn more if you create a positive relationship with the instructor. Research on adult thinking indicates that a college education is a very influential factor in cognitive development and that interacting with professors is one of the key influences. Here are some do's and don'ts that will help you get along and create a positive impression.

**Do's:**

1. Learn the instructor's name and appropriate title.
2. Attend every class and <u>be on time</u>.
3. Make an appointment to visit your instructor during office hours. Express an interest in the course and in your grades. Learn about the professor's interests.
4. Prepare for class by reading assignments ahead so that you can answer and ask informed questions.
5. Sit near the front of the room or down the center aisles.
6. Inform the instructor of any special problems or needs you may have. For example, if you are epileptic or have hearing or vision problems, the instructor should be informed.

**Don'ts:**

1. Don't do anything that will call negative attention to yourself, such as talking at inappropriate times or going late to class repeatedly.
2. If you miss class, NEVER ask, "Did we do anything in class today?"
3. Do not confess to the instructor that you have not read the assignments or prepared for class and do not offer excuses.
4. Do not miss an exam unless you are absolutely too ill to walk into the room, and in that event, try to let the instructor know ahead of time that you cannot be there.
5. Don't be afraid to approach your instructor with concerns about class — most of us are human.

# CHAPTER 9—MOTIVATION AND EMOTION

**Learning Objectives**

1. Discuss how instinct, drive, and incentive have been used to explain motivated behaviors.
2. Discuss cognitive dissonance theory.
3. Explain how the concept of balance or equilibrium can be used to explain motivated behaviors.
4. Describe how homeostasis relates to temperature regulation as a physiologically-based drive.
5. List the factors that may influence thirst.
6. Describe the ways in which the sex drive is a unique physiologically-based drive.
7. Discuss the internal and external factors that influence the drive to eat.
8. Discuss achievement motivation and explain how it is measured.
9. Discuss the needs for power and affiliation.
10. List four components that define emotional experience.
11. Name four theories of emotion and briefly describe each.
12. Describe the activities of the sympathetic division of the autonomic nervous system during states of emotionality.
13. Describe the various brain centers that are involved in emotionality.
14. Discuss the relationship between facial expressions and emotion.
15. Define homosexuality and discuss its possible causes.
16. Describe five sexually transmitted diseases.

**Chapter 9 Outline**

I. Preview
  A. Motivation can be explained in terms of physiologically-based drives, which are related to survival, and psychologically-based motives, which are learned and social in nature.
  B. Motivation is an important concept that affects virtually everything we do.

II. Approaches to Motivation
  A. An assumption about motivation is that it is made up of two subprocesses.
    1. Arousal is the activation of behavior and/or mental processes.
    2. It also provides direction or focus to one's behavior.
    3. Motivation is defined as the process that arouses, directs, and maintains behavior.
  B. In the early days of psychology, behaviors were often explained in terms of innate instincts.
    1. Instincts are unlearned, complex patterns of behavior that occur in the presence of certain stimuli.
    2. William McDougall (1908) suggested that human behaviors are motivated by 11 basic instincts.
      a. His list kept growing, as different behaviors required new explanations.
      b. This approach merely described or relabeled behaviors and did not explain them.
  C. An alternative explanation utilized needs and drives.
    1. Clark Hull defined a need as a shortage or lack of some biological essential required for survival.
    2. A drive is a state of tension, arousal, or activation.
    3. There are several complications with this approach.
      a. The relationship between the strength of a need and the strength of the resulting drive is not straightforward.
      b. To claim that drives arise only from needs that arise from biological deprivations seems unduly restrictive.
      c. This explanation does not account for behaviors that organisms engage in even after all their biological needs are met.
    4. Abraham Maslow believed that needs that ultimately motivate human action are limited in number and are hierarchically arranged.
      a. This is a stage theory.
      b. Maslow's arrangement of needs conforms to common sense.
      c. There is a problem with the idea that one can assign ranks to needs and put them in a neat order.
      d. Because of its intuitive appeal, Maslow's theory remains in favor both within and outside of psychology.

D. An approach based on incentives focuses on external stimuli as motivating agents or incentives.
   1. Incentives are external events that act to pull our behavior.
   2. This idea is similar to the principles of operant conditioning in the sense that we are motivated to do whatever leads to reinforcement and not to do whatever leads to punishment.

E. The basic idea of approaches based on balance or equilibrium is that we are motivated to maintain a state of balance.
   1. Homeostasis is a state of balance or equilibrium.
      a. When applied to physiological processes, this means that there is a set point and when this is upset we become motivated to return to it.
      b. This idea was developed by Walter Cannon (1932).
   2. Arousal theories of motivation claim that there is an optimal level of arousal that organisms are motivated to maintain.
      a. This view suggests that for any activity or situation, there is a best, most efficient level of arousal.
      b. Optimum levels of arousal vary with the nature or difficulty of the task.
      c. Optimum levels may vary considerably from individual to individual.
   3. The cognitive dissonance view proposes that we are motivated to maintain a state of balance among our ideas or beliefs as well as our physiological processes (called consonance).
      a. This approach is associated with Leon Festinger.
      b. Cognitive dissonance is a state of tension or discomfort that exists when we hold inconsistent cognitions.
      c. Dissonance leads to motivated behavior.

III. Physiologically-Based Drives

A. Whenever anything happens to elevate or depress our body temperature above or below its homeostatic level, we become motivated.
   1. Two centers in the hypothalamus in the brain act together as a thermostat.
   2. When automatic, physiological reactions fail, you may be motivated to take some voluntary action on your own.

B. We are motivated to drink by several cues.
   1. Internal, physiological cues are complex.
      a. About two-thirds of the fluid in our bodies is contained within our bodies' cells (intracellular).
      b. One-third is held in the spaces between cells (extracellular).
      c. Intercellular loss of fluid is monitored by regions of the hypothalamus.
      d. Extracellular fluid loss is monitored by the kidneys.
   2. External, psychological cues may also influence drinking behavior.

C. There are many factors that motivate a person to feel hungry and eat.
   1. Internal, physiological cues originate in the hypothalamus and the liver.
      a. Theories of hunger that focus on the role of the hypothalamus are called dual-center theories because two regions in the hypothalamus regulate food intake.
      b. One center is the eat center; the other is the no-eat center.
      c. The liver monitors levels of blood sugar in the blood.
      d. When blood sugar levels are low, we are stimulated to eat.
      e. We may also respond to levels of fat stored in our bodies.
      f. The concept of set point or homeostasis suggests a person's overall body weight is physiologically regulated.
      g. Research evidence suggests that there are powerful genetic forces at work that determine one's overall body size and fat distribution.
   2. We often respond to external cues that stimulate us to engage in eating behavior.
      a. We respond to the stimulus properties of food.
      b. We may eat from habit rather than need.
      c. We may eat simply because others around us are eating.
      d. Overweight people tend to be less sensitive to internal hunger cues from their bodies and more sensitive to external eating cues from the environment.

D. As a physiologically-based drive, the sex drive is unique in several ways.

1. Survival of the individual does not depend on its satisfaction.
2. Unlike most physiologically-based drives, the sex drive depletes rather than replenishes the body's energy.
3. It is not present at birth.
4. Internal and external influences have different degrees of impact depending on the species involved.
5. The importance of internal, physiological states is much greater in lower species than it is in primates and humans.
6. As the complexity of the organism increases, the role of internal cues becomes less certain and less noticeable.
7. In addition to the internal forces produced by the sex hormones, sex drives can be stimulated by a wide range of environmental stimuli.

E. Homosexuals are individuals who are sexually attracted to and aroused by members of their own sex.
   1. Many combinations of sexual orientation are possible.
   2. Kinsey found that about half of the males who responded to his surveys fell somewhere between the two end points of his seven-point scale of sexual orientation.
   3. Conservative estimates suggest that about 2 percent of American males are exclusively homosexual.
   4. Female homosexuality is about half as prevalent as male homosexuality.
   5. Sexual responsiveness is the same for homosexuals as for heterosexuals.
   6. There is no generally accepted theory of the causes of homosexuality.
      a. It is probably an interaction of genetic, hormonal, and environmental factors.
      b. There are no significant differences in hormone levels between heterosexuals and homosexuals.
      c. LeVay examined the brains of homosexual men, heterosexual men, and heterosexual women (post mortem) and found that an area of the hypothalamus is smaller in homosexual men.
      d. LeVay's study provides the best evidence to date of a biological correlate to homosexuality.
      e. Some psychologists still favor environmental explanations for homosexuality.

F. Sexually transmitted diseases (STDs) are contagious diseases that are transmitted through sexual contact.
   1. Chlamydia is one of the most common of the STDs in North America.
      a. It is a bacterial infection of the genital area.
      b. Symptoms include burning urination in men and women.
      c. Untreated in women, it may lead to pelvic inflammatory disease (PID), which may cause infertility.
      d. Treatment with an antibiotic is usually effective within one week.
   2. Gonorrhea, a bacterial infection of the moist tissue areas around the genitals, is one of the most common of all STDs.
   3. Syphilis is a disease caused by a bacterium.
      a. Untreated, it runs through four known stages.
      b. Untreated, it can lead to death.
      c. Treatment with penicillin or tetracycline is relatively simple.
   4. Genital herpes is a skin disease that affects the genital area, producing small sores and blisters.
      a. It is caused by a virus.
      b. There is no cure.
   5. Acquired immune deficiency syndrome (AIDS) is caused by a virus and is usually transmitted through sexual contact or contaminated needles.
      a. AIDS is caused by a virus called human immunodeficiency virus (HIV).
      b. The HIV directly attacks the body's immune system.
      c. AIDS is not highly contagious; there has to be an exchange of bodily fluids for AIDS to be transmitted.
      d. AIDS is fatal; there is no vaccine to prevent it, and there is no cure.
      e. Totally abstaining from sex (or using condoms), not sharing needles with IV drug users, and donating your own blood prior to surgery minimize the risk of AIDS.

f. AIDS is a psychological problem, too.

IV. Psychologically-Based Motivation
   A. Achievement motivation is defined as the acquired need to meet or exceed some standard of success or excellence in one's behaviors.
      1. Need to achieve, or nAch, was introduced in 1938 by Henry Murray.
      2. Murray developed the thematic apperception test (TAT), a projective test of achievement motivation.
      3. David McClelland found consistent differences between those with a high need for achievement and those without it.
         a. Achievers generally try tasks in which success is not guaranteed but for which there is a reasonable chance of success.
         b. Subjects with low nAch scores tend to either choose tasks where success is guaranteed or where there is almost no chance of success.
      4. Other researchers have proposed that some people are motivated by a fear of failure.
      5. Need to achieve appears to be learned in early childhood.
         a. These children have been positively encouraged to excel.
         b. They are generally encouraged to work things out independently.
   B. Power motivation consists of a need to be in control.
      1. Individuals with high power motivation need to be admired.
      2. They prefer situations in which they can control the fate of others, usually by manipulating access to information.
   C. Affiliation motivation involves a need to be with others, to work with others, and to form friendships and associations.
      1. This need is usually at odds with a need for power.
      2. Affiliation needs may be at least partly biologically based.
   D. Need for competence means managing to cope effectively, on one's own, with the challenges of everyday living.

V. The Nature of Emotions
   A. In defining emotion, one must look at four interactive components of the emotional reaction: feeling or affect, cognitive reaction, physiological reaction, and behavioral reaction.
      1. There has been considerable debate within psychology concerning the definition of emotion.
      2. A working definition of emotion is that it is a reaction that includes the subjective experience of feeling or affect, a cognitive interpretation, an internal physiological reaction, and some behavioral expression.
   B. Theories of emotion are attempts to state, in a systematic way, just how we become emotional and how the various components of an emotional state interact.
      1. The James-Lange approach suggests that one perceives an emotion-producing stimulus, experiences some appropriate emotion, and then behaves accordingly.
      2. The Cannon-Bard approach proposes that a lower brain center, the thalamus, receives emotion-producing stimulation and immediately sends messages to the cerebral cortex for interpretation and to get lower brain centers to initiate a physiological reaction.
      3. The Schachter-Singer approach claims that how we "feel" at any point in time is a result of a number of interacting factors.
         a. The three factors are:
            i. The stimulus in the environment.
            ii. The person's heightened physiological arousal.
            iii. The person's cognitive appraisal of the situation.
         b. The critical factor is how the person uses his or her cognitive skills to interpret the situation.
      4. The opponent-process approach claims that emotions tend to occur in pairs that are basically opposite in their nature.
      5. Psychologists continue to propose models or theories to account for the nature of an emotional reaction.
         a. Richard Lazarus proposed a new theory stressing the motivational role of emotionality.

    b. Lazarus believes that emotion is a result of specific relationships between people and their environment.

VI. Physiological Aspects of Emotion
  A. The autonomic nervous system is involved in emotional responses and consists of two parts.
    1. The parasympathetic division is actively involved in maintaining a relaxed, calm, and unemotional state.
    2. The sympathetic division is responsible for physiological responses to stress.
      a. The pupils of the eyes dilate.
      b. Heart rate and blood pressure are elevated.
      c. Blood is diverted away from the digestive tract toward the limbs and brain.
      d. Respiration increases.
      e. Perspiration forms.
      f. Blood sugar levels increase.
      g. There is loss of bladder and bowel control.
      h. Blood will clot more readily than usual.
    3. Part of the physiological component of emotion is hormonal.
  B. The brain ultimately controls all emotional responses.
    1. The activity of the autonomic nervous system is closely related to and coordinated by the central nervous system.
    2. The limbic system seems most involved in those emotional responses stimulated by threat, that call for defensive or attacking behaviors.
    3. The hypothalamus is very involved in many motivational states.
    4. The role of the cerebral cortex seems to be largely inhibitory.
      a. It modifies emotional reactions based on the impulses from the lower brain centers.
      b. It controls the cognitive aspect of emotion by interpretation and memory of emotional events.

VII. Outward Expressions of Emotion
  A. Language and facial expression are important ways of displaying one's emotions.
    1. Nonhuman animals have many ritualistic, complex, and instinctive patterns of behavior to communicate many emotional states.
    2. Verbal report can be used by humans to communicate emotion.
    3. Body language can also communicate emotional condition through postural cues and gestures.
  B. A growing body of evidence supports the idea that facial expressions of one's emotional state may be innate responses.
    1. Several studies by Paul Ekman demonstrate a reliable relationship between emotional state and facial expression cross-culturally.
    2. A follow-up study by Ekman has shown that simply moving one's facial muscles into positions associated with emotional expression can actually cause distinctive physiological changes associated with the emotional state.

**Learning Chapter 9 Vocabulary**

Write the definition for each of the following key terms on the lines provided at the right. Then fold the paper vertically so you can see only the term and try to say the definition. Practice this until you can say them all correctly.

MOTIVATION

AROUSAL

INSTINCTS

NEED

DRIVE

INCENTIVES

HOMEOSTASIS

SET POINT

COGNITIVE DISSONANCE

HYPOTHALAMUS

NEED TO ACHIEVE

THEMATIC APPERCEPTION TEST

NEED FOR POWER

NEED FOR AFFILIATION

HOMOSEXUALS

SEXUALLY TRANSMITTED DISEASES

CHLAMYDIA

GONORRHEA ______________________________
______________________________

SYPHILIS ______________________________
______________________________

GENITAL HERPES ______________________________
______________________________

AIDS ______________________________
______________________________

EMOTION ______________________________
______________________________

**IDIOMS AND DIFFICULT PHRASES**

**at least when compared to perceived "benefits"** (p. 308) It is important to note that the word benefits in this sentence refers to an individual's perceptions. There are NO BENEFITS gained from smoking.

**now more openly discussed than it was in the 1940s and 1950s (more "out of the closet")** (p. 317) The phrase "coming out of the closet" describes the process of homosexuals announcing their sexual preference to family and friends.

**gutlevel** (p. 327) Reacting to something at the gut level means reacting based on instinct or intuition. People sometime refer to their intuitive thoughts as "gut feelings."

**butterflies in your stomach** (p. 328) The light, nervous feeling you get in your stomach when you are nervous is sometimes described as feeling like "butterflies in your stomach." Perhaps you experienced this the first time you flew on an airplane or gave a speech or solo performance .

**Matching**

Match the following key terms from your text with the appropriate definition.

| | |
|---|---|
| ______ 1. cognitive dissonance | ______ 2. need for affiliation |
| ______ 3. motivation | ______ 4. syphilis |
| ______ 5. AIDS | ______ 6. arousal |
| ______ 7. bulimia | ______ 8. incentives |
| ______ 9. STDs | ______ 10. thematic apperception test |
| ______ 11. drive | ______ 12. instincts |
| ______ 13. hypothalamus | ______ 14. need to achieve |
| ______ 15. set point | ______ 16. homeostasis |
| ______ 17. need for power | ______ 18. need |
| ______ 19. homosexual | ______ 20. chlamydia |
| ______ 21. emotion | ______ 22. gonorrhea |

a. The process of arousing, maintaining, and directing behavior.
b. One's level of activation or excitement; indicative of a motivational state.
c. Unlearned, complex patterns of behavior that occur in the presence of particular stimuli.
d. A lack or shortage of some biological essential resulting from deprivation.
e. A state of tension resulting from a need that arouses and directs an organism's behavior.
f. External stimuli that an organism may be motivated to approach or avoid.
g. A state of balance or equilibrium among internal, physiological conditions.
h. A normal, optimum level of balance among physiological or psychological reactions.
i. A motivating discomfort or tension caused by a lack of balance or consonance among one's cognitions.

j. A small brain structure involved in many drives, including thirst, hunger, sex, and temperature regulation.
k. An STD caused by a bacterial infection, which may pass through four stages, ultimately resulting in death.
l. An eating disorder characterized by recurrent episodes of binge eating and then purging to remove the just-eaten food.
m. Contagious diseases that are usually transmitted through sexual contact.
n. The learned need to meet or exceed some standard of excellence in performance.
o. A projective personality test requiring a subject to tell a series of short stories about a set of ambiguous pictures.
p. The learned need to be in control of events or persons, usually at another's expense.
q. The need to be with others and to form relationships and associations.
r. A deadly disease caused by a virus (HIV) that destroys the body's natural immune system, and that can be transmitted by sexual behaviors.
s. Persons who are sexually attracted to and aroused by members of their own sex.
t. Very common STD; bacterial infection of the genital area.
u. An STD caused by a bacterial infection of moist tissues in the genital area.
v. A reaction involving subjective feeling, physiological response, cognitive interpretation, and behavioral expression.

**True-False Practice Test**

___ 1. According to Clark Hull's theory, when an organism is in a drive state, it is motivated.
___ 2. When the strength of a need increases, the strength of the accompanying drive always increases as well.
___ 3. Drive reduction theory appears to be a good explanation for all human behavior.
___ 4. One important aspect about incentive theory is that it offers an alternative to the biological concepts previously offered as explanations for behavior.
___ 5. Arousal is probably lowest when a person is in the deepest stages of sleep.
___ 6. There appears to be an optimum arousal level for most tasks which if exceeded will detract from the performance of the task.
___ 7. Shivering when you are too cold is a behavior that demonstrates arousal theory.
___ 8. The hypothalamus is involved in maintaining equilibrium in terms of body temperature.
___ 9. Involuntary actions that help the body maintain equilibrium can be supplemented by voluntary actions.
___ 10. In general, in the male of any species, sexual behavior is entirely controlled by the presence of the male hormones.
___ 11. As the complexity of the organism increases, from rats to dogs to humans, the role of internal cues in the sex drive becomes less important.
___ 12. One interesting thing about anorexia nervosa is its predominance among females.
___ 13. With treatment, the prognosis for patients with eating disorders is very good.
___ 14. Both power needs and the need for achievement are measured by the TAT.
___ 15. Conflict may arise if a person is high in both need for achievement and need for affiliation.
___ 16. Among psychologists, there is no consensus as to the definition of emotion.
___ 17. According to the opponent-process theory, the emotional response to the stimulus decreases with subsequent exposures, but the opposing emotion increases when the stimulus is removed.
___ 18. It may be possible to make yourself happy just by smiling.
___ 19. Contrary to popular opinion, most homosexuals are indistinguishable from heterosexuals in their appearance and mannerisms.
___ 20. AIDS is now considered to be at epidemic proportions in the United States.

**Fill-In Practice Test**

1. A person's level of activation or excitement is called ___________.
2. Unlearned, complex patterns of behavior that occur in the presence of certain stimuli are ___________.
3. The psychologist who suggested that human behavior is motivated by eleven basic instincts was ___________.
4. Drives based on learned responses are called ___________ drives.

5. Drives based on physiological, unlearned needs are called _______________ drives.
6. According to Maslow, the needs that motivate human behavior are limited in number and arranged in a/an _______________.
7. According to Maslow, once a person's basic needs for food, water, and shelter are met, the person will be motivated by the need for __________.
8. External events that act to pull our behavior are called _____________.
9. A person's most suitable or normal level of activity for certain functions is called ______ _________.
10. A person who needs very high levels of arousal is referred to by Zuckerman as a ____________ _________.
11. A state of tension or discomfort that exists when we hold inconsistent, dissonant cognitions is called ____________ ____________.
12. ___________ is an eating disorder characterized by repeated episodes of binge eating and purging.
13. The usual means for measuring the need for achievement is by administering the ________________ ________________ ___________.
14. Women who were said to back off from competition for fear of winning and thus losing popularity and femininity were said to be suffering from _______ ____ ___________.
15. The need to form friendships and associations is known as the need for ____________.
16. According to the ___________________ theory, when a fear-producing stimulus is removed, the opposite feeling, relief, will replace the fear.
17. The psychologist who believes that cognition is not a necessary component of emotion is _________.
18. The __________________ division of the autonomic nervous system is involved in maintaining a relaxed state.
19. The _________________ division of the autonomic nervous system is involved in arousal.
20. Persons who are sexually attracted to and aroused by members of their own sex are called _______________.
21. The STD that is incurable but not fatal is _____________.
22. The most deadly of the STDs is __________.

**Chapter 9 Multiple Choice Practice Test**

1. The biggest problem with using instincts to explain human behavior is that
   a. humans don't have instincts
   b. this approach simply renamed the behaviors and doesn't really explain anything
   c. the list of instincts becomes unmanageable
   d. it makes human behavior seem too much like animal behavior
2. Which of the following is an example of a secondary drive?
   a. A baby is crying because it is hungry.
   b. A toddler goes to the refrigerator and asks for "drink."
   c. An adolescent girl tells her mother she needs a new pair of shoes.
   d. A ten-year-old has a fever and asks his mother for aspirin.
3. Explaining motivated behavior based on incentives seems quite similar to the theory of
   a. Maslow's hierarchy
   b. operant conditioning
   c. drive reduction
   d. homeostasis
4. Which of the following situations is best explained by set point theory?
   a. A person feels bored and so he takes a nap.
   b. A person climbs a mountain because it is there.
   c. A person does a job so he will get paid.
   d. A person loses weight while ill and then quickly gains it back.
5. Which of the following is NOT a correct match?
   a. Cannon — achievement motivation
   b. Zuckerman — sensation seekers
   c. Maslow — needs hierarchy
   d. Festinger — arousal

6. The observation that some people will drink only Pepsi, while others drink Coke and still others prefer some other brand, supports the notion that:
   a. drives like the thirst drive are exclusively physiological in nature
   b. in blind taste-tests, those same people could not tell the difference between their favorite brand and the others
   c. learning and past experience can have a strong influence on how physiological drives are expressed
   d. in the long run, our bodies "know" what is best for us, a concept called the "wisdom of the body" by W. Cannon
7. Our most important physiological cues for eating come from
   a. the liver and the hypothalamus
   b. stomach contractions
   c. the sight of food
   d. the smell of food
8. The prognosis for anorexia nervosa is particularly poor with almost ______ percent relapsing within a year of the end of treatment.
   a. 20
   b. 35
   c. 50
   d. 60
9. Which of the following is the best explanation for homosexuality?
   a. It is the result of environmental influences.
   b. It may be the result of environmental or genetic influences but no one really knows for sure.
   c. It appears to run in families so it must be genetically determined.
   d. It is caused by a hormonal imbalance during prenatal development.
10. Which of the following STDs cannot be cured with penicillin or antibiotics?
    a. syphilis
    b. herpes
    c. gonorrhea
    d. chlamydia
11. The transmission of the AIDS virus from one person to another requires
    a. only casual contact
    b. direct physical contact such as kissing
    c. exchange of bodily fluids such as blood or semen
    d. intimate sexual contact such as mutual masturbation
12. Research by David McClelland on his concept of "need to achieve" would predict that someone with a high nAch, if given a choice, would choose a job:
    a. in which he or she was almost bound to be successful
    b. that was challenging, but that could be done well with effort
    c. that was so difficult that it almost certainly could not be done well
    d. in which he or she could succeed, but only at the expense of others
13. Beth wants to be a teacher because she believes it is important for the future of the world to help children become literate. She is motivated by
    a. need for power
    b. need for competence
    c. need for affiliation
    d. need for achievement
14. One problem with Maslow's theory is that
    a. people are not motivated by physiological needs
    b. there appear to be exceptions to the hierarchical structure or ordering of needs
    c. research seems to refute the theory
    d. drive reduction theory offers a better explanation of motivation

15. Which of the following is NOT a way that the sex drive differs from other physiological drives?
   a. The survival of the individual does not depend on it.
   b. The satisfaction of the sex drive depletes bodily energy whereas the satisfaction of other drives maintains bodily energy.
   c. It is not present at birth.
   d. It is motivated only by internal cues such as hormones.

16. Which of the following is LEAST likely to be a factor in the presence of an eating disorder?
   a. parenting and family style
   b. a strong need for achievement and approval
   c. a lower socioeconomic status
   d. cultural influences suggesting that "thin is in"

17. The most successful treatment for anorexia is one that
   a. involves behavior modification
   b. involves the patient's family
   c. combines hospitalization with behavior modification
   d. treats the psychological symptoms

18. Which of the following is NOT one of the components of emotional reaction?
   a. objective feeling
   b. cognitive reaction
   c. physiological reaction
   d. behavior

19. The James-Lange theory of emotion differs from the common sense interpretation of emotion in that
   a. James and Lange believe that the experience of emotion follows the behavioral response, whereas the common-sense approach suggests that the behavior follows the emotional experience
   b. James and Lange suggest a limited number of stimuli that produce particular emotions, whereas common sense denies a limit
   c. the common-sense approach omits the cognitive component
   d. James and Lange have proven their theory through research, and no such research exists to confirm the common-sense theory

20. Which of the following is the correct sequence for the James-Lange theory of emotion?
   a. stimulus, emotion, response
   b. response, emotion, consequence
   c. stimulus, response, emotion
   d. response, experience, emotion

21. Which of the following actions would NOT result from being in an emotional situation?
   a. the pupils dilate
   b. blood is transported from the periphery to the center of the body
   c. blood sugar levels increase
   d. respiration increases, making breathing deeper and more rapid

22. The part of the brain involved in the cognitive aspect of emotion is the
   a. hypothalamus
   b. amygdala
   c. limbic system
   d. cerebral cortex

23. Drives based on learned needs are called
   a. instincts
   b. secondary drives
   c. motives
   d. primary drives

24. Drives produced by biological needs are called
    a. base motives
    b. body needs
    c. primary drives
    d. instinctual drives

25. Which of the following is most closely associated with the concept of homeostasis?
    a. studying hard to do better on the next psychology test
    b. shivering when you are cold
    c. bleeding when you are cut
    d. gaining weight when you overeat

**Check Your Knowledge of the Learning Objectives**

The following questions are examples of what you should know when you have finished studying this chapter. Write the answers to these questions. Use your book to verify the answers. Page references are provided.

1. How do instinct, drive, and incentive explain motivated behaviors? p. 302-303

2. Explain cognitive dissonance theory. p. 308

3. How can the concepts of balance and equilibrium be used to explain motivated behaviors? p. 306-307

4. Describe how homeostasis relates to temperature regulation as a physiologically-based drive. p. 309-310

5. List the factors that may influence thirst. p. 311

6. Describe the ways in which the sex drive is a unique physiologically based drive. p. 314-316

7. Discuss the internal and external factors that influence the drive to eat. p. 312-313

8. Discuss achievement motivation and explain how it is measured. p. 321-322

9. Discuss the needs for power and affiliation. p. 322-323

10. List four components that define emotional experience. p. 324

11. Name four theories of emotion and briefly describe each. p. 325-326

12. Describe the activities of the sympathetic division of the autonomic nervous system during states of emotionality. p. 327-328

13. Describe the various brain centers that are involved in emotionality. p. 328

14. Discuss the relationship between facial expressions and emotion. p. 329

15. Define homosexuality and discuss its possible causes. p. 317-318

16. Describe five sexually transmitted diseases. p. 318-319

## Dr. G's Best Study Tips #9

**Taking Objective Tests**

1. Read instructions carefully and follow them.
2. Reading through the test, answer the questions you know immediately because this will give you a sense of confidence.
3. Once you have answered a question, NEVER change your answer unless you have a sudden insight and know another answer to be correct. Do not change just because you have begun to feel doubtful about your first response.
4. Use other questions to answer or at least give you hints about the questions you don't know.
5. On multiple choice exams, a good approach is to read only the statement and treat it as a fill-in-the-blank question, generating your own response. Then try to find the alternative that best matches your own answer.
6. Read all multiple choice options carefully before you mark an answer.
7. Pay close attention to words such as not, never, true, false, except, always, and only.
8. On true/false exams, guess true if you have no idea at all. It is more difficult to construct false statements, and studies show that the probability of true statements is higher than that of false statements.
9. Always answer every question, even if you just make a wild guess. You will surely get no credit if you leave an answer blank.
10. The absolute best test-taking skill is preparation. Studying will do more for your exam grades than any other suggestion or tip that you can employ.

# CHAPTER 10—PERSONALITY: THEORIES AND ASSESSMENT

**Learning Objectives**

1. Discuss the three levels of consciousness proposed by Freud.
2. List Freud's three structures of personality and the principles by which they operate.
3. Explain the contributions of Adler, Jung, and Horney to the psychoanalytic approach.
4. Describe the personality theories of Watson, Skinner, Dollard and Miller, and Bandura.
5. Discuss Rogers' and Maslow's humanistic approach to personality.
6. Define personality trait.
7. List the "Big Five" personality dimensions.
8. Discuss the strengths and weaknesses of the psychoanalytic, humanistic, trait, and behaviorist approaches to personality.
9. List the goals of personality assessment.
10. Describe how behavioral observations are used for assessing personality.
11. Discuss the advantages and disadvantages of the interview as a personality assessment technique.
12. Describe the MMPI and define multiphasic.
13. Describe the Rorschach and the TAT and describe the characteristics of projective techniques.

**Chapter 10 Outline**

I. Preview
   A. We have come to believe that knowing someone's personality is required if we are truly to understand that person.
   B. We have come to appreciate that knowing someone's personality is not easily done.
   C. A number of theories have emerged in psychology that describe the nature of personality.
      1. A theory is a series of assumptions.
         a. The assumptions that comprise a theory are reasonably and logically related to each other.
         b. The ideas of a theory can lead to specific, testable hypotheses.
      2. Personality is the sum of affect (feelings, moods, and emotions), behaviors, and cognitions (thoughts, beliefs, and ideas) that can characterize people in a number of situations over time.
      3. Theories of personality allow us to describe differences that we know exist among people.

II. The Psychoanalytic Approach
   A. The psychoanalytic approach is associated with Sigmund Freud and his students.
      1. Freud was the first to present a truly unified theory of personality.
      2. Freud's theory of personality has been one of the most influential and most controversial in all of science.
      3. Two basic points characterize the psychoanalytic approach: (1) reliance on innate, inborn drives as explanatory concepts of human behavior, and (2) acceptance of the power and influence of unconscious forces to mold and shape our behavior.
   B. Freud's approach in therapy and his theories about the nature of personality arose largely from observations of his patients and intensive self-examination.
   C. Freud believed that there are three levels of consciousness.
      1. Ideas, memories, motives, and desires of which we are actively aware are said to be conscious.
      2. Aspects of our mind that are not conscious at any one moment, but that can be easily brought to awareness, are stored at a preconscious level.
      3. Cognitions, feelings, and motives that are not available to the conscious mind are said to be at the unconscious level.
         a. Freud believed that the contents of the unconscious mind influence our daily behaviors.
         b. A good deal of Freudian psychoanalysis as a therapeutic technique is aimed at helping a patient get in touch with the contents of the unconscious mind.

D. According to Freudian theory, our behaviors, thoughts, and feelings are governed largely by the operation of a number of basic instincts.
   1. Life instincts (eros) are impulses of survival, in particular those that motivate sex, hunger, and thirst.
      a. Each instinct has its own energy that activates our behavior.
      b. Libido is the energy through which the sexual instincts operate.
   2. Death instincts (thanatos) are opposed to the life instincts.
   3. According to Freud, our goal in life is to resolve conflicts between these two instincts.

E. Freud also proposed that the human personality is composed of three separate, though interacting, structures or subsystems.
   1. The id is the totally inborn or inherited portion of personality.
      a. The id resides in the unconscious level of the mind.
      b. The driving force of the id is libido, or sensual energy.
      c. The id operates on the pleasure principle.
   2. The ego is that part of the personality that develops through our experience with reality.
      a. It is the rational, reasoning part of the personality.
      b. The ego operates on the reality principle.
      c. One of the ego's main jobs is to mediate between the id and the superego.
   3. The superego can be likened to one's sense of morality or conscience.
      a. It operates on the idealistic principle.
      b. It has no contact with reality.

F. The result of unresolved conflicts between the id and the superego is anxiety. In order to cope with anxiety, Freud suggested that we use ego defense mechanisms.
   1. Repression involves forgetting about some anxiety-producing desire or event.
   2. Denial is a mechanism in which a person simply refuses to acknowledge the realities of the anxiety-producing situation.
   3. Rationalization involves making up excuses for one's behavior rather than facing the anxiety-producing real reasons.
   4. Fantasy provides an escape from anxiety through imagination or daydreaming.
   5. Projection is a matter of seeing in others those very motives, or traits, that it would make one anxious to see in oneself.
   6. Regression involves a return to an earlier, more primitive, even childish, level of behavior.
   7. Displacement usually refers to aggression. It is a matter of a person directing motives or behaviors at some substitute person or object rather than expressing them directly.
   8. Using defense mechanisms is a normal reaction.
   9. Defense mechanisms can become maladaptive.

G. Freud suggested a stage theory of the development of personality.
   1. In the oral stage (birth to one year), the child derives pleasure from oral activities: feeding, sucking, and making noises.
   2. In the anal stage (ages 1 to 3 years), children develop the ability to control their bowel and bladder habits and can display aggression by either "going" at inappropriate times or refusing to "go" when placed on the potty chair.
   3. In the phallic stage (ages 3 to 5 years), the genitals replace the mouth as the child's source of pleasure.
      a. The Oedipus complex in boys occurs during this stage.
      b. The same phenomenon is described as the Electra complex in girls.
   4. During the stage of latency (ages 4 to 6), sexual development is on hold.
   5. The genital stage (from puberty on) involves a sexual reawakening and renewal of sexual impulses.

H. Neo-Freudians were bothered by the focus on biological instincts and libido and the lack of concern for social influences.
   1. Alfred Adler (1870-1937) proposed that we are very much products of the social influences on our personalities.
      a. Our major goal is the achievement of success or superiority.
      b. This goal is designed to overcome a childhood inferiority complex.
      c. Adler's view of people is much more upbeat and positive than Freud's.

2. Carl Jung (1875-1961) believed that our major goal in life is to bring together in unity all of the aspects of our personality.
    a. Jung accepted the idea of an unconscious mind.
    b. He called this the personal unconscious.
    c. The collective unconscious contains very basic ideas and notions that go beyond an individual's own experiences.
    d. Jung referred to the contents of our collective unconscious as archetypes, universal forms and patterns of thought.
3. Karen Horney (1885-1952) placed great emphasis on early childhood experiences.
    a. Basic anxiety develops when a child feels isolated and alone in a hostile environment.
    b. If parents are inconsistent, indifferent, or overly punishing, children may also develop basic hostility.
    c. Horney believed that people interact with each other in three distinct ways.
        i. They move away from each other, seeking independence and self-sufficiency.
        ii. They move toward others, tending to be compliant and dependent.
        iii. They move against others, where the effort is to be in control, to gain power and dominance.
    d. Horney was the first to take Freud to task over his male chauvinist ideas.

III. The Behavioral-Learning Approach
  A. John Watson (1878-1958) and his followers argued that psychology should turn away from the study of the mind and consciousness because they are unverifiable and ultimately unscientific.
    1. Psychology should study observable behavior.
    2. Personality theory is not needed; what matters is learning.
    3. He believed that instincts and innate impulses have little to do with the development of behavior.
  B. B. F. Skinner claimed to have proposed no particular theory of learning, much less of personality.
    1. He refused to refer to any sort of internal variables to explain behavior.
    2. Behavior is shaped by its consequences.
  C. John Dollard (1900-1980) and Neal Miller (b. 1909) tried to use the basic principles of learning theory to explain personality and how it develops.
    1. Personality grows out of the system of habits one develops in response to various cues in the environment.
    2. Behavior is motivated by primary drives and learned drives.
    3. Motivated by drives, the habits that are reinforced become part of one's personality.
    4. Miller proposed that conflict is explainable in terms of tendencies (habits) to approach or avoid goals.
  D. Albert Bandura (b. 1925) claims that many aspects of our behavior, of our personalities, are learned, but they are often learned through observation and social influence.
    1. Learning involves a cognitive rearrangement and representation.
    2. This theory suggests that we influence our environment just as it influences us.

IV. The Humanistic-Phenomenological Approach
  A. This approach is not deterministic; what matters most is how people view themselves and others,
    1. It tends to focus much more on the here and now.
    2. It tends to emphasize the wholeness or completeness of the personality.
  B. Carl Rogers' (1902-1986) view of personality is referred to as person-centered or self theory.
    1. He developed his views through the observation of clients in a clinical setting.
    2. He believed that the most overwhelming of human drives is the drive to become fully functioning.
        a. This involves an openness to oneself and one's feelings and desires.
        b. One should have positive self-regard.
    3. What is important is not what is but what is felt or perceived.
  C. Abraham Maslow (1908-1970) saw as our major goal in life the need to realize positive needs, to self-actualize; believed psychology was far too pessimistic and negative.

V. The Trait Approach
   A. Trait theories tend to be more concerned with the adequate description of personality than with the explanation of personality.
      1. A trait is any distinguishable, relatively enduring way in which one individual differs from others.
      2. Traits are descriptive dimensions.
         a. They are not simple either/or propositions.
         b. Traits fall along a continuum.
   B. Gordon Allport (1897-1967) proposed that a trait is a real force that exists within an individual and that can be used to explain the consistency in a person's behaviors.
      1. A personality trait might produce a range of different specific responses, but those responses would be, in their essence, very much alike.
      2. Personality traits are of two types:
         a. Common traits are shared by almost everyone.
         b. Personal traits are unique to the individual and are of three different subtypes.
            i. A cardinal trait is one trait that is so powerful that it influences virtually everything that the person does.
            ii. Central traits are the 5-10 traits that best characterize a person.
            iii. Secondary traits are characteristics that seldom govern our reactions and may be applied only in specific circumstances.
   C. Raymond Cattell (b. 1905) proposed an empirical approach to personality, relying on the results of psychological tests, questionnaires, and surveys.
      1. Cattell used a statistical technique called factor analysis.
      2. He said there are two types of personality traits.
         a. Surface traits are clusters of behaviors that go together, are easily observed, and are found in a number of settings.
         b. Source traits are fewer in number, are not directly observable, and are the source of surface traits.
      3. It is one's pattern of underlying source traits that determines which surface traits will be expressed as behavior.
   D. Hans Eysenck (b. 1916) claimed that personality can be divided into two main types.
      1. Extroversion-introversion is one personality dimension.
         a. Extroverts seek stimulation; they are active and sociable.
         b. Introverts are reserved, cautious, and withdrawn.
      2. Stability-instability (often called neuroticism).
         a. People high on stability are calm and easygoing.
         b. People at the other extreme are moody, anxious, and temperamental.
      3. Recently Eysenck proposed a third type of personality, psychoticism, which interacts with the first two.
      4. Eysenck claims that one's position on ghis 3 dimensions is largely inherited or instinctive.
   E. The Big Five is the five-factor model consisting of the traits personality theorists use to describe personality.
      1. Dimension I is Eysenck's "Extroversion/Introversion" dimension.
      2. Dimension II is "Agreeableness" or "Friendliness."
      3. Dimension III is most commonly called "Conscientiousness."
      4. Dimension IV is Eysenck's "Stability/Instability" dimension.
      5. Dimension V is simple "Intellect," "Intelligence," or "Openness."
      6. The Big Five traits have emerged from nearly 50 years of research.
      7. There is a lack of theoretical explanation for the how and the why of these dimensions.

VI. Evaluating the Four Approaches to Personality
   A. Psychoanalytic theory provides the most complex and comprehensive approach to personality.
      1. Among Freud's accomplishments, most psychologists agree that he:
         a. Focused attention on the importance of early childhood experiences.
         b. Suggested that some impulses affect our behaviors even though they are beyond awareness.

c. Drew attention to the impact of sexuality and sexual impulses as influences on behavior and personality.
2. But there remain two major criticisms of Freudian psychoanalytic theory.
a. It is largely derived from the observations of disordered patients.
b. Many of its assumptions are untestable.

B. The major strengths of a behavioral-learning approach to personality also constitute its major weaknesses.
1. Some argue that it totally dehumanizes personality.
2. Even social learning theory approaches are too deterministic.
3. They are really not theories at all.
a. They tend to be very specific and focused.
b. They avoid any mention of biologically determined characteristics.

C. The humanistic-phenomenological approach also includes both strengths and weaknesses.
1. It reminds us of the wholeness of the personality.
2. It warns us of the danger in analyzing something complex in artificial segments.
3. It is positive and upbeat.
4. It has considerable impact on therapists and counselors.
5. It is almost impossible to test any of its assumptions scientifically.
a. Terms are fuzzy and ill-defined.
b. It is more a philosophical theory than a psychological theory.

D. Trait theories have few advantages and several disadvantages.
1. They provide us with the means of measuring or assessing those characteristics.
2. They suggest that we look at organism variables when we try to make predictions about behavior or mental processes.
3. However, they offer little more than description.
4. There is disagreement about which traits are the most important.
5. These theories suppose a consistency of reaction over time and in different situations that may be more fictional than real.

VII. Personality Assessment

A. There are three goals in personality assessment.
1. One goal is to adequately diagnose a person's problem.
2. A second goal of assessment is theory building.
3. The third goal is determining whether a measured personality characteristic can be used to predict some other behavior.

B. Behavioral observation involves drawing conclusions about an individual's personality on the basis of observations of his or her behavior.
1. There may be problems with casual, unstructured observations.
a. Observations based on a small range of behaviors in a limited setting cannot be generalized to other groups or situations.
b. Behaviors observed may not be typical or characteristic.
2. The behavioral observations can be an excellent source of information, particularly when the observations being made are purposeful, careful, and structured.
3. Behavioral observations are commonly a part of any clinical assessment.
4. Rating scales provide many advantages over casual observation.
a. They focus the attention of the observer on a set of specified behaviors to be observed.
b. They yield a more objective measure of a sample of behavior.
c. Using the rating scales, one can have behaviors observed by a number of raters.

C. Interviews involve a conversational interchange between the interviewer and subject to gain information about the subject.
1. The basic idea of the interview is to focus on what people say about themselves rather than what they do.
2. A major advantage of the interview is its flexibility.

D. Paper-and-pencil tests are objective assessments of personality that yield quantifiable data.
1. The Minnesota Multiphasic Personality Inventory (MMPI) is a pencil-and-paper test used to assess a number of personality dimensions.
2. The MMPI was designed to help in the diagnosis of persons with mental disturbances and, thus, is not a personality test in the sense of identifying personality traits.

3. It is the most researched test in psychology and one of the most commonly used.
4. The MMPI was revised in 1989 and is now referred to as the MMPI-2. It is composed of 567 statements to which a subject responds true or false.
   a. The statements cover feelings, attitudes, physical symptoms, and past experiences.
   b. In its construction, only items that discriminated or differentiated among the different groups of subjects and patients were kept.
5. It is a criterion-referenced test in that each item on the test is referenced to one of the criterion groups-either normals or patients with a particular diagnosis.
6. The California Personality Inventory (CPI) was constructed with the same logic as the MMPI.
   a. The CPI was constructed using only normal subjects.
   b. The CPI assesses 18 normal personality traits.
7. Some multiphasic tests have been designed in conjunction with a particular personality theory.
   a. The 16 PF (PF stands for personality factors) Questionnaire was designed around Cattell's trait theory.
   b. Subjects respond yes or no to 100 statements.
8. A number of personality questionnaires or inventories are designed to measure just one trait and, thus, are not multiphasic; i.e., the Taylor Manifest Anxiety Scale.

E. Projective techniques are personality assessment techniques requiring subjects to respond to ambiguous stimuli, thus "projecting" some of their "selves" into their responses.
1. In the word association technique, there are no right or wrong answers, but insight is gained into the patient.
2. The unfinished sentence procedure consists of having subjects complete sentences in the way that they want.
   a. There are no right or wrong responses.
   b. Interpreting responses is rather subjective.
3. The Rorschach inkblot test is a famous projective technique in which the subject is asked to say what is seen in a series of inkblots.
   a. Many psychologists question the efficiency of the Rorschach as a diagnostic instrument.
   b The Rorschach inkblots seem neither very reliable nor valid.
4. The Thematic Apperception Test (TAT) is a projective technique in which the subject is asked to tell a story about a set of ambiguous pictures.
   a. It is designed to provide a mechanism to discover the subjects' hidden needs, desires, and emotions, which are projected into their stories.
   b. It is a thematic test because scoring depends largely on the interpretation of the themes of the stories.

**Learning Chapter 10 Vocabulary**

Write the definition for each of the following key terms on the lines provided at the right. Then fold the paper vertically so you can see only the term and try to say the definition. Practice like this until you can say them all correctly.

PSYCHOANALYTIC APPROACH

NEO-FREUDIANS

LIFE INSTINCTS (EROS)

LIBIDO

DEATH INSTINCTS (THANATOS)

ID

PLEASURE PRINCIPLE

EGO

REALITY PRINCIPLE

DEFENSE MECHANISMS

SUPEREGO

IDEALISTIC PRINCIPLE

INFERIORITY COMPLEX

PHENOMENOLOGICAL

TRAITS

BEHAVIORAL OBSERVATION

INTERVIEW

MMPI ______________________________

PROJECTIVE TECHNIQUE ______________________________

RORSCHACH INKBLOT TEST ______________________________

THEMATIC APPERCEPTION TEST (TAT) ______________________________

REPRESSION ______________________________

DENIAL ______________________________

RATIONALIZATION ______________________________

FANTASY ______________________________

PROJECTION ______________________________

REGRESSION ______________________________

DISPLACEMENT ______________________________

**Idioms and Difficult Phrases**

**feels that blowing her top at her boss** (p. 342) To "blow your top" means to become very angry and lose control, perhaps yelling or throwing things. Do people from your country "blow their tops" or keep their feelings "bottled up" inside themselves?

**say the first thing that pops into your head** (p. 361) The first thing that "pops into your head" is simply the first word or thought you have, that is, the first idea that "comes to mind."

**Matching**

Match the following key terms from your text with the appropriate definition.

| | | | |
|---|---|---|---|
| ______ | 1. MMPI | ______ | 2. psychoanalytic |
| ______ | 3. inferiority complex | ______ | 4. neo-Freudians |
| ______ | 5. death instincts | ______ | 6. libido |
| ______ | 7. projective technique | ______ | 8. superego |
| ______ | 9. behavioral observation | ______ | 10. projection |
| ______ | 11. fantasy | ______ | 12. regression |
| ______ | 13. life instincts | ______ | 14. ego |
| ______ | 15. interview | ______ | 16. Rorschach Inkblot Test |
| ______ | 17. idealistic principle | ______ | 18. phenomenological |
| ______ | 19. id | ______ | 20. reality principle |
| ______ | 21. pleasure principle | ______ | 22. defense mechanisms |

a. The approach to personality associated with Freud and his followers that relies on instincts and the unconscious as explanatory concepts.
b. Personality theorists (including Adler, Jung, and Horney) that kept many basic psychoanalytic principles, but differed from a strict Freudian view, adding new concepts of their own.
c. Inborn impulses proposed by Freud that compel one toward survival, including hunger, thirst, and sex.
d. The energy that activates the life (sexual) instincts (largely of the id).
e. Inborn impulses proposed by Freud that compel one toward destruction, including aggression.
f. The instinctive aspect of personality that seeks immediate gratification of impulses; operates on the pleasure principle.
g. The impulse of the id to seek immediate gratification to reduce tensions.
h. The aspect of personality that encompasses the sense of "self;" in contact with the real world; operates on the reality principle.
i. Force that governs the ego; arbitrating between the demands of the id, the superego, and the real world.
j. Unconsciously applied techniques that protect the self (ego) from feelings of anxiety.
k. The aspect of personality that refers to ethical or moral considerations; operates on the idealistic principle.
l. The force that governs the superego; opposed to the id, seeks adherence to standards of ethics and morality.
m. The Adlerian notion that as children dealing with our environment, we develop a sense of inferiority that needs to be overcome to reach maturity.
n. When under stress, a return to earlier, childish levels of previously productive behaviors.
o. Relating to an approach that emphasizes one's perception and awareness of events as being more important than the events themselves.
p. Seeing in others those very characteristics and motives that cause stress in oneself.
q. The personality assessment technique of drawing conclusions about one's personality based on observations of one's behaviors.
r. The personality assessment technique involving a conversational interchange between the interviewer and subject to gain information about the subject.
s. A paper-and-pencil inventory of 567 true-false questions used to assess a number of personality dimensions, some of which may indicate the presence of a psychological disorder.
t. A personality assessment technique requiring subjects to respond to ambiguous stimuli, thus projecting his or her "self" into their responses.
u. A projective technique in which the subject is asked to say what he or she sees in a series of inkblots.
v. An escape from stress through imagination and daydreaming.

**True-False Practice Test**

___ 1. Freud's personality theory rests on the two basic premises of innate drives and the power of the unconscious.
___ 2. Freud referred to the sexual instincts as eros.
___ 3. The basic structure of personality that operates on the pleasure principle is the ego.
___ 4. John Watson and B.F. Skinner were neo-Freudians.
___ 5. The behaviorists disagreed with the principles of psychoanalytic theory on the basis that the study of the unconscious was not observable or verifiable.
___ 6. Albert Bandura is a neo-Freudian who suggested that personality is learned by observing the behaviors of others and noting which of those behaviors are reinforced.
___ 7. The phenomenological approach to personality suggests that what matters most is how a person views himself and other people.
___ 8. Abraham Maslow criticized most of the current psychological theory of his time as being too negative and pessimistic.
___ 9. Allport, Eysenck, and Cattell all have in common the fact that they are trait theorists.
___ 10. One important aspect of psychoanalytic theory is that it helped us focus on the importance of adolescence.
___ 11. At present, there is no single theory that adequately explains personality without shortcomings.

___ 12. Interactionism refers to the fact that personality may best be explained as an interaction between stable personality traits and the individual's perception of a particular situation.
___ 13. The MMPI is the most researched test in all of psychology.
___ 14. The MMPI and the Rorschach are the same type of personality tests.
___ 15. In a projective test, subjects are asked to respond to ambiguous stimuli.

**Fill-in Practice Test**

1. An organized collection of testable ideas used to explain a particular subject matter is a/an __________.
2. The affects, behaviors, and cognitions of people that can characterize them in a number of situations over time are referred to as ______________.
3. Freud's technique of therapy that was derived from his personality theory is known as ________________.
4. Ideas, feelings, and motives of which we are aware are said to be ______________.
5. According to Freud, our behaviors, thoughts, and feelings are governed by _______ __________.
6. The impulses for survival are called life instincts or _______.
7. The impulses of destruction are referred to as death instincts or ____________.
8. According to Freud, people deal with anxiety by using __________ ____________.
9. The psychologist chosen by Freud to be his successor, and the man who developed the idea of the collective unconscious, was _______ _________.
10. Carl Jung believed that the unconscious contained universal patterns and forms called ____________.
11. Dollard and Miller argued that personality is determined by one's __________ which are formed in response to environmental cues.
12. A distinguishable, relatively enduring way in which one individual differs from another is a/an _________.
13. Gordon Allport described characteristics that are shared by almost everyone as __________ ________.
14. Using a technique called __________________, a psychologist may have a client act out a given life situation in order to learn more about the client's personality.
15. The most important instrument of clinical assessment is the ______________.

**Chapter 10 Multiple Choice Practice Test**

1. Which of the following is NOT included in the textbook definition of personality?
   a. affects
   b. behaviors
   c. preferences
   d. cognitions
2. Awareness is to consciousness as availability is to ____________.
   a. preconsciousness
   b. unconsciousness
   c. psychoanalysis
   d. affect
3. John is an alcoholic who at times feels suicidal. Which of the following terms would best describe in Freudian terms what motivates those thoughts?
   a. basic instincts
   b. the preconscious
   c. eros
   d. thanatos
4. The Freudian personality structure that keeps us in touch with reality is the
   a. id
   b. ego
   c. superego
   d. libido

5. Alfred Adler developed the idea of the
   a. inferiority complex
   b. defense mechanism
   c. collective unconscious
   d. phenomenological approach
6. Which of the following is NOT a correct match?
   a. Adler—inferiority complex
   b. Jung—archetypes
   c. Freud—defense mechanism
   d. Karen Horney—collective unconscious
7. The neo-Freudian who theorized that people have three ways of interacting-moving away, moving toward, and moving against-other people was
   a. Alfred Adler
   b. Carl Jung
   c. Karen Horney
   d. Anna Freud
8. Which of the following is NOT a correct match?
   a. Cattell—source trait
   b. Eysenck—extroversion
   c. Allport—common trait
   d. Maslow—factor analysis
9. Which of the following is NOT one of the "Big Five" dimensions of personality in the recently developed "Five-Factor Model"?
   a. extroversion-introversion
   b. psychoticism
   c. conscientiousness
   d. stability-instability
10. Of the following, which would NOT be considered to be a lasting contribution of Freud's psychoanalytic approach to personality?
   a. focusing on aggression as a central concern
   b. stressing the role of early experience and childhood
   c. introducing the notion of the unconscious
   d. attending to the impact of sexuality on personality
11. Which of the following personality theories was criticized for relying too heavily on the notion of biological drives and for concepts that are untestable?
   a. psychoanalytic approach
   b. trait theory
   c. behaviorist approach
   d. humanism
12. Which of the following would be the LEAST valid reason for personality assessment?
   a. theory construction
   b. genetic planning
   c. predicting other behaviors
   d. clinical diagnosis
13. When analyzing responses to the TAT, what does a psychologist look for?
   a. emerging themes or stories that provide insights about the subject
   b. the extent to which the subject attended to or ignored the colors in the stimulus card
   c. the average number of items correct for each subtest
   d. attention to detail and descriptions of animals

14. In what way is the MMPI a "criterion-referenced" test?
   a. Items were included only if they differentiated among diagnosed groups.
   b. The standardization groups, used to establish test norms, were very large.
   c. The test includes items that determine the extent to which the subject is taking the test seriously.
   d. The authors had a full and complete theory of personality traits in mind before they began writing test items.

15. If you meet someone new at a party, what personality assessment technique are you likely to use to evaluate that person?
   a. interview
   b. paper-and-pencil test
   c. projective
   d. behavioral observation

16. Which of the following is NOT one of the sources upon which Freud drew to form his theory of personality?
   a. great works of philosophy
   b. observations of his patients
   c. self-examination
   d. observation of his children

17. One of the goals of psychoanalysis is to help a person get in touch with his/her
   a. conscious
   b. preconscious
   c. unconscious
   d. conscience

18. Which of the following is NOT a correct match?
   a. id—pleasure principle
   b. ego—reality principle
   c. conscience—morality principle
   d. superego—idealistic principle

19. Alfred Adler, Carl Jung, and Karen Horney all have in common the fact that they
   a. had their beginnings in psychoanalytic theory
   b. were neo-Freudians
   c. offered alternate ideas to psychoanalytic theory
   d. all of the above

20. One of the first psychologists to accuse Freud of male chauvinism was
   a. Horney
   b. Jung
   c. Skinner
   d. Adler

21. The psychologist who believed that people strive to become fully functioning was
   a. Karen Horney
   b. Carl Rogers
   c. Carl Jung
   d. Neil Miller

22. Which of the following may be viewed as the major advantage of the so-called behavioral-learning approach to personality?
   a. Most of the psychologists who support this approach were already famous for other contributions.
   b. It focuses entirely on external forces, such as the environment and other people.
   c. It relies on concepts that are observable and measurable.
   d. It has given rise to the fullest, most comprehensive of theories.

23. What one thing most separates humanistic approaches to personality from behavioral and psychoanalytic approaches?
   a. The humanistic view is non-deterministic.
   b. The humanist position is based on research data.
   c. Humanism relies most heavily on cognitions.
   d. Humanism focuses on early childhood learning.

24. The psychologist who used factor analysis to examine traits was
   a. Eysenck
   b. Cattell
   c. Allport
   d. Dollard

25. Which of the Freudian defense mechanisms is marked by a return to childish behavior in the presence of stress?
   a. fantasy
   b. regression
   c. repression
   d. projection

**Check Your Knowledge of the Learning Objectives**

The following questions are examples of what you should know when you have finished studying this chapter. Write the answers to these questions. Use your book to verify the answers. Page references are provided.

1. Discuss the three levels of consciousness proposed by Freud. p .339

___

___

2. List Freud's three structures of personality and the principles by which they operate. p. 340

___

___

___

3. Explain the contributions of Alfred Adler to the psychoanalytic approach. p. 343

___

___

4. Explain the contributions of Carl Jung to the psychoanalytic approach. p. 344

___

___

___

5. Explain the contributions of Karen Horney to the psychoanalytic approach. p. 344-345

___

___

___

6. Describe the personality theories of John B. Watson. p. 345

___

___

___

7 Describe the personality theories of B.F. Skinner. p. 346

___

___

___

8. Describe the personality theories of Dollard and Miller. p. 346

___

___

___

9. Describe the personality theories of Albert Bandura. p. 347

___

___

___

10. Discuss the humanistic approach of Rogers and Maslow. p .347-348

11. List the "Big Five" personality dimensions. p. 352

12. Discuss the strengths and weaknesses of the psychoanalytic, humanistic, trait, and behaviorist approaches to personality. p. 352-355

13. List the goals of personality assessment. p. 356-357

14. Describe how behavioral observations are used for assessing personality. p. 357-358

15. Discuss the advantages and disadvantages of the interview as a personality assessment technique. p. 358-359

16. Describe the MMPI and define multiphasic. p. 359-360

17. Describe the Rorschach and the TAT. p. 361

18. Describe the characteristics of projective techniques. p .361

## Dr. G's Best Study Tips # 10

**Suggestions for Taking Notes**

1. At the start of class, date your notes and give them a title that corresponds to the chapter to be presented in lecture. Be sure to number the pages as you go and date each page.
2. Don't try to write every word the professor says; just get the important facts and details. Listen for key words that alert you to what's coming. Numerical terms signal a list, e.g., "three" reasons for taking good notes. Other possible key words and phrases are "if," "then," "when," "next," "as a result," "leading up to," and "because of." I am sure you get the idea.
3. If the professor writes something on the board or an overhead projector, write it down.
4. Write your notes in your own words. It is important that you understand what you write and not just memorize words that have no real meaning for you.
5. Try to write in complete thoughts or sentences as much as possible.
6. Ask your instructor to clarify any points you don't understand.
7. Review your notes as soon after class as possible, definitely the same day. The longer you wait, the more difficult it will be to add any ideas, clarify, or rewrite.
8. Use your textbook or handouts to add or clarify points you don't understand.
9. Use abbreviations only to the extent that you can understand or remember the symbols and short forms you are using and interpret them later.
10. Do not rely solely on your notes for studying. You must also read your text and other assigned material.

# CHAPTER 11—STRESS AND HEALTH

**Learning Objectives**

1. Define stress and stressors.
2. Discuss the SRRS as a measure of the stress of everyday life.
3. Define environmental and personal frustration and give an example of each.
4. Name four types of motivational conflict and give an example of each.
5. Discuss effective and ineffective strategies for coping with stress.
6. Describe the general adaptation syndrome.
7. Explain the frustration-aggression hypothesis.
8. Describe the theories of Lazarus and Hobfoll regarding life-induced stress.
9. Describe the type A behavior pattern and discuss its relationship to health.
10. List eight strategies used by health psychologists to help patients maintain treatment.

**Chapter 11 Outline**

I. Stressors: The Causes of Stress
  A. Stress includes physiological reactions and unpleasant feelings.
    1. Stress is defined as a complex set of reactions made by an individual under pressure to adapt.
    2. Stressors are the sources of stimuli for stress.
  B. Behind the study of frustration-induced stress is the assumption that all behavior is goal-directed.
    1. It is often difficult to directly infer goals and behavior from each other.
    2. Organisms don't always reach all of their goals.
    3. Frustration is the blocking of goal-directed behavior.
    4. It is helpful to be able to recognize what is blocking us from our goals in order to respond adaptively.
      a. Environmental frustration implies that the blocking of goal-directed behavior is being done by something or someone in the environment.
      b. Personal frustration results when internal reasons prevent us from reaching our goals.
  C. Stress may result because our own motivational system is causing a conflict.
    1. Approach-approach conflicts produce the least amount of stress because the organism is caught between two potentially desirable alternatives.
    2. Avoidance-avoidance conflicts are characterized by two alternatives, each of which is negative or punishing.
    3. Approach-avoidance conflicts are typified by vacillation between being motivated to approach and motivated to avoid.
    4. Multiple approach-avoidance conflicts arise when an individual is faced with a number of alternatives, each of which is in some way positive and negative at the same time.
  D. Sources of stress that do not fit neatly into our descriptions of either conflict or frustration are called life-induced stress.
    1. Holmes and Rahe studied the stress caused by changes in one's life using their Social Readjustment Rating Scale (SRRS).
      a. Psychologists have reported positive correlations between scores on the SRRS and the incidence of physical illness and disease.
      b. This scale concentrates on big life changes.
    2. Richard Lazarus argues that big crises or major events are often too large to have an impact on us directly.
      a. What may cause us to feel stressed are the ways in which these big events produce little changes in our lives.
      b. These big events create a ripple effect of change in our lives.
    3. Another view suggests that stressors are perceived threats to our resources.

II. Reacting to Stressors
  A. How people perceive stressful situations and how they respond to them varies from person to person.
    1. Some people, labeled as having "hardy personalities," seem to be very resistant to the negative effects of stress.

a. Hardy types are optimistic and feel in control of their own lives.
b. Hardy types view stressful situations as opportunity for growth.

B. By reacting to stress through learning, we adapt in such a way as to reduce or eliminate the source of the stress.
1. Much everyday learning is motivated by frustration-induced stress.
2. Learning through experience with stress may also teach the value of escape and avoidance.
3. The stress we experience might be unpleasant, but it may produce positive consequences by forcing us to learn new options.

C. Some reactions to stressors are maladaptive and ineffective.
1. Continuing to accept the same stress and not change is to fixate.
2. The frustration-aggression hypothesis claims that aggression is always caused by frustration.
3. Anxiety, another maladaptive reaction to stress, is a general feeling of tension or apprehension that often accompanies a perceived threat to one's well-being.

III. Stress produces physiological reactions.

A. Selye's description of the general adaptation syndrome (GAS) is the most widely accepted description of the physiological reactions to stressors.
1. The GAS occurs in three stages: alarm, resistance, and exhaustion.
2. In the alarm stage, there are rapid changes in the sympathetic nervous system.
   a. Heart rate and blood pressure increase.
   b. Pupils dilate.
   c. Digestion ceases and the blood supply is rerouted to the extremities of the body.
   d. The adrenal glands secrete norepinephrine and mobilize the body's resources.
   e. These levels of sympathetic activity are usually maintained for only a few minutes.
3. In resistance, the stressor remains present and resistance to the stressor remains above normal levels, so the drain on the body's resources continues.
4. In the final stage, exhaustion, the bodily resources are nearly depleted and both physical and psychological breakdown are eminent.

IV. Health psychology is the study of psychological or behavioral factors that affect physical health and illness.

A. Involving psychologists in the medical realm of physical health is based on four assumptions.
1. Certain behaviors increase the risk of certain chronic diseases.
2. Changes in behaviors can reduce the risk of certain diseases.
3. Changing behaviors is often easier and safer than treating many diseases.
4. Behavioral interventions are comparatively cost-effective.

B. There seems to be a positive correlation between some personality variables and physical health.
1. Type A behavior pattern (TABP) is a collection of behaviors often associated with coronary heart disease.
   a. Many studies have linked heart disease with Type A behaviors.
   b. Some recent studies have called this into question.
   c. Type A is complex and difficult to diagnose accurately.
   d. Type A as currently defined may be too global a pattern of behaviors, and only a subset of these behaviors are diagnostic of heart disease.
2. Logan Wright defines the Type A personality as follows:
   a. Time urgency: concern over wasting small bits of time.
   b. Chronic activation: the tendency to stay alert and ready all of the time.
   c. Multiphasia: having a number of projects going at once.
3. More research on diagnosis of Type A behavior patterns is needed.

C. One role of the health psychologists is to intervene to bring about changes in dangerous lifestyle behaviors.
1. Seven of the 10 leading causes of death in the U.S. are, in large part, behaviorally determined.
2. Interventions have been developed to change a wide range of behaviors.
3. New strategies for smoking are aimed at discouraging youth from beginning to smoke.
   a. Nearly 80 percent of quitters relapse within a year.

b. Most smokers who quit permanently do so without any special program.

4. One area of intervention has to do with assisting patients in complying with physician orders, including:
   a. Specific assignments
   b. Skill training
   c. Cueing specific behaviors
   d. Tailoring the regimen to meet schedule and other needs
   e. Behavioral contracts
   f. Shaping behaviors toward the desired treatment regimen
   g. Self-monitoring
   h. Reinforcement of desired behaviors

**Learning Chapter 11 Vocabulary**

Write the definition for each of the following key terms on the lines provided at the right. Then fold the paper vertically so you can see only the term and try to say the definition. Practice this until you can say them all correctly.

GENERAL ADAPTATION SYNDROME ______________________

STRESS ______________________

STRESSORS ______________________

FRUSTRATION ______________________

HEALTH PSYCHOLOGY ______________________

TYPE A BEHAVIOR PATTERN ______________________

CONFLICT ______________________

COGNITIVE REAPPRAISAL ______________________

FRUSTRATION-AGGRESSION HYPOTHESIS ______________________

**Idioms and Difficult Phrases**

**while some try to "marry money"** (p. 371) To "marry money" means to marry someone who is rich or comes from a wealthy family. The practice of paying a dowry is very unusual in the United States.

**he or she is going to "get burned"** (p. 373) In very informal speech, the phrase "getting burned" means to be deceived, injured, or defeated.

**being caught in slow moving traffic may drive you up the wall**. (p. 376) Although in this sentence the phrase "drive you up the wall, is used to describe traffic the phrase has nothing to do with driving. To "drive someone up the wall" is to aggravate or frustate them until they are ready to "blow their top" (see idioms in chapter 10).

**might consider breaking off the relationship** (p. 380 To break off a relationship means to end the relationship. Couples who are ending a relationship are said to be "breaking up." My sister recently "broke up with" her boyfriend.

**Matching**

Match the following key terms from your text with the appropriate definition.

______ 1. health psychology
______ 2. frustration
______ 3. type A behavior pattern
______ 4. stress
______ 5. conflict
______ 6. stressors
______ 7. cognitive reappraisal
______ 8. general adaptation syndrome
______ 9. frustration-aggression hypothesis

a. A collection of behaviors (competitive, achievement-oriented, impatient, easily aroused, often hostile or angry) often associated with coronary heart disease.
b. A complex pattern of reactions to real or perceived threats to one's sense of well-being that motivates adjustment.
c. Real or perceived threats to one's sense of well-being; sources of stress.
d. A stressor; the blocking or thwarting of goal-directed behavior.
e. A stressor in which some goals can be satisfied only at the expense of others.
f. Re-thinking a stressful situation to consider it in a more positive light, for example, determining if a stressor is real or imagined.
g. The view (now discredited) that all aggression stems from frustration.
h. The field of applied psychology that studies psychological factors affecting physical health and illness.
i. A pattern of physiological reactions to stressors, including alarm, resistance, and exhaustion.

**True-False Practice Test**

___ 1. One thing about stress is that everyone experiences it.
___ 2. It may be possible to make oneself happy just by smiling.
___ 3. Stress that results from frustration is somewhat pathological.
___ 4. Environmental frustration implies that goal-directed behavior is being blocked by something or someone in the environment.
___ 5. As difficulty in decision making increases, stress level will also increase.
___ 6. The approach-approach conflict creates the greatest amount of stress.
___ 7. The positive correlation between scores on the SRRS and physical illness indicates that stress causes illness.
___ 8. Both stressors and reactions to stress vary considerably from person to person.
___ 9. One positive result of stress is that we may learn new ways to attain our goals.
___ 10. The correct order for stages in the general adaptation syndrome is alarm, reaction, and exhaustion.
___ 11. "If at first you don't succeed, try, try, again," is good advice for a person trying to reduce stress.

___ 12. According to the frustration-aggression hypothesis, aggression is always caused by frustration.

___ 13. Logan Wright suggests that time urgency, chronic activation, and multiphasia are the key components of type A behavior related to coronary heart disease.

___ 14. One role of the health psychologist is to bring about changes in potentially dangerous or unhealthy behaviors.

___ 15. Health psychologists can do little to promote healthy behaviors, and must be content to work on reducing harmful behaviors.

**Fill-In Practice Test**

1. The stimuli for stress are called __________.
2. The blocking of goal-directed behavior results in ______________.
3. A choice between two equally desirable goals is called a/an ____________________________ conflict.
4. The most stressful type of conflict is the _________________________.
5. The Social Rating Readjustment Scale measures stress brought about by __________.
6. Richard Lazarus argued that stress doesn't result from the big life changes, but more from the everyday little events or _____________.
7. The SRRS was developed by ____________ and Rahe.
8. In the context of stress reduction, _________________ __________________ refers to a rethinking of the nature of the situation so as to cast it in the best possible light.
9. A general feeling of tension, apprehension, and dread that involves predictable physiological changes refers to ___________.
10. At one time, ____________________ was believed to be the only cause of aggression.
11. _____________ behavior pattern is associated with coronary heart disease.
12. The stages of the general adaptation syndrome are alarm, resistance, and ______________.
13. The tendency to have a number of projects all going at once is called ________________.
14. Maladaptive responses to stress include anxiety, fixation, and ____________________.
15. Health psychologists work toward the understanding, treatment, and _____________ of disease.

**Chapter 11 Multiple Choice Practice Test**

1. Which of the following is NOT considered one of the sources of stress?
   a. life events
   b. frustration
   c. aggression
   d. conflict

2. The relationship between environmental frustration and personal frustration may also be characterized as
   a. stimulus vs. response
   b. need vs. drive
   c. social vs. nonsocial
   d. external vs. internal

3. Aretha wants an ice cream cone, but she does not want to make the long walk to the store to buy one. She will probably experience the frustration of a/an __________ conflict.
   a. approach-approach
   b. avoidance-avoidance
   c. approach-avoidance
   d. multiple approach-avoidance

4. According to Richard Lazarus, which of the following events would be more stressful?
   a. retirement
   b. divorce
   c. moving to another city
   d. a series of small breakdowns that put your car in the shop

5. Which of the following is NOT likely to reduce stress?
   a. relaxation
   b. exercise
   c. cognitive reappraisal
   d. focusing on a smaller hassle

6. According to Dollard's frustration-aggression hypothesis,
   a. frustration and aggression always go together
   b. both frustration and aggression can be reduced by exercise
   c. aggression may produce many different types of frustration
   d. aggression is always caused by frustration

7. The type of conflict that creates the most stress is
   a. avoidance-avoidance
   b. approach-approach
   c. multiple approach-avoidance
   d. approach-avoidance

8. Jolan wants to play basketball for the UNLV "Running Rebels" when he grows up. However, current predictions of his height indicate that he will be only about five feet eight inches tall. This situation is an example of
   a. environmental frustration
   b. personal frustration
   c. approach-avoidance conflict
   d. approach-approach conflict

9. "Out of the frying pan and into the fire" is a cliche' that refers to a/an __________ conflict.
   a. avoidance-avoidance
   b. approach-approach
   c. multiple approach-avoidance
   d. approach-avoidance

10. According to the SRRS, the single most stressful life event is
   a. divorce
   b. marriage
   c. death of a spouse
   d. death of a parent

11. In coping with stress, the opposite of change is
   a. stagnation
   b. fixation
   c. frustration
   d. adaptation

12. Which of the following reactions or responses to stress would be considered maladaptive?
   a. relaxation
   b. cognitive reappraisal
   c. aggression
   d. exercise

13. You are vulnerable to physical illness and infection to a greater degree than normal. Although the sympathetic response seems to have returned to normal, the physiological systems continue to mobilize bodily reserves. You are in the __________ stage of the general adaptation syndrome.
   a. alarm
   b. resistance
   c. fixation
   d. exhaustion

14. Which of the following is NOT an assumption for the basis of health psychology?
   a. Certain behaviors increase the risk of certain chronic diseases.
   b. You can change any behavior using humanistic principles.
   c. Changes in behaviors can reduce the risk of certain diseases.
   d. Behavioral interventions are comparatively cost-effective.

15. According to Logan Wright, which of the following is NOT a part of type A behavior pattern associated with coronary heart disease?
    a. time urgency
    b. chronic activation
    c. multiphasia
    d. achievement-orientation

**Check Your Knowledge of the Learning Objectives**

The following questions are examples of what you should know when you have finished studying this chapter. Write the answers to these questions. Use your book to verify the answers. Page references are provided.

1. Define stress and stressors. p. 370

2. Discuss the SRRS as a measure of the stress of everyday life. p. 374-375

3. Define environmental and personal frustration and give an example of each. p. 371-372

4. Name four types of motivational conflict and give an example of each. p. 372-374

5. Discuss effective and ineffective strategies for coping with stress. p. 376-378

6. Describe the general adaptation syndrome. p. 379

7. Explain the frustration-aggression hypothesis. p. 378

8. Describe the theories of Lazarus and Hobfoll regarding life-induced stress. p. 374-375

9. Describe the type A behavior pattern and discuss its relationship to health. p. 383-384

10. List eight strategies used by health psychologists to help patients maintain treatment. p. 385-386

## Dr. G's Best Study Tips #11

**Using 3X5 Cards**

An excellent way to study the extensive vocabulary that psychology presents is to use 3x5 cards. Prepare the cards by writing the term you want to learn on one side and a definition or related fact on the other side. Take the cards with you in your purse or pocket and study them whenever you have a few minutes. You might be stuck in traffic or waiting in the dentist's office, or you might even get out of class a few minutes early. Remember, we have already discussed the benefits of short, frequent study periods.

Tape a few of the cards around your bathroom mirror and study them while you shave, brush your teeth, or comb your hair. You will be surprised how much you gain from these few minutes. Ten minutes a day for six days means one hour that you don't have to spend in the library or sitting at your desk.

When you study the cards, look at the term and say the definition aloud. If you can define the term, place the card in a discard pile. If you cannot, then read the definition three times and place the card on the bottom of the stack. When you have gone through the cards once, shuffle them just as you would playing cards. This prevents you from learning the definitions in some sort of order and becoming dependent on that order as a memory cue. A real benefit of this study method is that you have evidence that it works: just look at the discard pile. That represents the terms you have already learned. In addition, the studying task has been reduced. Each time you study, you are focusing on the information you do not know and you are reducing the learning task as you discard the terms you do know.

# CHAPTER 12—ABNORMAL PSYCHOLOGY: THE PSYCHOLOGICAL DISORDERS

**Learning Objectives**

1. Explain how psychological abnormality is defined.
2. Describe the DSM-III-R and discuss its advantages and disadvantages.
3. Characterize phobic disorders.
4. Define panic disorder.
5. Compare and contrast generalized anxiety disorder and panic disorder.
6. Distinguish between obsessions and compulsions.
7. Describe posttraumatic stress disorder.
8. Distinguish between hypochondriasis and conversion disorder.
9. Characterize dissociative disorders.
10. Characterize personality disorders.
11. Distinguish between psychogenic amnesia and psychogenic fugue.
12. Discuss the use of the term "insanity."
13. Define mood disorders and discuss their prevalence and causes.
14. Discuss the major symptoms of schizophrenia.
15. Distinguish between process and reactive schizophrenia.
16. Distinguish between positive and negative schizophrenia.
17. Describe the distinguishing characteristics of catatonic, disorganized, paranoid, undifferentiated, and residual schizophrenia.
18. Describe the factors suspected as causes of schizophrenia.

**Chapter 12 Outline**

I. Preview
   A. Mental disorders are much more common than any of us would like to think.
   B. A 1984 NIMH study reported that approximately 40 to 50 million adult Americans were suffering from some sort of psychological disorder.
   C. Psychological disorders have an impact on all of us.

II. Definition and Classification
   A. Abnormal means statistically uncommon and maladaptive cognitions, affect, and/or behaviors that are at odds with social expectations and that result in distress and discomfort.
      1. Literally, abnormal means "not of the norm" or "not average."
      2. The reactions of people who are suffering from a psychological disorder are also maladaptive.
      3. Abnormality may show itself at a number of different levels of functioning including : affect, behaviors, and cognitions.
      4. What may be clearly abnormal and disordered in one culture may be viewed as quite normal, if not commonplace, in another.
      5. Psychological disorders involve distress or discomfort.
      6. Normal and abnormal are endpoints on a continuum.
      7. Abnormal does not mean dangerous.
      8. Abnormal does not mean bad.
   B. The classification of abnormal reactions involves diagnosis as the recognition of a disorder on the basis of the presence of particular symptoms.
      1. In 1883, Emil Kraepelin published the first classification scheme for mental disturbances based on the idea that each disorder has its own collection of symptoms and its own cause.
      2. The American Psychiatric Association published a classification for mental disorders called the Diagnostic and Statistical Manual of Mental Disorders.
         a. The DSM-III-R is the system of classification most widely used in all mental health fields.
         b. It recommends that the diagnosis of a disorder be sensitive to the individual's physical well-being, recent stress, and level of adaptation over the past three years.
         c. The DSM tries to avoid any reference to etiology, or causes, of disorders.
         d. The DSM-IV is in preparation, to be available in the mid-1990s.

3. There are many advantages to having a single classification scheme.
   a. It provides a basis for communication about the disorder with other professionals.
   b. Once disorders are classified, we can begin to think about appropriate treatments.
4. There are problems associated with any scheme of classifying disorders.
   a. Applying labels to people is often dehumanizing.
   b. It is easy to fall into the habit of believing that labels explain.
   c. Labels often create unfortunate and lasting stigmas, or negative attitudes, about people.
   d. Systems of classification tend to focus on the person and not on the larger contexts in which individuals live.
5. Insanity is not a psychological term; it is a legal term.
   a. Insanity is the diminished capacity and inability to tell right from wrong.
   b. Definitions vary from state to state.

III. Anxiety Disorders

A. Anxiety is a general feeling of apprehension or dread accompanied by predictable physiological changes.
   1. Anxiety involves two levels of reaction: subjective feelings and physiological responses
   2. Anxiety disorders are among the most common of all psychological disorders.

B. With anxiety disorders, the major symptom is real, felt anxiety, often coupled with what is called "avoidance behavior," or the attempt to resist or avoid the stimulus situation that produces the anxiety reactions.
   1. Phobic disorders involve persistent, irrational fear that leads a person to avoid the feared object, activity, or situation.
      a. The fear is intense enough to be disruptive or debilitating.
      b. Intensity is an important factor in separating phobias from fears.
      c. The prognosis for treatment of phobias is good.
      d. Agoraphobia, a commonly treated phobia, is a fear of open places, of being alone, or of being in public places from which escape might be difficult.
   2. Panic disorder is characterized by anxiety attacks that are sudden and unpredictable.
      a. These are experienced much like a phobic reaction, but without any particular stimulus.
      b. Panic attacks are not uncommon among people under stress.
      c. To qualify as a psychological disorder, attacks must have occurred at a rate of at least four within a four-week period and be accompanied by physiological symptoms.
      d. Most people who are diagnosed as having a panic disorder are also agoraphobic.
      e. A panic disorder can be accompanied by intermittent feelings of depression, which may explain the high rate of suicide and suicide attempts in persons with this disorder.
   3. Generalized anxiety disorder is characterized by persistent, chronic, and distressingly high levels of unattributable anxiety.
      a. It does not seem to be brought on by anything specific in the person's environment.
      b. People with this disorder are always in some state of uneasiness.
      c. People with this disorder usually have no good explanations for their feelings of anxiety.
      d. Although people with this disorder often can continue to function in social situations, they are particularly prone to drug and alcohol abuse.
   4. Obsessions are ideas or thoughts that involuntarily and persistently intrude into awareness.
      a. Obsessions are pointless and groundless thoughts.
      b. They may be acting as defense mechanisms against some repressed, anxiety-producing idea, desire, or memory.
   5. Compulsions are constantly intruding acts or behaviors.
      a. They are repetitive.
      b. They serve no real purpose and provide no genuine sense of satisfaction.
      c. Persons may engage in these pointless behaviors in order to prevent some other behaviors from taking place.
   6. Obsessive-compulsive disorder is a combination of obsessions and compulsions.

a. Recent evidence suggests a biological basis for OCD.
b. Drug treatment is often successful in alleviating the symptoms of OCD.

7. Posttraumatic stress disorder (PTSD) involves several symptoms that arise at some time well after the experiencing of a traumatic, highly stressful event.
   a. Some of the symptoms include disruptive recollections, distressing dreams, flashbacks, and anxiety.
   b. Anxiety qualifies as a symptom when it occurs persistently and traumatically along with other symptoms.
   c. People with PTSD see themselves as special, detached from others who cannot "share their experience."
   d. PTSD is not uncommon.

C. Somatoform disorders in some way involve physical, bodily symptoms or complaints.
   1. Psychosomatic disorders are not somatoform disorders.
   2. Hypochondriasis is the appropriate diagnosis for someone preoccupied with the fear of developing or having some serious disease.
      a. The person now has a way to explain otherwise unexplainable anxiety.
      b. The illness may be used to excuse the person from those activities that he or she finds anxiety-producing.
      c. The illness or disease may be used as a way to gain attention or sympathy.
   3. Conversion disorder is the display of a severe physical disorder for which there is no medical explanation and which is often accompanied by an apparent lack of concern on the part of the patient.
      a. The loss in physical functioning is typically of great significance.
      b. Medical explanations may run contrary to the symptoms.
      c. La belle indifference-an inappropriate lack of concern over one's condition-is a remarkable secondary symptom.
      d. This disorder intrigued Sigmund Freud.

D. A person with a dissociative disorder dissociates or escapes from some aspect of life or personality that is seen as the source of stress, discomfort, or anxiety.
   1. Psychogenic amnesia is a psychologically caused inability to recall important personal information.
      a. There is a large range in the type and extent of the forgetting associated with this disorder.
      b. Cases of this disorder tend to be more common in wartime, when traumatic experiences are more common.
   2. Psychogenic fugue is a condition of amnesia accompanied by unexplained travel or change of location.
      a. The persons usually have no reasonable explanation for how they got to where they are.
      b. This disorder may involve an escape from stressful situations.
   3. Multiple personality is the existence within an individual of two or more distinct personalities, each of which is dominant at a particular time.
      a. This is not schizophrenia.
      b. This disorder is extremely rare.
      c. The change in personality is usually dramatic, complete, and extreme.
      d. Changes in personality usually take place without warning, predicted by no particular environmental cue.
      e. Individuals with a multiple personality disorder are unable to control or predict which personality will be dominant at any one time.

IV. Personality Disorders

A. Personality disorders are enduring patterns of perceiving, relating to, and thinking about the environment and oneself that are inflexible and maladaptive.

B. The DSM-III-R lists 11 different personality disorders, organized into three groups.
   1. Group 1 includes disorders in which the individual can be characterized as odd or eccentric.
   2. Group 2 includes disorders in which the individual appears overly dramatic, emotional, or erratic, and where behaviors are quite impulsive.

3. Group 3 adds the dimension of anxiety or fearfulness to the standard criteria for personality disorder.

C. The prognosis is usually quite poor for personality disorders.

D. A person with antisocial personality disorder has a history of disregard for the rights and property of others.

1. The prognosis for antisocial personality disorder is very poor.
2. There are several hypotheses attempting to explain the cause of antisocial personality disorder.
   a. There is a biologically based lack of adequate emotional arousal.
   b. There is an unusually high need to seek stimulation.
   c. There is some genetic basis for the disorder.
   d. There is a high incidence of parental loss.
   e. There was an inappropriate (or lack of ) bonding or attachment with parents in childhood.
   f. Interaction of two or more of these factors seems to be important.

V. Mood Disorders

A. Mood disorders (affective disorders) clearly demonstrate some disturbance in one's emotional behaviors or feelings.

B. Mood disorders are defined in terms of extremes of mood.

1. Depression is the more common of the two extremes.
   a. Depression is usually found alone.
   b. Mania is almost always associated with episodes of depression.
2. Depression is recognized as a prevalent disorder.
   a. It occurs twice as often in women as in men.
   b. Approximately 1 person in 20 has suffered a major depressive episode.
3. Mania is a condition of mood that cannot be maintained for long because it is too tiring.
   a. Persons usually also show signs of depression as well as mania.
   b. Bipolar disorder is still commonly referred to as manic-depression.

C. Depression is caused by a number of different, but potentially interrelated, causes.

1. There is evidence that there is a genetic predisposition for bipolar mood disorder.
   a. If one identical twin has the disorder, the chance that the other twin will be diagnosed with it is 70 percent.
   b. For unipolar mood disorder (depression only), the data is 40 percent for identical twins and 11 percent for fraternal twins.
   c. A number of neurotransmitters called biogenic amines seem to directly influence mood.
   d. A current theory is that depression is caused by a reduction in biogenic amines and that mania is caused by an overabundance of these chemicals.
   e. Stress causes changes in the neurotransmitters in the brain.
2. Learning theorists have attributed depression to a number of experiential phenomena, including most importantly, a lack of effective reinforcers.
3. Other theorists, such as Aaron Beck, argue that although depression is displayed as a disorder of affect, its causes may be largely cognitive.
4. The psychoanalytic view claims that depression is a reflection of early childhood experiences that lead to anger directed inward.

VI. Schizophrenia

A. Schizophrenia is the label given to a number of specified disorders that share a distortion of reality and a retreat from others, accompanied by disturbances in perception, thinking, affect, and behavior.

1. It seems to involve virtually every aspect of living.
2. There is usually a disturbance of thinking.
3. Schizophrenics may engage in a number of unusual behaviors, typically ritualized, stereotyped, and meaningless.
4. One of the most obvious behavioral consequences of schizophrenia is found in language behavior.
5. Schizophrenics have flattened affect.
   a. The average schizophrenic patient is usually quite colorless, withdrawn, and of very little danger.

b. Schizophrenia means "split of the mind."
c. The term has never been used to describe multiple personality.

B. Schizophrenia can be classified as process and reactive.
1. Process schizophrenia describes symptoms that have developed gradually, usually over a period of years.
2. Reactive schizophrenia has a sudden onset of symptoms.
3. These two types should be seen as extremes on a continuum.
4. Schizophrenia could be divided into two types depending on the nature of the symptoms described at diagnosis.
a. In positive schizophrenia, symptoms such as hallucinations, delusions, muscular rigidity, and/or bizarre behaviors are added to the normal behaviors.
b. In negative schizophrenia symptoms result in the lack of or the disappearance of behaviors that once were present. The person becomes withdrawn and apathetic and experiences reduced energy and motivation.
c. This positive/negative distinction is useful in that it may provide alternative explanations of the disease or alternative treatments.
5. The DSM-III-R lists five categories of schizophrenia (summarized in Figure 12.7 of the text).

C. The causes of schizophrenia are tentative and multidimensional.
1. There is a higher risk of being diagnosed as a schizophrenic if there is a history of the disorder in one's family.
a. Adult children of schizophrenics are significantly more likely to develop schizophrenia than are the adult children of nonschizophrenic parents.
b. The odds of being diagnosed as schizophrenic in the general population are about 1 in 100.
c. The odds for those who are identical twins of schizophrenics are nearly 1 in 2.
2. The role of dopamine in schizophrenia has recently come to light from several lines of research.
a. Abuse of amphetamines often leads to development of many symptoms found in schizophrenia.
b. Amphetamines are chemically very similar to dopamine and may actually cause an increase in dopamine levels in the brain.
c. Drugs that alleviate schizophrenic symptoms commonly block receptor sites for dopamine in the brain.
d. There is little evidence that schizophrenics have elevated levels of dopamine in their brains.
e. Schizophrenics may have a heightened sensitivity in their brains to dopamine.
f. Schizophrenics may have unusually large ventricles.
g. Recent evidence suggests a lack of balance between the two hemispheres of the brain.
3. A standard view of the social factors leading to schizophrenia is that it develops in response to early experiences within the family unit.
a. Early childhood experiences of schizophrenics seem filled with conflict, anxiety, doubt, and emotional tension.
b. There is an unusually high incidence of double messages and double binds being presented to children who later tend to become schizophrenic.
c. Many people raised in such homes never develop any schizophrenic symptoms.

**Learning Chapter 12 Vocabulary**

Write the definition for each of the following key terms on the lines provided at the right. Then fold the paper vertically so you can see only the term and try to say the definition. Practice this until you can say them all correctly.

ABNORMAL ______________________________
______________________________

DIAGNOSIS ______________________________
______________________________

INSANITY

ANXIETY

PHOBIC DISORDER

PROGNOSIS

AGORAPHOBIA

PANIC DISORDER

GENERALIZED ANXIETY DISORDER

OBSESSIONS

COMPULSIONS

OBSESSIVE-COMPULSIVE DISORDER

SOMATOFORM DISORDER

HYPOCHONDRIASIS

CONVERSION DISORDER

DISSOCIATIVE DISORDER

PSYCHOGENIC AMNESIA

PSYCHOGENIC FUGUE

MULTIPLE PERSONALITY DISORDER

PERSONALITY DISORDERS

POSTTRAUMATIC STRESS DISORDER

PSYCHOTIC DISORDERS ______________________________

ORGANIC MENTAL DISORDERS ______________________________

REACTIVE SCHIZOPHRENIA ______________________________

MOOD DISORDERS ______________________________

SCHIZOPHRENIA ______________________________

PROCESS SCHIZOPHRENIA ______________________________

**IDIOMS AND DIFFICULT PHRASES**

**a large gray area between the two where distinctions get fuzzy** (p. 395) The context of this sentence provides a nice definition of the phrase "gray area." This phrase can be used to describe something that does not neatly fit into opposing categories. Opposing ideas are sometimes referred to as black and white. Therefore, gray is somewhat a blending of the two colors and a blending of the opposing ideas.

**that every wrong number** (p. 409) "Geting a wrong number" means dialing the wrong telephone number or receiving a telephone call from someone who has dialed the wrong number.

**this disorder tends to run in families** (p. 409 This phrase usually refers to genetic traits or (as in the case of antisocial personality disorder) learned qualities, habits, or traditions that are passed from one family member to another.

**think of themselves in a poor light** (p. 413) To think of something "in a poor light" is to think of it negatively.

**a chicken and egg problem** (p. 421) The "chickenandegg problem is trying to determine which came first. Which did come first, the chicken or the egg?

**Matching**

Match the following key terms from your text with the appropriate definition.

______ 1. compulsions
______ 2. prognosis
______ 3. psychogenic fugue
______ 4. somatoform disorders
______ 5. diagnosis
______ 6. hypochondriasis
______ 7. posttraumatic stress disorder
______ 8. personality disorders
______ 9. psychogenic amnesia
______ 10. multiple personality
______ 11. conversion disorder
______ 12. abnormal
______ 13. obsessive disorder
______ 14. mood disorders
______ 15. panic disorder
______ 16. agoraphobia
______ 17. schizophrenia
______ 18. generalized anxiety disorder
______ 19. phobic disorder
______ 20. anxiety
______ 21. reactive schizophrenia
______ 22. process schizophrenia

a. Statistically uncommon, maladaptive cognitions, affect, and/or behaviors that are at odds with social expectations and that result in distress or discomfort.
b. The act of recognizing a disorder on the basis of the presence of particular symptoms.
c. Schizophrenia in which the onset of the symptoms is comparatively slow and gradual.
d. Schizophrenia in which the onset of the symptoms is comparatively sudden.
e. A general feeling of apprehension or dread accompanied by predictable physiological changes.
f. An intense, irrational fear that leads a person to avoid the feared object, activity, or situation.
g. The prediction of the future course of an illness or disorder.
h. A phobic fear of open places, of being alone, or of being in public places from which escape might be difficult.
i. A disorder in which anxiety attacks suddenly and unpredictably incapacitates; there may be periods free from anxiety.
j. Persistent, chronic, and distressingly high levels of unattributable anxiety.
k. Ideas or thoughts that involuntarily and persistently intrude into awareness.
l. Constantly intruding, stereotyped, and essentially involuntary acts or behaviors.
m. Psychological disorders that result in physical or bodily symptoms or complaints.
n. A mental disorder involving the fear of developing some serious disease or illness.
o. The display of a severe physical disorder for which there is no medical explanation; often accompanied by an apparent lack of concern on the part of the patient.
p. Complex psychotic disorders characterized by impairment of cognitive functioning, delusions and hallucinations, social withdrawal, and inappropriate affect.
q. A psychologically caused inability to recall important personal information.
r. A condition of amnesia accompanied by unexplained travel or change of location.
s. The existence within one individual of two or more distinct personalities, each of which is dominant at a particular time.
t. Enduring patterns of perceiving, relating to, and thinking about the environment and oneself that are inflexible and maladaptive.
u. Disorders of affect or feeling; usually depression; less frequently, mania and depression occurring in cycles.
v. An anxiety disorder in which disruptive recollections, distressing dreams, flashbacks, and felt anxiety occur well after the experience of a traumatic event.

**True-False Practice Test**

___ 1. The question of abnormality should be considered in a cultural context.
___ 2. Mental illness is so pervasive in the U.S. that all of us will experience it either in ourselves or in someone we know.
___ 3. In psychology, it is appropriate to consider normal and abnormal as two distinct categories.
___ 4. Most abnormal behavior is dangerous.
___ 5. It is most accurate to say that there are both advantages and disadvantages to classifying mental disorders.
___ 6. The DSM-III-R attempts to overcome the disadvantages of classifying mental disorders by offering suggestions for treatment.
___ 7. Anxiety disorders are more common in men than in women.
___ 8. Healthy individuals may exhibit some of the same behaviors as people with obsessive-compulsive disorder, with less intensity or frequency.
___ 9. Conversion disorder is quite rare among the anxiety disorders.
___ 10. Paralysis, deafness, and blindness are classic examples of hypochondriasis.
___ 11. Conversion disorder was the most commonly diagnosed psychological disorder among military personnel during World War I.
___ 12. One difference between hypochondriasis and conversion disorder is that in conversion disorder, there is a real medical problem.
___ 13. In psychogenic amnesia, the person usually forgets the trauma that leads up to the amnesia.
___ 14. Multiple personality is commonly confused with schizophrenia by the popular press.
___ 15. Multiple personality is a psychotic disorder.
___ 16. In general, psychotic disorders are more severe and debilitating than anxiety disorders.
___ 17. A person suffering from a psychotic disorder may require hospitalization.
___ 18. Psychotic disorders are different from anxiety disorders in that they impair affect, cognition, and behavior.

___ 19. In mood disorders, it is equally likely that a person will suffer from depression alone, mania alone, or both depression and mania.
___ 20. According to the DSM-III-R, depression is twice as likely in women as in men.
___ 21. Recurrences are common in both mania and depression.
___ 22. Schizophrenic individuals rarely suffer from both delusions and hallucinations.
___ 23. Although schizophrenics usually lose touch with reality, their affect is generally appropriate.
___ 24. Actually, schizophrenia is a label that refers to many different disorders.
___ 25. The prognosis is better for process schizophrenia than for reactive schizophrenia.
___ 26. Although process-reactive and positive-negative are descriptors of schizophrenia that provide useful information, neither is actually a dimension or type of diagnosed schizophrenia.
___ 27. An adopted person who is diagnosed schizophrenic is more likely to have adoptive parents who are schizophrenic than biological parents who are.

**Fill-In Practice Test**

1. Recognizing a disorder on the basis of the presence of a set of symptoms is referred to as ______________.
2. The _____________ is the most widely used classification system in all of mental health.
3. The legal term for mental disorders that is not used in psychology is __________.
4. ______________ is a general feeling of apprehension or dread accompanied by predictable physiological changes such as increased muscle tension, shallow rapid breathing, and drying of the mouth.
5. Phobic disorders are characterized by persistent _______.
6. Unrealistic, excessive, and persistent worry or anxiety characterizes _________________ _____________ disorder.
7. Hand washing, grooming, counting, and checking behaviors are common ________________.
8. Victims of kidnapping or rape are likely to suffer from _________________ _________ disorder.
9. The __________________ disorders involve physical or bodily complaints and symptoms.
10. A person preoccupied with the fear of developing or having some serious disease is suffering from ___________________.
11. __________________ disorder occurs when an individual experiences a loss or alteration of physical functioning that appears to be an expression of psychological conflict or need.
12. When a person suffering from amnesia finds himself in a different location, it is referred to as _____________ __________.
13. ____________ disorders are those that involve a gross impairment of functioning and a loss of contact with reality.
14. What were once described as affective disorders are now referred to as ________ disorders.
15. The opposite of depression is _________.
16. People who swing back and forth between depression and mania, with interspersed periods of normal affect, are said to have _______________ ___________.
17. The most devastating, puzzling, and frustrating of all mental illnesses is __________________.
18. A person who suffers only from depression and does not also have periods of mania is said to have _________________ disorder.
19. Schizophrenics often make up meaningless words called _______________.
20. Schizophrenic symptoms that have developed gradually over a period of years are referred to as __________ schizophrenia.
21. _____________ schizophrenia refers to the sudden onset of schizophrenic symptoms.
22. One hypothesis about the cause of schizophrenia has to do with the presence of an abundance of the neurotransmitter ,______________ , in the brain.
23. The type of schizophrenia characterized by periods of extreme withdrawal and a tendency to remain motionless for hours is the ________________ type.
24. The type of schizophrenia which occurs at the earliest age is the ________________ type.

**Chapter 12 Multiple Choice Practice Test**

1. Statistically speaking, if there are 100 students in your psychology class, how many are likely to suffer from a psychological disorder sometime in their lives?
   a. 10
   b. 15
   c. 20
   d. 30
2. A person's behavior that is strange or bizarre must also be ____________ in order to be considered abnormal.
   a. infrequent
   b. maladaptive
   c. creative
   d. destructive
3. When Kraepelin published the first classification scheme for mental disturbances, the cause of mental illness was thought to be
   a. biological
   b. sociological
   c. environmental
   d. hereditary
4. Which of the following is NOT one of the disadvantages or problems associated with classifying mental disorders?
   a. Classification explains the disorders, but does not offer treatment suggestions.
   b. Labeling people is dehumanizing.
   c. All the attention is focused on the individual and none on the family or society.
   d. Labels create lasting stigmas and negative attitudes about people.
5. For which of the following phobias is a person most likely to seek treatment?
   a. fear of cats
   b. fear of bees
   c. fear of heights
   d. fear of open places
6. Maria has sudden, unpredictable, unprovoked attacks of intense anxiety. She is most likely suffering from
   a. panic disorder
   b. agorophobia
   c. hypochondriasis
   d. generalized anxiety disorder
7. Which of the following disorders is commonly first diagnosed in childhood or adolescence?
   a. panic disorder
   b. obsessive-compulsive disorder
   c. hypochondriasis
   d. generalized anxiety disorder
8. The difference between compulsive behavior such as gambling or eating and the compulsions associated with OCD is in the
   a. anxiety associated with the compulsive behavior
   b. individual's ability to control or decrease the behavior
   c. pleasure associated with the compulsive behavior
   d. intensity of the person's guilt about the behavior
9. In posttraumatic stress disorder, the likelihood of recovery is related to
   a. the extent to which there are complicating factors such as alcoholism
   b. the extent to which the patient experienced psychological problems before the event
   c. the extent to which social support is available
   d. all of the above

10. It is quite possible, of course, for an individual to experience two (or more) psychological disorders at the same time. Which of the following pairs of disorders is MOST LIKELY to occur together?
    a. generalized anxiety disorder — conversion disorder
    b. psychogenic amnesia — compulsive disorder
    c. agoraphobia — panic disorder
    d. hypochondriasis — multiple personality

11. Freud developed the treatment technique of psychoanalysis in order to deal with
    a. conversion disorder
    b. phobias
    c. hypochondriasis
    d. obsessive-compulsive disorder

12. One plausible explanation for psychogenic fugue and psychogenic amnesia is that they are
    a. an attempt to avoid stress
    b. an attempt to get attention
    c. a way of dealing with anxiety
    d. a means of avoiding responsibility

13. Unusually high incidences of child abuse, sexual abuse, and drug abuse are related to
    a. schizophrenia
    b. obsessive-compulsive disorder
    c. multiple personality
    d. psychogenic fugue

14. Personality disorders can be distinguished from other disorders on many grounds, but which of the following enables us to differentiate personality disorders from anxiety-based disorders? As opposed to anxiety-based disorders, personality disorders
    a. are more commonly a reaction to frustration and stress
    b. involve a long-standing history of symptoms
    c. are usually found more in children and adolescents
    d. involve some degree of loss of contact with reality

15. Demetri seems to overreact to everything and constantly seeks attention and approval. At a party, he is the first to put a lampshade on his head. He describes all his experiences as "peak, the best" and all his troubles as "the worst." He is most likely suffering from _____________ personality disorder.
    a. passive-aggressive
    b. schizoid
    c. histrionic
    d. antisocial

16. Which of the following statements about psychotic disorders is TRUE?
    a. People who suffer from psychotic disorders rarely require hospitalization.
    b. Psychoses and neuroses are the same thing.
    c. Psychotic disorders are not discussed in the DSM-III-R.
    d. Psychotic disorders are characterized by a loss of contact with reality.

17. Psychiatrist Aaron Beck offers an explanation for mood disorders that is largely
    a. behaviorist
    b. cognitive
    c. biological
    d. situational

18. Which of the following statements concerning schizophrenic patients is TRUE?
    a. They are usually colorless, socially withdrawn, and not at all dangerous.
    b. They usually exhibit wild, crazed behavior, and may be violent.
    c. Even though they may be having delusions, they are usually able to communicate clearly.
    d. The most common affect is extreme moods, either mania or depression.

19. Factors such as an excess of dopamine, normal brain configuration, severe disruptions early in family life, and a relatively good response to treatment are correlated to ____________ schizophrenia.
    a. reactive
    b. process
    c. positive
    d. negative

20. Everything else being equal, which person will have the greatest chance of being diagnosed with schizophrenia?
    a. someone who knows and interacts with many schizophrenics on a regular basis
    b. someone who has an identical twin diagnosed as having the disorder
    c. someone with abnormally large ventricles in their cerebral cortex
    d. someone whose mother is generally cold, aloof, and unaffectionate

**Check Your Knowledge of the Learning Objectives**

The following questions are examples of what you should know when you have finished studying this chapter. Write the answers to these questions. Use your book to verify the answers. Page references are provided.

1. Explain how psychological abnormality is defined. p. 395

_______________________________________________
_______________________________________________
_______________________________________________
_______________________________________________
_______________________________________________

2. Describe the DSM-III-R and discuss the advantages and disadvantages of a classification system for disorders. p. 396-397

_______________________________________________
_______________________________________________
_______________________________________________
_______________________________________________

3. Describe phobic disorders. p. 399

_______________________________________________
_______________________________________________
_______________________________________________
_______________________________________________
_______________________________________________
_______________________________________________
_______________________________________________

4. Define panic disorder. p. 400

_______________________________________________
_______________________________________________
_______________________________________________
_______________________________________________
_______________________________________________

5. Compare and contrast generalized anxiety disorder and panic disorder. p .. 400-401

_______________________________________________
_______________________________________________
_______________________________________________
_______________________________________________
_______________________________________________

6. Distinguish between obsessions and compulsions. p. 401-402

_______________________________________________
_______________________________________________
_______________________________________________
_______________________________________________
_______________________________________________
_______________________________________________

7. Describe posttraumatic stress disorder. p. 403

8. Distinguish between hypochondriasis and conversion disorder. p. 404-405

9. Characterize dissociative disorders. p. 405

10. Characterize personality disorders. p. 407-409

11. Distinguish between psychogenic amnesia and psychogenic fugue. p. 406

12. Discuss the use of the term "insanity." p. 398

13. Define mood disorders and discuss their prevalence and causes. p. 410-413

14. Discuss the major symptoms of schizophrenia. p. 413

15. Distinguish between process and reactive schizophrenia. p. 416

16. Distinguish between positive and negative symptoms of schizophrenia. p. 417

17. Describe the distinguishing characteristics of catatonic, disorganized, paranoid, undifferentiated, and residual schizophrenia. p. 418

18. Describe the factors suspected as causes of schizophrenia. p. 417-420

## Dr. G's Best Study Tips # 12

**Taking Essay Exams**

1. Read through the instructions to make sure you know how many questions to answer and what the scoring system will be. Plan which questions you will answer and in what order and budget your time for each question.
2. Organize and outline your answers to make sure you don't leave out any important information.
3. Read each question carefully and answer only what is asked. Look for key words: describe, define, list, explain, compare and contrast, illustrate.
4. Answer the questions that you know first. This will build your confidence.
5. Start your essay with a CHAPTER sentence, present the facts, and follow with a conclusion.
6. Use the vocabulary covered in class and in your text. Give specifics when possible.
7. Use examples to back up your judgments and opinions.
8. Leave space after each answer so you can go back and add details if you have extra time or remember additional facts.
9. Go back and reread each answer to be sure you didn't omit anything. Proofread for spelling and grammatical errors and correct them.
10. Prepare for the test by constructing your own essay questions and writing practice answers. The learning objectives in this study guide will be very helpful in anticipating essay questions.

**********************************************************************************

Below are two essay questions that cover abnormal psychology. Use them to practice your essay writing techniques.

1. Discuss the advantages and disadvantages of diagnosis in abnormal psychology.
2. List and describe five subclassifications of schizophrenia.

# CHAPTER 13 — TREATMENT AND THERAPY FOR PSYCHOLOGICAL DISORDERS

**Learning Objectives**

1. Trace the history of the treatment of people with psychological disorders.
2. Define prefrontal lobotomy and discuss its use, both past and present.
3. Describe ECT and its current use.
4. Discuss treatment with antipsychotic drugs, listing the various drugs and their effects.
5. Discuss treatment with antidepressant drugs.
6. Discuss treatment with antianxiety drugs and the dangers of their use.
7. Describe Freudian psychoanalysis and define its major features.
8. Explain how psychoanalysis is different today from how it was practiced by Freud.
9. Discuss the essential characteristics of client-centered therapy.
10. Describe the techniques used in behavior therapy, including systematic desensitization, flooding, aversion therapy, contingency management, contracting, and modeling.
11 Describe rational-emotive therapy and cognitive restructuring therapy.
12. Discuss the advantages of group therapy.
13. List the two assumptions underlying family therapy.
14. Discuss the effectiveness of psychotherapy in general and whether any one type is more effective than others.

**Chapter 13 Outline**

I. Preview
   A. Nearly one-quarter of all the days that Americans spend in the hospital can be accounted for by mental disorders.
   B. The basic premise that persons with psychological disorders should be treated humanely is remarkably recent in our history.
   C. The idea of active intervention to improve the quality of life of persons suffering from mental disorders is more recent still.
   D. This history is important to help understand why some persons have strong negative attitudes and beliefs about those with psychological disorders.

II. A Historical Perspective
   A. How people have been treated has been consistent with the prevailing view of what caused the disorder.
      1. Greeks and Romans believed that mentally disturbed individuals had offended the gods.
         a. They might just be temporarily out of favor.
         b. Severely disturbed patients were seen as being physically possessed by evil spirits.
         c. Ancient therapists exorcised the evil spirits.
         d. Many persons died of the treatment or were killed if the treatment failed.
      2. Hippocrates (460-377 B.C.) believed that mental disorders had physical causes.
         a. He identified epilepsy as being a disorder of the brain.
         b. His impact was slight and short-lived at that time.
      3. The Middle Ages (A.D. 1000-1500) was a period in history during which the oppression and persecution of the mentally ill were at their peak.
         a. During that period, the mentally ill were seen as possessed by or in league with the devil.
         b. Treatment consisted of torture.
      4. When not tortured or killed, the insane were put in asylums.
         a. The first asylum was probably St. Mary of Bethlehem Hospital in London (known as Bedlam).
         b. Patients were treated by bleeding to remove "bad blood."
      5. Philippe Pinel (1745-1826) was named director of an asylum for the insane in Paris.
         a. Pinel ordered the chains and shackles removed from about 50 inmates.
         b. The conditions of the patients in many cases improved dramatically.
         c. Pinel's humane treatment can be viewed as the beginning of a very gradual enlightenment concerning mental illness.

III. Who Provides Treatment and Therapy?
   A. Many professions are equipped to help, to provide psychotherapy.
      1. Clinical psychologists usually have a Ph.D. in psychology.
         a. They spend a year in internship.
         b. They usually have extensive training in psychological testing.
      2. Psychiatry is a specialty area in medicine.
         a. Psychiatrists serve an internship and a residency at a mental hospital.
         b. They are the only therapists who can use biomedical treatments.
      3. Counseling psychologists usually have a Ph.D. in psychology.
      4. A licensed professional counselor will have a degree in counselor education and will meet state requirements for a license to perform psychotherapy.
      5. Psychoanalyst is a special label given either to a clinical psychologist or a psychiatrist who has also received intensive training in the methods of Freudian psychoanalysis.
      6. Clinical social workers engage in a variety of psychotherapies, but their traditional role has been involvement in family and group therapy.
   B. Psychotherapy may be offered by a number of other professionals and paraprofessionals.
      1. Some have master's degrees in psychology.
      2. Occupational therapists aid the psychologically and physically handicapped.
      3. Psychiatric nurses often work in mental hospitals and clinics.
      4. Pastoral counseling is a specialty of many with a religious background and a master's degree in either psychology or educational counseling.
      5. Mental health technicians are involved in the delivery of many mental health services, though they usually do not provide unsupervised psychotherapy.

IV. Biomedical Treatments of Psychological Disorders
   A. Psychosurgery refers to surgical procedures designed to affect psychological or behavioral reactions.
      1. A prefrontal lobotomy severs the major neural connections between the prefrontal lobes and the lower brain centers.
         a. Lobotomy was first used in 1935 by Egas Moniz, a Portuguese psychiatrist.
         b. The logic behind the operation was that the frontal lobes influence the more basic emotional centers of the brain.
         c. An instrument was inserted through the eye socket, on the nasal side, and pushed into the brain.
      2. This technique had terrible side effects.
         a. One to 4 percent of patients died.
         b. Survivors had seizures, memory loss, an inability to plan ahead, and a general listlessness and loss of affect.
      3. Prefrontal lobotomies are not done now because they are no longer needed.
   B. Electroconvulsive therapy (ECT), introduced in 1938, involves passing an electric current (70 to 150 volts) across a tranquilized patient's head for a fraction of a second.
      1. There is a physical seizure, followed by a short loss of consciousness.
         a. The procedure takes about five minutes.
         b. Side effects include memory loss for events just preceding the shock and for the shock itself.
      2. ECT often alleviates the symptoms of depression and sometimes other psychotic symptoms.
         a. Beneficial effects may be long-lasting.
         b. No more than 12 treatments should be given, and these should be spread over a long period of time.
         c. There is evidence of brain damage and permanent memory loss with ECT.
      3. ECT is still in use.
         a. About 100,000 patients receive ECT yearly.
         b. The numbers are on the rise.
      4. The introduction of psychoactive, antidepressant medications has lessened the need for ECT.
   C. The use of drug therapy is a recent development and is one of the most significant scientific achievements of the last half of the twentieth century.

1. Antipsychotic drugs reduce the severity of, and occasionally may even eliminate, psychotic symptoms.
    a. The introduction of phenothiazines in the mid-1950s was a breakthrough.
    b. The first of these, chlorpromazine, was discovered in France.
    c. A neurosurgeon, Henri Laborit, was looking for a drug that would calm patients before surgery.
    d. Most of the antipsychotics are only good for treating positive symptoms.
    e. Clozapine is a new drug that seems to be effective in treating negative symptoms as well as positive ones.
    f. Lithium has been found to be very effective in treating patients with bipolar mood disorders.
    g. The antipsychotic drugs have many negative side effects.
    h. Medicated patients may be released from hospitals, stop taking their medication, and have their psychotic symptoms return.
2. Antidepressant drugs elevate mood.
    a. MAO inhibitors increase levels of neurotransmitters.
    b. Tricyclics are also widely used today.
    c. Tricyclics have side effects of intellectual confusion, increased perspiration, and weight gain.
    d. Patients taking MAO inhibitors must adhere to a strict diet.
    e. Dosages need to be carefully monitored.
    f. Flouxetine (Prozac) was introduced in 1987 and is currently the single most prescribed antidepressant.
3. Antianxiety drugs (or tranquilizers) help reduce the felt aspect of anxiety.
    a. They are the most commonly prescribed of all drugs.
    b. Meprobamates (Miltown or Equanil) are basically muscle relaxants.
    c. Benzodiazepines (Librium, Valium) act on the central nervous system.
    d. The tranquilizing effects of the drugs are not long-lasting.
    e. Patients may rely on these drugs to alleviate even the slightest fears and worries.

V. Psychoanalytic Techniques
    A. Psychoanalysis is based on a number of assumptions, most of them having to do with the nature of conflict and the unconscious mind.
    B. A number of procedures and processes are used in Freudian psychoanalysis.
        1. In free association patients are told to say out loud whatever comes into their minds.
            a. Patients are not to edit their associations.
            b. To aid in relaxation, Freud had his patients lie down, be comfortable, and avoid eye contact with the analyst.
        2. Resistance-the inability or unwillingness to freely discuss some aspect of one's life-is analyzed in therapy as one clue to the source of emotional problems.
        3. Analyzing a patient's dreams is an important part of psychoanalysis.
            a. Freud called dreams the "royal road to the unconscious."
            b. Freud analyzed dreams at two levels: manifest and latent content.
        4. Transference occurs when the patient unconsciously comes to view and feel about the analyst much the same way he or she feels about some other important person in his or her life.
            a. Feelings become more accessible in this way.
            b. Countertransference occurs when the therapist allows his or her own feelings and past experiences to interfere with neutral and objective interaction with patients.
    C. Freudian psychoanalysis today is typified by a concern for shortening the length of analysis.
        1. Today's analyst will also take a more active, directive role than Freud did.
        2. The couch as a requirement is usually gone.
        3. Modern psychoanalysts tend to spend more time exploring the present.

VI. Humanistic Techniques
    A. There are many different types of humanistic psychotherapies and their closely allied cousins, the existential therapies.
        1. They are all concerned with self-examination.
        2. They try to foster psychological growth and development.

B. Client-centered, or Rogerian, therapy is probably the therapy that best typifies the humanistic approach.
   1. The client is the center of the client-therapist interaction.
   2. For Rogers, therapy provides a special opportunity for a person to engage in self-discovery.
   3. The following ideas characterize the client-centered approach.
      a. The focus is on the present.
      b. The focus is on one's feelings or affect.
      c. The therapist will attempt to reflect, rather than interpret, how the client is feeling.
      d. The therapist will be an active, empathetic listener.
      e. Unconditional positive regard will be given.

C. Gestalt therapy is associated with Fritz Perls and shares many of the same goals as client-centered therapy.
   1. One goal of gestalt therapy is to help the individual to integrate his or her thoughts, feelings, and actions.
   2. Gestalt therapy differs from client-centered therapy in that the therapist is more actively involved and challenges the client.

VII. Behavioral Techniques

A. Behavior therapy is a collection of many specific techniques based on principles of learning rather than a single unified approach.

B. Systematic desensitization is the application of classical conditioning procedures to alleviate extreme feelings of anxiety.
   1. This was one of the first applications of learning principles to meet with success.
   2. It was introduced by Joseph Wolpe in the late 1950s.
   3. There are three stages involved in systematic desensitization in its standard form.
      a. The subject is instructed in methods of relaxation.
      b. The second step is to construct an anxiety hierarchy.
      c. The subject then relaxes and focuses on each item in the hierarchy sequentially.
   4. It is based on the logic that a person cannot be relaxed and anxious at the same time-they are incompatible responses.

C. Flooding is another procedure that is aimed at eliminating fears or anxieties based on specific stimuli.
   1. Flooding is an in vivo, or real life, procedure.
   2. The subject, accompanied by the therapist, is actually placed in his or her most fear-arousing situation and prohibited from escaping.

D. In aversion therapy, a stimulus that produces a pleasant response is paired with an aversive, painful, unpleasant stimulus until the stimulus becomes unpleasant.
   1. Aversion is very effective at suppressing a specific behavior.
   2. It is seen as the lesser of two evils.
   3. It has probably given behavior therapy a bad reputation with the general public.

E. Contingency management and contingency contracting borrow heavily from the principles of operant conditioning.
   1. Appropriate behaviors lead to rewards and opportunities to do valued things.
   2. Inappropriate behaviors lead to aversive stimulation and fewer opportunities.
   3. It is called contingency management when the therapist controls rewards and punishments.
   4. Contingency contracting amounts to establishing a token economy of secondary reinforcers.

F. Modeling involves the acquisition of a new, appropriate response through the imitation of a model.
   1. Modeling often amounts to having patients watch someone else perform a certain appropriate behavior.
   2. Some phobias, especially in children, can be overcome through modeling.
   3. Assertiveness training involves many processes and often relies on modeling.

VIII. Cognitive Techniques

A. The principle is that to change how one feels and acts, therapy should first be directed at changing how one thinks.

B. Rational-emotive therapy (RET), associated with Albert Ellis, has as its basic premise that psychological problems arise when a person tries to interpret what happens in the world on the basis of irrational beliefs.
   1. Disturbed behaviors and feelings arise from maladaptive cognitions.
   2. When compared with client-centered techniques, RET is quite directive.
   3. Cognitive therapists claim that client-centered therapists hold a number of irrational beliefs.
      a. For example, client-centered therapists feel a person should always be loved for everything they do.
      b. Cognitive therapists also disagree with the belief that it is better to avoid problems than to face them.

C. Cognitive restructuring therapy, associated with Aaron Beck, is similar to RET but is much less confrontational and direct.
   1. According to Beck, people with psychological disorders share certain characteristics.
      a. They tend to have very negative self-images.
      b. They tend to take a very negative view of life experiences.
      c. They overgeneralize.
      d. They actually seek out experiences that reinforce their negative expectations.
      e. They have a negative outlook.
      f. They avoid seeing the bright side.
   2. A therapist offers the patient an opportunity to test or demonstrate his or her beliefs.

IX. Group Approaches

A. Group therapy is a general label applied to a variety of situations in which a number of people are involved in a therapeutic setting at the same time.
   1. In standard group therapy, a number of clients are brought together at one time (with a therapist's guidance) to share their feelings and experiences.
   2. Group therapy provides an economic advantage over individual psychotherapy.
   3. Most groups are quite informal, and no particular form of therapy is dominant.
   4. Group approaches have a number of benefits.
      a. Clients become aware that they are not the only ones with problems.
      b. Clients have a sense of support from other group members.
      c. Helping others is a therapeutic process.
      d. The client may learn new and more effective ways of interacting with others.

B. Family therapy is a variety of group therapy that focuses on the roles, interdependence, and communication skills of family members.
   1. Family therapy is often implemented after one member of a family enters therapy.
   2. Underlying this approach are two related assumptions.
      a. Each individual family member is a part of a system, and he or she has an impact on other family members.
      b. Difficulties within families stem from improper methods of communication.

X. Evaluating Psychotherapy

A. Evaluating psychotherapy has proven to be a very difficult task.
   1. Psychotherapy is effective compared to doing nothing.
   2. More treatment is better than less treatment.
   3. There is no evidence, in general, that one type of therapy is significantly better than any other.

B. There are several problems involved with doing research on the effectiveness of psychotherapy.
   1. There is little data on how people respond without therapy.
   2. We can't agree on what we mean by recovery.
   3. There is often concern about how to measure or assess outcomes.

C. When comparing psychotherapy methods, in general, there are no differences.

**Learning Chapter 13 Vocabulary**

Write the definition for each of the following key terms on the lines provided at the right. Then fold the paper vertically so you can see only the term and try to say the definition. Practice this until you can say them all correctly.

PSYCHOSURGERY

LOBOTOMY

ELECTROCONVULSIVE THERAPY

ANTIPSYCHOTIC DRUGS

ANTIDEPRESSANT DRUGS

ANTIANXIETY DRUGS

PSYCHOTHERAPY

COGNITIVE RESTRUCTURING THERAPY

FREE ASSOCIATION

RESISTANCE

TRANSFERENCE

CLIENT-CENTERED THERAPY

EMPATHIC

BEHAVIOR THERAPY

SYSTEMATIC DESENSITIZATION

FLOODING

FAMILY THERAPY

AVERSION THERAPY ______________________________
______________________________

CONTINGENCY MANAGEMENT ______________________________
______________________________

CONTINGENCY CONTRACTING ______________________________
______________________________

MODELING ______________________________
______________________________

RATIONAL-EMOTIVE THERAPY ______________________________
______________________________

**IDIOMS AND DIFFICULT PHRASES**

**put them away** (p. 430.) To put someone away means to put them in jail or an insane asylum or isolate them in some way.

**We've already touched on this matter** (p. 432) To touch on a matter is to discuss it or give it your attention.

**So big deal** (p. 443) In informal speech, to say that something is a big deal is to say that it is important. The phrase is often said sarcastically (as it is in this case) to express that someone is exaggerating an event.

**My old man** (p. 443) This is a slang expression that can mean father (as in this case) or husband. The expression "my old lady" refers to a person's wife or mother.

**Matching**

Match the following key terms with the appropriate definitions.

______ 1. lobotomy
______ 2 resistance
______ 3. electroconvulsive therapy
______ 4. psychosurgery
______ 5. antianxiety drugs
______ 6. antidepressant drugs
______ 7. antipsychotic drugs
______ 8. empathic
______ 9. rational-emotive therapy
______ 10. family therapy
______ 11. flooding
______ 12. modeling
______ 13. aversion therapy
______ 14. systematic desensitization
______ 15. free association
______ 16. client-centered therapy
______ 17. transference
______ 18. behavior therapy
______ 19. psychotherapy
______ 20. contingency contracting
______ 21. cognitive restructuring therapy
______ 22. contingency management

a. The treatment of mental disorders through psychological means, effecting change in cognitions, affect and/or behavior.
b. A psychosurgical technique in which the prefrontal lobes of the cerebral cortex are severed from lower brain centers.
c. The procedure in psychoanalysis in which the patient is to express whatever comes to mind without editing responses.
d. In psychoanalysis, the inability or unwillingness to freely discuss some aspect of one's life.
e. In psychoanalysis, the situation in which the patient comes to feel about the analyst in the same way he or she once felt about some other important person.
f. The humanistic psychotherapy associated with Rogers, aimed at helping the client grow and change from within.

g. Able to understand and share the essence of another's feelings; to view from another's perspective.
h. Techniques of psychotherapy founded on principles of learning established in the psychological laboratory.
i. The application of classical conditioning procedures to alleviate anxiety in which anxiety-producing stimuli are paired with a state of relaxation.
j. A technique of behavior therapy in which a subject is confronted (in vivo) with the object of his or her phobic fear while accompanied by the therapist.
k. Chemicals, such as the meprobamates and benzodiazepines, that alleviate the symptoms of anxiety.
l. A technique of behavior therapy in which an aversive stimulus, such as a shock, is paired with an undesired behavior.
m. Bringing about changes in one's behaviors by controlling rewards or punishments.
n. Establishing a token economy of secondary reinforcers to reward appropriate behaviors.
o. The acquisition of new responses through the imitation of another who responds appropriately.
p. A form of cognitive therapy associated with Ellis, aimed at changing the subject's irrational beliefs or maladaptive cognitions.
q. A form of cognitive therapy, associated with Beck, in which patients are led to overcome negative self-images and pessimistic views of the future.
r. A variety of group therapy focusing on the roles, interdependence, and communication skills of family members.
s A surgical procedure designed to affect one's psychological or behavioral reactions.
t. A treatment, usually for the symptoms of depression, in which an electric current passed through a patient's head causes a seizure and loss of consciousness.
u. Chemicals, such as chlorpromazine, that are effective in reducing psychotic symptoms.
v. Chemicals, such as MAO inhibitors and tricyclics, that reduce and/or eliminate the symptoms of depression.

**True-False Practice Test**

___ 1. The systematic, humane treatment of people with psychological problems is a twentieth-century phenomenon.
___ 2. A study of the history of the treatment of people with psychological disorders can help us understand why these problems are viewed with such strong negative attitudes today.
___ 3. The ancient Greeks and Romans believed that psychological disorders were the result of being possessed by evil spirits or angering the gods.
___ 4. In the early history of psychological disorders, many people either died as a result of treatment or were killed outright if treatment failed.
___ 5. In Greek and Roman times, the treatment for psychological disorders was done by shepherds.
___ 6. Unfortunately, even the enlightened scientists like Hippocrates had little lasting impact on the manner of treatment for individuals with psychological problems.
___ 7. For hundreds of years, the treatment for mental illness was torture for those who would not confess.
___ 8. The distinction between the mentally ill and the mentally retarded is a fairly recent one (since the 1800s).
___ 9. Bedlam was really an exceptionally bad institution, and most of the other asylums were really quite good in their treatment of the insane.
___ 10. At the present time, lobotomies are illegal.
___ 11. One of the problems with ECT is that the beneficial effects are very short-lived.
___ 12. The use of drugs to treat mental illness has been hailed as one of the most significant scientific achievements of the last half of the twentieth century.
___ 13. Most of the antipsychotic drugs work through some effect on neurotransmitters.
___ 14. In all, there are only a few different types of psychotherapies.
___ 15. In the past 30 years, psychotherapy has become more common.
___ 16. Freud referred to a patient's unwillingness to discuss certain aspects of life as resistance.
___ 17. The humanistic and existentialist therapies share a concern for self-examination, personal growth, and development.
___ 18. Aversion therapy is most effective when used in conjunction with another form of therapy.

___ 19. The contingency contracting technique is most effective with older adults in an open environment.
___ 20. Cognitive therapists believe that a change in how a person thinks can bring about a change in the way the person acts.
___ 21. Aaron Beck would be likely to describe his clients as optimists.
___ 22. Beck's theory was most similar to Albert Ellis' cognitive theory.
___ 23. Depression responds well to cognitive restructuring therapy.
___ 24. Only a trained psychoanalyst should conduct group therapy sessions.
___ 25. About the only benefit to group therapy is saving a little money.
___ 26. The applications of family therapy are usually limited to working with cases of alcoholism.
___ 27. According to family therapists, it is very difficult for a therapist to bring about change in a child whose parents will not take part in therapy.
___ 28. In general, there is some indication that family therapy is a better approach for many problems than individual therapy.

**Fill-In Practice Test**

1. A therapist who does an internship at a psychiatric hospital or mental health center and has extensive background in psychological testing is a __________ __________.
2. Perhaps the first person to suggest that psychological disorders had physical causes was ________________, around 400 B.C.
3. The persecution and oppression of the mentally ill peaked during the __________ ______.
4. The idea that mentally ill people were in league with the devil or possessed by evil spirits continued well into the _______ century.
5. The first insane asylum became known as ___________.
6. The man known for unchaining the people at an asylum in France is __________.
7. The reform identified as the mental health movement began in the early ______ century.
8. Surgical procedures designed to affect psychological reactions are called ________________.
9. _____________ is a surgical procedure which severs the connections between the prefrontal lobes and the lower brain centers.
10. Electroconvulsive therapy is the more formal term for what are commonly called __________ ______________.
11. Chemicals that have their effect on the person's affect or behavior are collectively referred to as _____________ _______.
12. Most antipsychotic drugs are prescribed for patients suffering from _________________.
13. The difference between a Ph.D. and a Psy.D. is generally that a Psy.D. program emphasizes clinical work more and ____________ less.
14. The difference between a psychologist and a psychiatrist is that the psychiatrist is trained in _____________ as well as in psychology.
15. Freud referred to the symbolic representation of the contents of the unconscious in dreams as __________ content.
16. According to Freud, _________________ occurs when the patient unconsciously begins to feel about the analyst the same way he or she feels about some other important person.
17. A therapist who lets his or her feelings and past experiences interfere with their neutral and objective interactions with a patient is experiencing _______________________.
18. Carl Rogers founded ______________________ therapy.
19. _______________ therapy could be described as methods of psychotherapeutic change founded on principles of learning established in the psychological laboratory.
20. In ____________ _________________ therapy, the therapist controls rewards and punishments in an attempt to modify the patient's behavior.
21. A behavioral technique based on a token economy is called __________ _________________.
22. The client's thoughts, perceptions, attitudes, and beliefs about himself are key factors in ________________ therapies.
23. Aaron Beck's ______________ __________________ therapy is similar to RET, but less direct and confrontational.
24. Beck's cognitive approach has proven very effective in the treatment of______________.
25. When a number of people are involved in a therapeutic setting at one time, it is referred to as _________ therapy.

**Chapter 13 Multiple Choice Practice Test**

1. The first insane asylum was in
   a. London
   b. Rome
   c. Paris
   d. Athens
2. The turning point in the history of the treatment of the mentally ill that marked the beginning of enlightenment and better treatment was
   a. Hippocrates' declaration that mental illness has physical causes
   b. the burning of the last witches early in the 17th century
   c. an exorcism performed by Johann Sprenger
   d. the unchaining of inmates in a French asylum
3. The first person to perform a lobotomy was
   a. Pinel
   b. Dix
   c. Moniz
   d. Freeman
4. Which of the following results or side effects of lobotomy was not considered to be a problem?
   a. the fact that it was irreversible
   b. the fact that 1 to 4 percent of the patients died
   c. the fact that patients suffered memory loss and seizures
   d. the fact that patients suffered a loss of affect
5. Which of the following therapists may also be a psychoanalyst?
   a. licensed professional counselor
   b. clinical social worker
   c. psychiatrist
   d. pastoral counselor
6. The patients best suited for ECT (those who seem to benefit most) are those suffering from
   a. depression
   b. depression and other psychotic symptoms, such as hallucinations
   c. anxiety-based disorders
   d. schizophrenia
7. Most antipsychotic drugs are used to treat
   a. anxiety-based disorders
   b. depression
   c. schizophrenia
   d. suicidal patients
8. Which of the following is NOT a problem regarding the use of antipsychotic drugs?
   a. There are certain patients for whom the drugs have no effect.
   b. The antipsychotic drugs can produce unpleasant and dangerous side effects.
   c. The symptoms are likely to return if the drugs are discontinued.
   d. In many cases the drugs actually cause symptoms to worsen.
9. Lithium is to _______________ as clozapine is to schizophrenia.
   a. bipolar mood disorder
   b. depression
   c. anxiety-based disorders
   d. unipolar mood disorder
10. One difference between antipsychotic drugs and antidepressants is that
    a. antidepressants have no side-effects
    b. antidepressants are more likely to bring about long-term cures
    c. antidepressants have a shorter duration of effect
    d. antidepressants can be bought over the counter without a prescription

11. One real problem associated with antianxiety drugs is that they
   a. just aren't very effective
   b. have tremendous negative side-effects
   c. can only be used with the mildest disorders
   d. are so effective that the patient isn't motivated to deal with the source of the anxiety

12. Which psychologist characterized a good therapist as being well-adjusted, warm, empathic, and supportive?
   a. Freud
   b. Beck
   c. Rogers
   d. Beutler

13. Which of the following therapies is associated with unconditional positive regard and a nondirective approach by the therapist?
   a. psychoanalysis
   b. client-centered therapy
   c. rational-emotive therapy
   d. cognitive therapy

14. Which of the following therapies was made popular by Albert Ellis?
   a. psychoanalysis
   b. client-centered therapy
   c. rational-emotive therapy
   d. cognitive therapy

15. Joseph's father wants to help him get over his fear of the water, so he takes him to the local pool and gets into the water with him and will not let him out. This is an example of
   a. systematic desensitization
   b. flooding
   c. aversion therapy
   d. parent training

16. Benito went to a smoking cessation clinic where they had him chain-smoke until he became ill. This would be an example of
   a. systematic desensitization
   b. flooding
   c. aversion therapy
   d. parent training

17. Albert Bandura is associated with the behavioral therapy approach known as
   a. contingency management
   b. flooding
   c. implosive therapy
   d. modeling

18. Two related assumptions guide the course of much family therapy. One assumption views each family member as a part of a system, while the other assumption stresses:
   a. an even distribution of power and control
   b. mutual attempts at reinforcing appropriate behaviors
   c. the extent to which one's happiness depends on the other members of the family group
   d. a concern for improved, open, and honest communication among family members

19. Different forms of psychotherapy have different intermediate goals, but when all is said and done, the "bottom line" final goal of all psychotherapy is to:
   a. help the individual appreciate oneself and enhance oneself esteem
   b. bring about a relatively permanent change in affect, behavior, and/or cognition
   c. provide insight about the nature of whatever problem underlies the disorder being treated
   d. see to it that each patient receives proper medication

20. One advantage of group therapy is saving
    a. money
    b. time
    c. energy
    d. research

**Check Your Knowledge of the Learning Objectives**

The following questions are examples of what you should know when you have finished studying this chapter. Write the answers to these questions. Use your book to verify the answers. Page references are provided.

1. Trace the history of the treatment of people with psychological disorders. p. 429-430

2. Define prefrontal lobotomy and discuss its use, both past and present. p. 434

3. Describe ECT and its current use. p. 435

4. Discuss treatment with antipsychotic drugs, listing the various drugs and their effects. p. 436-437

5. Discuss treatment with antidepressant drugs. p. 437-438

6. Discuss treatment with antianxiety drugs and the dangers of their use. p. 438

7. Describe Freudian psychoanalysis and define its major features. p. 439-440

8. Explain how psychoanalysis is different today from how it was practiced by Freud. p. 441

9. Discuss the essential characteristics of client-centered therapy. p. 442

10. Describe the techniques used in behavior therapy, including systematic desensitization, flooding, aversion therapy, contingency management, contracting, and modeling. p. 444-446

11. Describe rational-emotive therapy and cognitive restructuring therapy. p. 447-448

12. Discuss the advantages of group therapy. p. 448-449

13. List the two assumptions underlying family therapy. p. 449

14. Discuss the effectiveness of psychotherapy in general and whether any one type is more effective than others. p. 450-452

## Dr. G's Best Study Tips #13

**Stressed about the Test**

Some people suffer from test anxiety so severe that it produces psychosomatic symptoms. Others experience poor performance along with anxiety. Whatever form it takes, test anxiety is unpleasant, but something can be done about it.

Research indicates that an overwhelming majority of test anxiety is related to poor preparation. The other study tips in this guide should help you to overcome this source of anxiety. If you are sure that you are preparing as well as possible and still experience test anxiety, try the following suggestions.

1. Get control of your breathing by focusing on it and counting as you inhale. Then exhale to the same slow count. You should feel much more in control and more relaxed.
2. Close your eyes and visualize a quiet, relaxing place, maybe a beach or a mountain scene. Think about how quiet and soothing the place is and how wonderful it is to be there in your mind. Repeat this as often as needed.
3. Spend some time thinking about why the exam is making you so anxious. What is it that you fear? Failure? Success? Being the last one finished? Disappointing someone? Disappointing yourself?
4. Listen to your self-talk. Is it negative? Do you say things to yourself like, "I'll never pass this test." or "I've always done poorly on essay exams." If so, stop this negative self-talk and replace it with positive messages, such as "I am well prepared and know my material." "It doesn't matter if I finish last." "I know I can get this even if it takes a second try."
5. Finally, seek help for the test anxiety. Talk with your instructor or visit the student counseling center. Our counseling center runs free seminars every semester on test anxiety. Perhaps there is similar help available on your campus.

# CHAPTER 14 — SOCIAL PSYCHOLOGY

**Learning Objectives**

1. Define stereotypes and norms and describe how they are cognitive.
2. Define attitude and list the three components of an attitude.
3. Explain how attitudes are acquired.
4. Define cognitive dissonance and explain how it relates to attitude change.
5. List the two basic types of attribution and explain how attribution becomes distorted or biased.
6. Describe the four theoretical models of interpersonal attraction.
7. Know the four determinants of interpersonal attraction and their effects.
8. Discuss the methodology and findings of Asch's studies.
9. Discuss Milgram's studies of obedience.
10. Explain how the presence of others affects helping behavior and list the three factors that account for these effects.
11. Describe how social influence affects quality of performance.
12. Describe how social influence affects group decision-making.

**Chapter 14 Outline**

I. Preview
   A. Social psychology is the field of psychology that is concerned with how people influence the thoughts, feelings, and behaviors of one another.
   B. Many other areas of psychology are also interested in reactions that are essentially social in nature.

II. The Social-Psychological Perspective
   A. We are all naive social psychologists.
      1. Social psychology tends to be perceived as interesting and relevant because it deals with familiar, everyday situations.
      2. Many people are willing to accept common sense, personal experience, and even folklores as the basis for explaining and making assumptions about social behavior.
   B. The social psychologist is distinguished by a perspective that relies on experimentation and other scientific research strategies as sources of knowledge about social behavior.
   C. Social psychology has taken on a clearly cognitive flavor in the past few years.
      1. Psychologists are attempting to understand social behavior by examining the mental structures and processes that are reflected in such behavior.
      2. An example of how mental processes are reflected in social behavior is a stereotype.
         a. A stereotype is a generalized mental representation of members of a group that is based on limited experience and that does not allow for individual differences.
         b. When stereotypes are based on accurate information, they are useful tools that help one simplify and deal more efficiently with a complex world.
      3. Prescriptions or expectations about how to behave and deal with social interactions are called social norms.
         a. Like stereotypes, they are cognitions that we may use to help simplify our social world.
         b. Because of social norms, we know how to act in a wide variety of social situations.

III. Attitudes
   A. An attitude is a relatively stable and general evaluative disposition directed toward some object. It consists of beliefs, feelings, and behaviors.
   B. An attitude has three components.
      1. The affective component consists of our feelings or emotions about the attitudinal object.
      2. The behavioral component consists of our response or action tendencies toward the object of our attitude.
      3. The cognitive component consists of our beliefs or thoughts about the attitudinal object.
      4. Predicting any single behavior on the basis of a person's attitude is very difficult.
   C. Attitude formation appears to occur through learning.
      1. Some attitudes are acquired through the simple associative process of classical conditioning.
         a. Some advertising attempts to work in that way.

b. Advertising with sexual connotations operates along the same lines.
2. Attitudes can also be formed as a result of the direct reinforcement of behaviors consistent with some attitudinal position.
3. When we observe others gaining reinforcers for having and expressing some attitude, we are likely to adopt that attitude ourselves (vicarious reinforcement).

D. Conscious, planned attempts to change someone's attitude are called persuasion.
1. Leon Festinger proposed that attitudes may follow behavior.
a. Festinger's theory refers to a condition he called cognitive dissonance.
b. Dissonance means discord, discomfort, or distress that is due to things being out of balance or not fitting together well.
2. The effectiveness of a persuasive communication is almost always influenced by its source.
a. A highly credible source will induce more change than a less credible source.
b. Especially important are expertise and trustworthiness.

IV. Social Perception

A. Attribution theory has to do with understanding the cognitions we use in trying to explain behavior, both our own and that of others.

B. Social psychologists have found it useful to distinguish between two basic types of attributions.
1. Internal attributions explain the source of behavior in terms of some characteristic of the person, often a personality trait or disposition, sometimes called dispositional attributions.
2. External attributions explain the sources of behavior in terms of the situation or social context outside the individual; they are referred to as situational attributions.

C. The evidence indicates that people tend to rely on certain types of information when making judgments about the sources of behavior: distinctiveness, consensus, and consistency.

D. An active area of research deals with the errors we tend to make in our social thinking.
1. The fundamental attribution error is an example of a cognitive bias.
a. This is the basic tendency when observing others to favor internal, personal attributions for their behavior rather than external, situational explanations.
b. This error is more common in Western cultures.
2. The just world hypothesis consists of people taking on the belief that we live in a just world where good things happen to good people and bad things happen to bad people.
3. Self-serving bias is the tendency to attribute our successes to our own effort and abilities and our failures to situational, external sources.
4. The actor-observer bias is a basic discrepancy between the way we explain our behavior and the way we explain someone else's.
a. External attributions are given when we talk about why we do things.
b. When we explain someone else's behaviors we tend to use internal attributions and refer to characteristics of the person whose behaviors we have been observing.

V. Interpersonal Attraction

A. Attraction can be seen as an attitude-a favorable and powerful attitude about another person.

B. Social psychologists have put forth a number of theoretical models to explain the bases of interpersonal attraction.
1. The reinforcement model claims that we tend to be attracted to people we associate with rewards.
2. The social exchange model emphasizes the comparison of the costs as well as the benefits of establishing or maintaining a relationship.
3. The equity model, an extension of the social-exchange theory, applies the appraisal of rewards and costs to both members of a social relationship.
a. Both members of a relationship have to share rewards equally.
b. If one person were to feel that he or she was getting less from a relationship than was deserved, the relationship would not be equitable and would be jeopardized.
4. The attachment theory suggests that interpersonal relationships can be classified into one of three types, depending on the attitudes that one has about such relationships.
a. Secure

b. Avoidant
c. Anxious/ambivalent

C. The following are four of the most common principles of interpersonal attraction.
  1. Reciprocity means that we tend to value and like people who like us back.
    a. We are most attracted to people who like us now, but who may have been neutral originally.
    b. We are likely to attribute initial liking to the way the person is-someone who likes everyone.
  2. Physical closeness, or proximity, tends to produce liking.
    a. The mere exposure phenomenon indicates that with a variety of novel social and nonsocial stimuli, liking tends to increase with repeated exposure to stimuli.
    b. Apparently there is some truth to the adage that familiarity breeds liking, not contempt.
  3. Physical attractiveness communicates something about us.
    a. For both men and women, the more physically attractive their date, the more they like the person and the more they want to go out again with that individual.
    b. Eventually subjects in a study started selecting partners whose level of physical attractiveness was more similar to their own (the matching phenomenon).
    c. Attractive persons are assumed to have other desirable characteristics as well-a phenomenon called the physical attractiveness stereotype.
  4. There is a very positive relationship between liking and the proportion of attitudes people hold in common.

V. Social Influence
  A. We modify our behavior so that it is consistent with the behavior of others, a process called conformity.
  B. The Asch studies showed that conformity occurred 37 percent of the time, and 75 percent of Asch's subjects conformed to group pressure at least once.
    1. The level of conformity increased as the size of the majority increased.
    2. Conformity decreased to 10 percent when there was one dissenter among the six confederates.
  C. Milgram's research on obedience to authority has become among the most famous and controversial in all of psychology.
    1. The original impetus for his research was his interest in the extreme obedience to Nazi authority displayed by many German military personnel during World War II.
    2. The original goal of his research was to determine if people of different nationalities differ in the degree to which they will obey a request to inflict pain on another person.
    3. His results were astonishing.
      a. Sixty-five percent obeyed the experimenter's demands and went all the way to the highest shock value.
      b. No subject stopped prior to the 300-volt level.
    4. A later replication with adult women as subjects produced precisely the same results.
  D. Attribution errors consist of attributing the subject's behavior to personality characteristics instead of recognizing the powerful situational forces at work.
    1. People tend to rely on others for help in determining social reality when ambiguity is present.
    2. We tend to accept perceived authority without questioning it.
  E. Milgram was severely criticized for placing people in such an extremely stressful situation.
    1. Milgram took great care to debrief his subjects after each session.
    2. Milgram also indicated that a follow-up study performed a year later with some of the same subjects showed that no long-term adverse effects had been created by his procedure.
    3. One of the effects of his research was to establish in the scientific community a higher level of awareness of the need to protect the well-being of human research participants.
  F. The tragic case of Kitty Genovese stimulated public concern and sparked a good deal of commentary in the media.
    1. This incident prompted a program of research that helped to establish a basic understanding of the social factors that can influence people to intervene.
    2. Latané and Darley were convinced that situational factors make such events possible.

a. People generally are not prepared to deal with emergencies.
b. A good predictor of who will intervene in an emergency turns out to be previous experience with similar emergency situations.
c. The risk of physical injury is an understandable deterrent to helping.
d. People may fail to help because they genuinely want to avoid the legal consequences that might follow.

G. Latané and Darley (1968) proposed a cognitive model for a bystander to intervene in an emergency.
1. The bystander must notice what is going on.
2. He or she must interpret the event as an emergency.
3. The bystander must decide that it is his or her responsibility to do something.

H. There are a number of psychological processes that account for what is called social inhibition helping, or bystander effect.
1. Audience inhibition refers to our tendency to hesitate to do things in front of others, especially strangers.
2. Pluralistic ignorance refers to group paralysis caused by the fact that no one is doing anything, thereby leading others to believe that there is no emergency.
3. Diffusion of responsibility refers to the fact that the greater the number of other people present, the smaller is each individual's personal obligation to intervene.

I. The situational determinants of helping behavior are present in all situations.

J. Social loafing refers to the tendency to work less as the size of the group in which one is working becomes larger.

K. Social facilitation means that performance improves due to the presence of others.

L. Social interference refers to impaired performance due to the presence of others.

M. Many of the decisions that we face are the sort that must be made in groups.
1. There is logic in the belief that group efforts to solve problems should be superior to the efforts of individuals.
2. Stoner found that the decisions rendered by groups were generally much riskier than those that the individual group members had made prior to the group decision-a risky shift.
3. The risky shift is simply a specific case of a more general group polarization phenomenon.
   a. This effect can occur in the opposite direction as well.
   b. Group polarization suggests that open discussion gives group members an opportunity to hear persuasive arguments they have not previously considered, leading to a strengthening of their original attitudes.
4. Groupthink is a style of thinking used by cohesive groups concerned with maintaining agreement to the extent that independent ideas are discouraged.
   a. Alternate courses of action are not considered realistically.
   b. It is characterized by a cohesive decision-making group that is relatively isolated from outside judgments.
   c. There is a directive leader who supplies pressure to conform to his or her position.
   d. There is an illusion of unanimity.

**Learning Chapter 14 Vocabulary**

Write the definition for each of the following key terms on the lines provided at the right. Then fold the paper vertically so you can see only the term and try to say the definition. Practice this until you can say them all correctly.

STEREOTYPE ______________________________
______________________________

NORMS ______________________________
______________________________

ATTITUDE ______________________________
______________________________

SOCIAL PSYCHOLOGY

COGNITIVE DISSONANCE

CONFORMITY

ATTRIBUTION

INTERNAL ATTRIBUTION

EXTERNAL ATTRIBUTION

FUNDAMENTAL ATTRIBUTION ERROR

JUST WORLD HYPOTHESIS

GROUPTHINK

ACTOR-OBSERVOR BIAS

MERE EXPOSURE PHENOMENON

MATCHING PHENOMENON

GROUP POLARIZATION

SOCIAL INTERFERENCE

AUDIENCE INHIBITION

PLURALISTIC IGNORANCE

DIFFUSION OF RESPONSIBILITY

SOCIAL LOAFING

SOCIAL FACILITATION

**IDIOMS AND DIFFICULT PHRASES**

**victims of rape often ask for it by the way they dress** (p. 471) In informal speech, this phrase (he/she asked for it) is often used to describe someone who has been injured or gotten into trouble. It means that this person behaved in such a way that they deserved to be injured. Does a woman deserve to be raped because she dresses in a certain (seductive) manner?

**Similarity is probably the glue that holds together romances**. (p. 475) This is a common metaphor that means that people who are alike will probably stay together. Opposites may attract, but similarities keep people together.

**they were in on the experiment** (p. 475) In informal speech to be "in on" something is to be a part of it. Confederates are part of an experiment. They are like actors and know what is being done in the experiment, unlike subjects who are usually not fully informed of the intent of the experiment until the experiment is finished.

**sometimes "choking" in front of home crowds** (p. 483) If a team or individual plays a very bad game, they are said to be "choking."

**Matching**

Match the following key terms with the appropriate definitions.

| | | | |
|---|---|---|---|
| ______ | 1. attribution | ______ | 2. internal attribution |
| ______ | 3. matching phenomenon | ______ | 4. mere exposure phenomenon |
| ______ | 5. social loafing | ______ | 6. stereotype |
| ______ | 7. social interference | ______ | 8. cognitive dissonance |
| ______ | 9. just world hypothesis | ______ | 10. attitude |
| ______ | 11. fundamental attribution error | ______ | 12. social psychology |
| ______ | 13. norms | ______ | 14. social facilitation |
| ______ | 15. external attribution | ______ | 16. actor-observer bias |
| ______ | 17. diffusion of responsibility | ______ | 18. conformity |
| ______ | 19. groupthink | ______ | 20. audience inhibition |
| ______ | 21. group polarization | ______ | 22. pluralistic ignorance |

a. A generalized mental representation of someone that minimizes individual differences and is based on limited experience.
b. Rules or expectations that guide our behavior in certain social situations by prescribing how we ought to behave.
c. A relatively stable and general evaluative disposition directed toward some object, consisting of feelings, behaviors, and beliefs.
d. The scientific study of how others influence the thoughts, feelings, and behaviors of the individual.
e. Improved performance due to the presence of others.
f. The tendency for a person to work less hard when part of a group in which everyone's efforts are pooled.
g. A motivating discomfort or tension caused by a lack of balance or consonance among one's cognitions.
h. The cognitions we generate when we attempt to explain the sources of behavior.
i. An explanation of behavior in terms of something within the person; a dispositional attribution.
j. An explanation of behavior in terms of something outside the person; a situational attribution.
k. The tendency to overuse internal attributions when explaining behavior.
l. The belief that the world is just and that people get what they deserve.
m. A style of thinking of cohesive groups concerned with maintaining agreement to the extent that independent ideas are discouraged.
n. Overusing internal attributions to explain the behaviors of others and external attributions to explain our own behaviors.
o. The tendency to increase our liking of people and things the more we see of them.

p. The tendency to select partners whose level of physical attractiveness matches our own.
q. Changing one's behavior, under perceived pressure, so that it is consistent with the behavior of others.
r. Reluctance to intervene and offer assistance in front of others.
s. A condition in which the inaction of others leads each individual in a group to interpret a situation as a nonemergency, thus leading to general inactivity.
t The tendency to allow others to share in the obligation to intervene.
u. Impaired performance due to the presence of others.
v. The tendency for members of a group to give more extreme judgments following a discussion than they gave initially.

**True-False Practice Test**

___ 1. Social psychologists are the only psychologists interested in reactions or behaviors that are social in nature.
___ 2. Social cognition involves the perception and evaluation of oneself and other people in social situations.
___ 3. Stereotypes can be helpful in that they help us to simplify and deal more efficiently with a complex world.
___ 4. Stereotypes and norms are the same thing.
___ 5. An attitude can be defined by the presence of any two of the three components of beliefs, behaviors, or cognitions.
___ 6. According to the theory of cognitive dissonance, beliefs follow behaviors.
___ 7. When a person experiences cognitive dissonance, it is likely that he will change either his behavior or his attitude in order to reduce the dissonance.
___ 8. When trying to create an attitude change, if the message is rather weak, one would be concerned with the peripheral route of persuasive communication.
___ 9. Research subjects from Eastern cultures are more likely to explain behavior in terms of external attributions than are people from Western cultures.
___ 10. According to attachment theory, one's style of relating to others is very stable throughout the lifespan.
___ 11. According to the principle of reciprocity, we are most attracted to the people who like us now but did not like us originally.
___ 12. No harm comes from the fact that physically attractive people are judged more favorably.
___ 13. The old adage that opposites attract is probably not true.
___ 14. Conformity is always undesirable and negative.
___ 15. Asch found that conformity increased as the size of the incorrect majority increased.
___ 16. Asch found that subjects were more likely to trust their own judgment if one other person among the confederates agreed with them.
___ 17. Milgram initially hypothesized that the Nazis' obedience might actually be a part of their character rather than a situational or external attribute.
___ 18. The astonishing results of Milgram's study indicated that the subjects responded to the authority figures and were not at all distressed when required to administer what they thought were painful shocks.
___ 19. People tend to rely on others for help in determining social reality when ambiguity is present.
___ 20. Following his study, Milgram provided reasonable care for his subjects, doing all that was necessary for them.
___ 21. There are really no reasonable excuses for failure to help in an emergency.
___ 22. According to Latané and Darley, the victim is unlikely to get help in an emergency because of all the steps in deciding to render assistance and the potential costs of intervention.
___ 23. The psychosocial law suggests that each person added to a group increases the likelihood that the target person will not respond to the emergency.
___ 24. Social loafing tends to decline when individuals believe that their effort is special or that it can be identified and evaluated.
___ 25. Group polarization refers to the fact that group discussion usually leads to a more conservative conclusion than the opinions of the individuals in the group.

**Fill-In Practice Test**

1. Social psychologists focus on the _______________, whereas sociologists would focus on the group.
2. ___________ ___________ involves the study of how other people affect the psychological reactions of the individual.
3. A _______________ is a generalized set of cognitions about members of a group that is based on limited experience and that does not allow for individual differences.
4. Shared expectations about how the members of a group ought to behave are called social ________.
5. A relatively stable and general evaluative disposition toward some object consisting of beliefs, feelings, and behaviors defines a/an ____________.
6. Conscious, planned attempts to change someone's attitude are referred to as ____________.
7. According to cognitive response theory, the power of a persuasive message can be reduced by the presence of _____________.
8. In attribution theory, ___________ attributions explain the source of behavior in terms of some characteristic of the person.
9. __________ attributions explain the sources of behavior in terms of the situation or social context.
10. The ________________ ________________ error is the tendency to disregard dispositional factors when we make judgments about behavior.
11. According to the ______________ model of interpersonal attraction, we are attracted to people that we associate with rewards.
12. ______________ theory suggests that interpersonal relationships can be classified into one of three types depending on the attitudes one has about such relationships.
13. Liking and valuing people who like and value us is referred to as ______________.
14. Modifying behavior under pressure in order to be consistent with the behavior of others is known as ______________.
15. Sherif used the _______________ __________ to show how social norms can develop and induce conformity in an ambiguous situation.
16. Yielding to the perceived pressure of peers is conformity, but yielding to the perceived pressure of an authority figure is _____________.
17. The Yale psychologist who became interested in and did research on obedience was ___________.
18. After a study such as Milgram's, it is very important that subjects be ____________, explaining to them the deceptions involved and why they were necessary.
19. First attempts at explaining why no one intervened to help Kitty Genovese used labels such as __________ ________ and alienation.
20. According to Latané and Darley, the first step in bystander intervention is for the bystander to ________ the situation.
21. The tendency to be hesitant to do things in front of others is referred to as ____________ _______________.
22. ______________ ______________ is the belief on the part of the individual that only she or he doesn't know what to do and that everyone else is doing nothing for a good reason.
23. The _____________ law specifies that each person that is added to a group has less impact on the target individual than the previous person to join the group.
24. __________ __________ refers to the tendency to work less as the size of the work group increases.
25. When the presence of others improves an individual's performance, it is called __________ _______________.

**Chapter 14 Multiple Choice Practice Test**

1. Social psychology can be defined as the study of
    a. how people influence the thoughts, feelings, and behaviors of an individual
    b. how people interact in groups
    c. a person's behavior in social situations
    d. why people form institutions and join groups or associations

2. A relatively stable and general evaluative disposition toward some object consisting of beliefs, feelings, and behaviors defines a/an
   a. norm
   b. stereotype
   c. attitude
   d. opinion

3. Your beliefs that imported foreign products are a threat to American jobs, priced too low for American goods to compete, and so on, illustrates the ___________ component of attitudes.
   a. affective
   b. cognitive
   c. intentional
   d. behavioral

4. Advertising that relies on testimonials from satisfied customers is relying on forming attitudes through
   a. operant conditioning
   b. classical conditioning
   c. observational learning
   d. persuasion

5. Which of the following individuals is likely to be the most persuasive?
   a. a celebrity selling a product related to his fame
   b. a celebrity selling a product unrelated to his fame
   c. an unknown expert, such as a doctor, selling a related product
   d. an unknown expert with a very persuasive message

6. Rachel left her door unlocked and her house was subsequently burglarized. Some of the neighbors said, "she got what she deserved." The neighbors' attitudes exemplify the
   a. self-serving bias
   b. actor-observer bias
   c. fundamental attribution error
   d. just world hypothesis

7. A student who attributes his good grades to his own brilliance and hard work, and his bad grades to poor teachers, illustrates the
   a. self-serving bias
   b. actor-observer bias
   c. fundamental attribution error
   d. just world hypothesis

8. Ben was interested in agriculture and wanted to become a rancher. While in high school, he dated a girl that he nicknamed, "five hundred acres" because her father owned a lot of land. One explanation for his attraction to her would be the _________ model.
   a. social exchange
   b. reinforcement
   c. equity
   d. attachment

9. The matching phenomenon suggests that when rejection is a real possibility, people choose partners who are similar to themselves in
   a. ethnicity
   b. socioeconomic status
   c. physical attractiveness
   d. age

10. Which of the following is NOT one of the four determinants of interpersonal attraction?
   a. proximity
   b. similarity
   c. reciprocity
   d. generosity

11. In the study of social influence, psychologists are most interested in how
  a. an individual influences another individual
  b. an individual influences a group of people
  c. groups of people influence individuals
  d. groups of people influence other groups of people

12. A confederate in a research study is someone who is
  a. "in on the experiment" and assists the researcher
  b. in the control group
  c. in the experimental group
  d. observing the study in order to maintain ethical standards

13. Asch is to conformity as Milgram is to __________.
  a. obedience
  b. perception
  c. social influence
  d. authority

14. Milgram's initial goal in his obedience research was to determine whether obedience differed among
  a. different ethnic groups
  b. different socioeconomic groups
  c. people with different amounts of education
  d. people in positions of authority

15. It is very unlikely that Milgram's studies will ever be repeated because
  a. it is unnecssary when research results are so conclusive
  b. some of the subjects in the learner role were permanently impaired
  c. ethical standards have been raised and would prohibit such a study today
  d. no one would voluntarily participate in such a study

16. Which of the following people is most likely to render aid in an emergency?
  a. a single bystander
  b. a single bystander with experience in similar emergencies
  c. a member of a large crowd of bystanders
  d. the first person who happens by

17. Scottie participates in speed skating events. His father, Bob, has been keeping records of his performances and notes that he skates faster when competing against other skaters as opposed to skating against the clock. The best explanation for this is
  a. bystander effect
  b. social facilitation
  c. social interference
  d. social loafing

18. A jury enters the jury room to deliberate with all of its members having moderate confidence in the defendant's guilt. After deliberations, and having found the defendant guilty, indeed, the jurors are even more convinced of the defendant's guilt. This illustrates the phenomenon known as
  a. group polarization
  b. groupthink
  c. social facilitation
  d. opinion drift

**Check Your Knowledge of the Learning Objectives**

The following questions are examples of what you should know when you have finished studying this chapter. Write the answers to these questions. Use your book to verify the answers. Page references are provided.

1. Define stereotypes and norms and describe how they are cognitive. p. 460-461

2. Define attitude and list the three components of an attitude. p. 461-462

3. Explain how attitudes are acquired. p. 463

4. Define cognitive dissonance and explain how it relates to attitude change. p. 463-465

5. List the two basic types of attribution and explain how attribution becomes distorted or biased. p. 469

6. Describe the four theoretical models of interpersonal attraction. p. 472-473

7. Know the four determinants of interpersonal attraction and their effects. p.473-475

8. Discuss the methodology and findings of Asch's studies. p. 475-476

9. Discuss Milgram's studies of obedience. p. 477

10. Explain how the presence of others affects helping behavior and list the three factors that account for these effects. p. 479-482

11. Describe how social influence affects quality of performance. p. 482

12. Describe how social influence affects group decision-making. p. 484

## Dr. G's Best Study Tips #14

**Social Cognition: Studying with Other People**

There appear to be three options for studying in terms of a social context: studying with better students, studying with students at about your same level, and tutoring or helping weaker students. Let's examine these options in a little more detail.

Your first step should be an honest evaluation of yourself as a student or "studier." Do you have good skills? Are you self-motivated? Are you well-organized? Are you able to stay on task or easily distracted? Do you make good grades? What do you have to offer a study partner? Once you have answered some of these questions, you are ready to think about whether you would benefit from a study group or study partner and what kind of person/people you should seek.

If you are a weak student, you should seek out a stronger student who will help you to select the main points, get organized, motivated, and stay on task. I believe there is little to be gained by assembling a group of weak students.

A strong student can really benefit by tutoring or helping others. Research indicates that peer tutors benefit more from the experience than the person who receives the tutoring. The best explanation for this is that the process of organizing the information and understanding it well enough to explain it to someone else enhances the tutor's own understanding and memory.

If you are an average student, you should seek out other average students or stronger students as study partners. Whatever your level, the following guidelines should be helpful.

1. Try to meet several people on the first day of class and get their phone numbers. You will want to call them about notes and assignments if you should be unable to attend class.
2. Look around to see who is taking notes. Try to find someone who appears to be organized. Listen for someone who asks intelligent, thought-provoking questions or offers relevant, interesting comments in class. Another hint: good students tend to sit near the front of class.
3. Once you have formed a study group, always have a definite plan as to what you want to accomplish when the group meets. If necessary, set an agenda just like a business meeting and stick to it. Do NOT let the study session turn into a "bull" session.
4. Go to the group well-prepared. Read assignments and write out questions ahead of time. Make notes about issues you want to clarify or discuss with the group. This should not be a substitute for individual effort, rather a way to enhance your own preparation.
5. Reward yourselves if you are successful. Raise your test grades? Then go out and celebrate.

# CHAPTER 15 — PSYCHOLOGY APPLIED: I/O, ENVIRONMENTAL, AND SPORTS PSYCHOLOGY

**Learning Objectives**

1. Explain what is involved in doing a job analysis.
2. Describe some of the information sources that can be used in making personnel decisions.
3. List some of the factors that need to be considered in the design, implementation, and evaluation of a training program.
4. Summarize some of the factors that affect motivation of workers to do a good job.
5. Define job satisfaction and the quality of work life.
6. Describe the relationship between job satisfaction and job productivity.
7. Define environmental psychology and list some of the issues that environmental psychologists study.
8. Define the concepts of personal space and territoriality.
9. Explain the difference between population density and crowding.
10. List the positive and negative aspects of city living.
11. Describe the effects of noise, extreme temperature, and neurotoxins have on behavior.
12. Explain what environmental psychologists can do to have a positive impact on the environment.
13. Discuss some of the ways that psychologists can become involved in sports and athletics.

**Chapter 15 Outline**

I. Preview
   A. Industrial-organizational psychologists specialize in the study of affect, behavior, and cognitions in the workplace.
   B. Industrial-organizational psychology is one of the fastest growing of psychology's specialty areas.
   C. Environmental psychologists are concerned about interactions between the physical environment and one's psychological state of well-being.
   D. Psychologists also apply their knowledge to the world of sports and athletics.
II. Industrial-Organizational Psychology
   A. Fitting the person to the job
      1. A job analysis is a process that results in a complete and specific description of a job.
         a. The first step of this process consists of compiling a complete description of what a person in that job is expected to do.
         b. The second step involves translating these duties into terms of measurable personal characteristics.
            i. Performance criteria may be "hard criteria," which include available data and are objective.
            ii. "Soft criteria" require some degree of subjective judgment, such as sense of humor, creativity, and congeniality.
   B. Picking people who can do good work requires a variety of techniques and sources of information.
      1. A job application form can serve three functions.
         a. It can be used as a rough screening device.
         b. It can supplement and/or provide cues for interviewing.
         c. It provides biographical data.
         d. Some I/O psychologists believe that biographical data are the best source of data for predicting success on the job.
      2. The employment interview is the most widely used employee selection procedure in this country.
         a. Unstructured interviews are subject to many sources of error.
         b. Validity studies for interviews are dismal.
         c. There are considerable individual differences in interviewer skill.
         d. Structured interviews are much more valid than unstructured interviews.
   C. Personnel selection often involves the administration and interpretation of psychological tests.
      1. Tests may be narrow in their application and assess only one skill.

2. Other tests assess a number of different skills and abilities.
3. The most useful tests appear to be those that measure some sort of cognitive ability.

D. The training and development of employees is one of the major concerns of business, industry, and government.
   1. Training activities are the most frequently reported approach to productivity improvement.
   2. Training consists of a systematic and intentional process of altering the behaviors of employees to increase organizational effectiveness.
   3. One must first do an assessment of training needs.
      a. The first step is to state the general goals of the training program.
      b. These must then be translated into actual training objectives.
      c. Specific statements are required stating what the training program is expected to accomplish.
      d. Evaluation criteria must then be developed.
      e. Specific training techniques must be developed.
      f. Training effectiveness must be evaluated.
         i. Training programs can be evaluated at a number of different levels.
         ii. Training programs that do not include ways and means of evaluating short- and long-term effectiveness will generally be of little value.
         iii. Evaluation is easier if effort is put into assessment of needs, job analysis, performance criteria, and training objectives at the beginning.

E. I/O psychologists have long been interested in how to motivate employees to do good work.
   1. Expectancy theory takes the view that workers make logical choices to do what they believe will result in their attaining outcomes of highest value.
      a. Employers should see that outcomes that follow good work are truly valued by workers.
      b. It is very important for workers to understand the relationship between their behaviors and outcomes.
   2. Equity theory takes the view that workers are motivated to match their inputs and outcomes with those of fellow workers in similar positions.
      a. Workers judge how much they are getting from the organization compared to what they are putting into it.
      b. This ratio of inputs to outcomes is compared to the ratio of another, similarly placed employee.
      c. The worker may increase or decrease input based on this comparison.
   3. Goal-setting assumes that workers are best motivated to perform a task for which the goals are clearly and specifically detailed.
      a. The goal must be clear.
      b. The employee must accept that goal as something worth working for.
      c. Difficult but achievable goals tend to increase productivity more than easy goals.
      d. Specific goals are better than general ones.
      e. Feedback about the nature of the work is important in maintaining motivation.
      f. Goals that are set by both the employer and the employee tend to be most effective.

F. Job satisfaction is an attitude or a collection of feelings about one's job or job experiences.
   1. Research on job satisfaction and personal characteristics suggests the following:
      a. There is a strong correlation between job satisfaction and age. Younger workers tend to be more dissatisfied.
      b. Data on sex differences in job satisfaction tend to be inconsistent.
      c. Racial differences tend to be small, although whites have more positive attitudes than nonwhites.
      d. Satisfaction is positively related to the perceived level or status of one's job or occupation.
   2. Quality of worklife (QWL) consists of a group of factors concerning one's work that influence one's attitude toward one's job. These include:
      a. A sense of respect from supervisors
      b. Employee security
      c. Income adequacy and equity
      d. A sense of self-esteem, challenge, and independence

e. Opportunities for social interaction
f. A sense of contribution
g. A relationship between life on the job and life off the job
h. Active participation in decision making

3. Concern for the welfare of workers and their sense of satisfaction is a relatively new phenomenon.

G. Job satisfaction and productivity may be related, but the relationship is complex and weak.
1. Increased productivity may have the effect of increasing satisfaction rather than vice versa.
2. Measures of job satisfaction can be used to aid the prediction of which workers are likely to be absent from work and which are likely to quit.
3. The relationship between dissatisfaction with one's job and turnover seems to be stronger.

III. Psychology and the Environment
A. Environmental psychology is the field of applied psychology that studies the effect of the general environment on organisms within it.
B. Personal space is the mobile "bubble" of space around you reserved for people with whom you have intimate relationships, and into which others may enter only by invitation.
1. The extent of one's personal space depends on the situation and other factors such as:
a. Who is the other person?
b. Is the other person about your age?
c. Is the person an attractive member of the opposite sex?
2. The extent of one's personal space is culturally determined.
3. Edward Hall (1966) claimed that personal space can be subdivided into four different distances.
a. Intimate distance-contact to 18 inches.
b. Personal distance-18 inches to 4 feet, reserved for friends and acquaintances.
c. Social distance-4 to 12 feet, for individuals whom we do not know well.
d. Public distance-12 to 25 feet, by which personal contact is minimized but communication is still possible.
4. We tend to feel uncomfortable whenever these distances are violated.
5. Territoriality is the setting off and marking of a piece of territory (a location) as one's own.
a. This was first studied in nonhumans.
b. In humans, primary territories are ours alone.
c. Secondary territories are more flexible and less well-defined and are not used for expressing personal identity.
d. Public territories are those we tend to occupy for only a short time.
e. Territories help to define our identity, promote privacy, and promote a sense of structure.

C. From research on rats (Calhoun, 1962), interest in crowding in cities grew.
1. Population density is a quantitative measure of the number of persons per unit of area.
2. Crowding is the subjective feeling of discomfort caused by a sense of lack of space.
a. Crowding is a negative condition.
b. Crowding may be independent of the number of persons involved.
3. There is increasing evidence to support the claim that living in the city is healthier, in a number of physical and psychological ways, than is living in the country.
4. The challenge of environmental psychologists is to help urban planners and architects to design living spaces in areas of high density that minimize the subjective experience of crowding.

D. Noise, temperature, and environmental toxins can have a profound effect on behavior.
1. Noise is any intrusive, unwanted, or excessive experience of sound.
a. Noise becomes most stressful when it is loud, high-pitched, and unpredictable.
b. Exposure to noise increases levels of stress, anxiety, and aggressive behaviors.
c. Unpredictable and uncontrollable noise causes performance levels to drop.
2. Extremes of temperature can have adverse effects on behavior.
a. Aggressive behaviors tend to increase during hot weather.
b. Violent crime increases during hot months and hot years.

c. Differences in crime rates among cities are better predicted by temperature than by social, demographic, and economic variables.
d. Riots tend to occur during moderately high temperatures (75 to 90 degrees Fahrenheit).

3. Environmental psychologists are concerned with toxins in the environment.
   a. Neurotoxins are chemicals (poisons) that affect psychological processes through the nervous system.
   b. Psychologists are concerned with educating the public about toxins.
   c. They are also involved with the diagnosis of effects of toxins.
   d. Refer to Figure 15.3 in the text for a list of neurotoxins and their effects.

E. Environmental psychologists are active in helping to establish programs aimed at changing the behaviors of large numbers of people in such a way as to ultimately benefit the environment.
   1. Applied behavior analysis (ABA) is an approach, based on operant conditioning, that attempts to find solutions to human environment problems in the real world.
   2. This is a three-stage process.
      a. The behaviors to be changed must be defined.
      b. Antecedent strategies (prompting procedures) are developed.
      c. Reinforcement for compliance should be given.

IV. Psychology and Sports
   A. Sports psychology is the application of psychological principles to sport and physical activity at all levels of skill development.
   B. Research analyzing the psychological characteristics of athletes has been less than satisfactory and tends to confirm the obvious.
      1. Successful athletes tend to score higher than nonsuccessful athletes on tests of assertion, dominance, aggression, and need for achievement.
      2. They score lower on such traits as anxiety level, depression, and fatigue.
      3. Hockey and football players are more tolerant of pain than are athletes in other sports, although this may be an outcome.
   C. The athlete in competition needs to be fully aroused and motivated to perform.
      1. Too much arousal may interfere with performance.
      2. Home fans may raise arousal levels of the home team beyond the point of maximum efficiency.
      3. Peak performance can be attained through a combination of mental and physical practices.
      4. Mental practice is useful in:
         a. Mentally rehearsing a particular behavioral pattern
         b. Reducing negative thoughts that may interfere with performance
         c. Rehearsing one's role in a team sport and setting realistic goals.

**Learning Chapter 15 Vocabulary**

Write the definition for each of the following key terms on the lines provided at the right. Then fold the paper vertically so you can see only the term and try to say the definition. Practice this until you can say them all correctly.

JOB ANALYSIS

PERFORMANCE CRITERIA

TRAINING

EXPECTANCY THEORY

EQUITY THEORY

JOB SATISFACTION

QUALITY OF WORK LIFE

TYPE A BEHAVIOR PATTERN

ENVIRONMENTAL PSYCHOLOGY

PERSONAL SPACE

TERRITORIALITY

POPULATION DENSITY

CROWDING

NEUROTOXINS

APPLIED BEHAVIOR ANALYSIS

SPORTS PSYCHOLOGY

**IDIOMS AND DIFFICULT PHRASES**

**OSHA will be by soon** (p. 490) The Occupational Safety and Hazard Administration is the government agency responsible for regulating workplace safety.

**taken simply on faith or face value** (p. 498) To accept something at face value is to accept it with only a very limited evaluation. Accepting an idea on faith is much the same as accepting it at face value.

**Matching**

Match the following key terms from your text with the appropriate definitions.

| | | | |
|---|---|---|---|
| ______ | 1. training | ______ | 2. population density |
| ______ | 3. expectancy theory | ______ | 4. neurotoxins |
| ______ | 5. equity theory | ______ | 6. performance criteria |
| ______ | 7. job satisfaction | ______ | 8. job analysis |
| ______ | 9. quality of work life | ______ | 10. sport psychology |
| ______ | 11. personal space | ______ | 12. environmental psychology |
| ______ | 13. territoriality | ______ | 14. crowding |
| ______ | 15. applied behavior analysis | ______ | 16. type A behavior pattern |

a. A complete and specific description of a job, including the qualities required to do it well.
b. Specific behaviors or characteristics that a person should have in order to do a job as well as possible.
c. Chemicals that affect psychological processes through the nervous system.
d. An approach, based on operant conditioning, that attempts to find solutions to human environment problems in the real world.
e. A systematic and intentional process of altering the behaviors of employees to increase organizational effectiveness.
f. The view that workers make logical choices to do what they believe will result in their attaining outcomes of highest value.
g. The view that workers are motivated to match their inputs and outcomes with those fellow workers in similar positions.
h. An attitude; a collection of feelings about one's job or job experiences.
i. A group of factors concerning one's work that influence one's attitude toward one's job.
j. The application of psychological principles to sport and physical activity at all levels of skill development.
k The subjective feeling of discomfort caused by a sense of lack of space.
l. A collection of behaviors often associated with coronary heart disease.
m. The field of applied psychology that studies the effect of the general environment on organisms within it.
n. The mobile "bubble" of space around you reserved for intimate relationships into which others may enter only by invitation.
o. The setting off and marking of a piece of territory as one's own.
p. A quantitative measure of the number of persons per unit of area.

**True-False Practice Test**

___ 1. A job analysis describes the actual behaviors done on the job in more detail than a job description.
___ 2. Most job analyses involve the use of both hard and soft criteria.
___ 3. The goal of a job analysis is to find the best available person to do a job as well as possible.
___ 4. A job analysis is really the first step in the selection, training, and motivation process.
___ 5. Research indicates that interviews are very successful techniques for selecting the right employee for the job.
___ 6. Unstructured interviews tend to be more valid than structured interviews.
___ 7. One problem with structured interviews is that they take away the interviewer's freedom to explore different issues.
___ 8. An I/O psychologist might be called on to construct a test to assess some unique ability or characteristic for which a valid measure does not already exist.
___ 9. In the decade of the 70s, training was the most frequently used approach to improving productivity.
___ 10. One crucial decision to be made about training is whether or not it is really needed.
___ 11. Although evaluating a training program is important, usually one evaluation immediately after the training session is sufficient.
___ 12. Motivation is of concern to the I/O psychologist because being able to do a job well and wanting to do a job well are not the same thing.
___ 13. One reason why employees are not motivated is that so few believe that they are actually compensated for their work performance.
___ 14. According to equity theory, the reality of fairness is more important than the perception of fairness.
___ 15. The concept of concern for worker satisfaction, safety, and quality of work life are products of the twentieth century.
___ 16. Many of the components of Type A behavior are actually very positive, productive traits that are valued in our society.
___ 17. Although a health psychologist would intervene with lifestyle behaviors associated with increased risk for certain diseases, there would not be similar intervention related to safety behaviors.
___ 18. Smoking is one case where preventive measures seem clearly advantageous over changing established habits.
___ 19. Personal space and territory are the same thing.
___ 20. Environmental psychologists have concluded that living in a densely populated city produces negative consequences such as increased stress.
___ 21. Noise is considered most stressful when it is loud, high-pitched, and unpredictable.
___ 22. Total absence of noise can also prove stressful.
___ 23. Although the presence of noise has been proven to disrupt performance on problem-solving tasks, the performance returns to normal as soon as the noise stimulus is removed.
___ 24. It seems clear that extreme temperatures have adverse effects on behavior.
___ 25. Although some environmental toxins affect physical health, there are none known that affect mental health or behavior.

**Fill-In Practice Test**

1. A _______ ____________ is a systematic study of the tasks, duties, and responsibilities of a job and the knowledge, skills, and abilities needed to perform it.
2. A list of characteristics that a person should have in order to do a job as well as possible is called ________________ ___________.
3. The ______________ is the most widely used employee selection procedure in this country.
4. When applicants are asked to role play the task they may be hired to do, it is referred to as ________________ ___________.
5. When choosing a test for use in personnel selection, _____________ of the test is a very important consideration.
6. The first nongovernmental use of the assessment center approach was by ________.
7. In the ______________ technique, applicants are provided a number of tasks, memos, and assignments of the sort they might encounter in a typical day at the office.

8. _____________ is a systematic intentional process of altering behavior of organizational members in a direction that contributes to organizational effectiveness.
9. _______________ proposed a system for implementing effective training programs.
10. The first step in designing and implementing a training program is _________ _______________.
11. According to ________________ theory, workers behave rationally and logically, making decisions based on their judgments, beliefs, and expectations.
12. According to ___________ theory, what matters most to workers is their perception of the extent to which they are being treated fairly compared to other workers.
13. _______ _________________ refers to a person's attitude toward work, usually a pleasurable or positive feeling.
14. The _________________ approach to safety is based on the notion that some people are more accident prone than others.
15. The ___________________ approach to safety is based on the idea that safety can be enhanced by designing safe equipment and procedures.
16. ___________ psychology is the study of psychological or behavioral factors affecting physical health and illness.
17. A person who is competitive, achievement-oriented, and impatient, probably could be characterized as having a /an _____________ behavior pattern.
18. _____________ could be considered to be the single greatest behavioral health risk.
19. ______________________ psychology is the subfield that studies how the general environment affects the behavior and mental processes of those living in it.
20. The imaginary bubble of space that surrounds a person and into which others may enter comfortably only by invitation is called ______________ ________.
21. The smallest amount or bubble of personal space is between actual contact and about 18 inches and is referred to as _________ distance.
22. A distance of 4 to 12 feet is referred to as _____________ distance.
23. __________________ involves the setting off and marking of a piece of territory as one's own.
24. A teenager's bedroom is a prime example of ____________ territory.
25. The number of persons or animals per unit of area is referred to as ________________ ____________.
26. Substances harmful to the nervous system are called __________.
27. The specific techniques of applied behavior analysis derive from the work of _______________.
28. _____________ psychology is the application of psychology to sport and physical activity at all levels of skill development.
29. __________ __________, a writer, might legitimately be referred to as the "mother of the environmentalist movement."
30. Psychologists are likely to help athletes with the __________ aspects of their game.

**Chapter 15 Multiple Choice Practice Test**

1. All psychologists are interested in the ABCs-affect, behavior, and cognitions. Which of the following distinguishes the work of an industrial psychologist from psychologists in other fields?
   a. an interest in the ABCs as applied to work settings
   b. using the ABCs to train good employees
   c. applying the ABCs to institutions
   d. a focus more on behavior and less on affect and cognition

2. The two steps in writing a job analysis are
   a. interviewing people in the job and reporting their ideas about the job
   b. making a complete description of what the person is expected to do and translating the duties into measureable criteria
   c. measuring what the person actually does and determining what changes should be made
   d. making a survey of the supervisors and compiling the survey results

3. Which of the following functions of a job application is believed by some industrial-organizational psychologists to be the best source for predicting success on the job?
   a. It can be used as a rough screening device.
   b. It can help determine how an employee will fit in with fellow workers.
   c. It can supplement the interview.
   d. It provides biographical data.
4. Which of the following can be positively influenced by training?
   a. quality of work
   b. quantity of work
   c. accent reduction
   d. all of the above
5. When I/O psychologists use psychological tests, it is usually to:
   a. screen out job applicants who have psychological disorders
   b. find psychological traits known to be correlated with job success
   c. ensure that only the most intelligent applicants will be considered for the job
   d. help determine which criteria of the job analysis are going to be most useful
6. The techniques most commonly used to increase productivity are:
   a. employee training programs
   b. attempts to increase worker satisfaction
   c. improved employee selection methods
   d. programs to motivate employees to work harder
7. Which of the following would typically be used to evaluate a training program?
   a. ask participants how they feel about the training
   b. measure the behavioral changes that follow the training
   c. measure increases in profit or productivity
   d. all of the above
8. In order for goal-setting to have a positive influence on a worker's behavior, which of the following criteria must be met?
   a. the employee must set the goal himself or herself
   b. the goal must be clear to the employee
   c. the employee must think of the goal as worth the effort
   d. both b and c
9. Which of the following is NOT true of goal-setting as a means of motivating employees?
   a. Difficult but achievable goals increase productivity more than easy goals.
   b. Specific goals are better than general ones.
   c. Periodical feedback is not necessary with highly motivated workers.
   d. It doesn't especially matter who sets the goal, as long as the employee thinks it is reasonable and worthwhile.
10. Which of the following workers is likely to experience the highest level of job satisfaction?
    a. a young black man with a high-status job
    b. a middle-aged white woman with a high-status job
    c. a young white man with a low-status job
    d. a middle aged black man with a high-status job
11. Factors such as a sense of respect from supervisors, income adequacy, job security, self-esteem, challenge, and independence, opportunities for social interaction, and a sense of making a real contribution are part of
    a. quality of work life
    b. motivation
    c. goal-setting
    d. job satisfaction
12. Which of the following work behaviors is most related to job satisfaction?
    a. productivity
    b. efficiency
    c. absenteeism
    d. motivation

13. Most smokers who quit permanently use
    a. the cold turkey method
    b. hypnosis
    c. behavior modification and nicotine gum
    d. no formal program or intervention

14. Which of the following activities are health psychologists likely to engage in?
    a. investigate the relationships between psychological variables and disease
    b. use psychological methods to help ease the symptoms of physical illness
    c. help people change behaviors in order to prevent health problems
    d. all of the above

15. Which of the following is the least influential factor related to personal space?
    a. who the intruder is
    b. your age
    c. your sex
    d. your cultural background

16. You are being audited by the IRS and have never met the auditor. Which of the descriptors below indicates the amount of personal space with which you are most likely to be comfortable. (Note that being in Brazil is not an option.)
    a. intimate distance
    b. personal distance
    c. social distance
    d. public distance

17. Hose's family has rented a pavillion in a local park to use for a family reunion. This is an example of
    a. primary territory
    b. secondary territory
    c. public territory
    d. private territory

18. Which of the following are functions of various territories that we devise?
    a. They provide a sense of structure and continuity.
    b. They help us claim some sense of identity.
    c. They regulate and reinforce our need for privacy.
    d. All of the above.

19. When comparing the costs and the benefits of city life, it appears that
    a. city life is definitely inferior to country living
    b. city life is worse for those who don't have other options
    c. city life really has no advantages over country life
    d. city life would be fine if the noise and air pollution problems were solved

20. Two important factors in whether noise disrupts performance are
    a. predictability and control
    b. pitch and predictability
    c. control and frequency of the noise
    d. ear protection and frequency of exposure

21. The common perception that high temperatures are associated with more aggressive behavior and displays of violence is
    a. a myth promoted by policemen to get more recruits during summer months
    b. an opinion not supported by research
    c. largely supported by research
    d. none of the above

**Check Your Knowledge of the Learning Objectives**

The following questions are examples of what you should know when you have finished studying this chapter. Write the answers to these questions. Use your book to verify the answers. Page references are provided.

1. Explain what is involved in doing a job analysis. p. 493

2. Describe some of the information sources that can be used in making personnel decisions. p. 494-495

3. List some of the factors that need to be considered in the design, implementation, and evaluation of a training program. p. 495-497

4. Summarize some of the factors that affect motivation of workers to do a good job. p. 499-501

5. Define job satisfaction and the quality of work life. p. 501-502

6. Describe the relationship between job satisfaction and job productivity. p. 502

7. Define environmental psychology and list some of the issues that environmental psychologists study. p. 503

8. Define the concepts of personal space and territoriality. p. 505-507

9. Explain the difference between population density and crowding. p. 508

10. List the positive and negative aspects of city living. p. 508

11. Describe the effects of noise, extreme temperature, and neurotoxins have on behavior. p. 509-511

12. Explain what environmental psychologists can do to have a positive impact on the environment. p. 511-513

13. Discuss some of the ways that psychologists can become involved in sports and athletics. p. 513-515

## Dr. G's Best Study Tips #15

**Add Some Color to Your Studying**

You may already be aware that the single most effective study strategy is highlighting or underlining in textbooks. Here are some hints for making this technique even more effective.

1. Don't underline mindlessly. Read carefully before you highlight or underline anything. Then limit your marking to those things you do not know. There is no sense marking a key term if it is one with which you are already familiar.
2. Use color-coding to identify different kinds of information. When you go back for a study session, you may find that you wish to review only key terms on one occasion and important people in psychology on another. To prepare for this, use one color to highlight key terms and another for important figures.
3. Another area that might be identified with a different color is important research studies and their results.
4. Can you think of additional ways to segment information for studying? If so, incorporate them into your new color-coding system.
5. When you study each segment that you have color-coded, you should begin to identify information that you know and other segments that still need more study. Develop a system for separating these by marking what you know with an asterisk or a check mark. When you study again, focus on the material that is not marked. In this manner, you are constantly making your learning task smaller and revealing to yourself the proven results of your previous study sessions.

# STATISTICAL APPENDIX

**Learning Objectives**

1. Define a frequency distribution and a histogram, and explain what each is used for.
2. List and define three measures of central tendency.
3. Define standard deviation.
4. Explain what is meant by "test of statistical significance."
5. Explain the normal curve and the percentage of cases at each standard deviation.

**Outline Statistical Appendix**

I. Introduction
   A. Statistics help us to summarize, describe, and make judgments about measurements.
   B. Statistics are tools to help us understand our subject matter.
   C. Statistics help us to analyze and understand measurements once we have made them.
   D. Statistical manipulations are more useful (even necessary) when we have collected many more than 100 numbers.

II. Organizing Data
   A. A frequency distribution lists, in order, all of the numbers, or scores, that have been collected and indicates the frequency with which each occurs.
   B. Graphs of frequencies of scores are among the most common types of graphs in psychology.
      1. A histogram is a bar graph in which the frequency of each x-score is indicated by the height of the bar above that score.
      2. A simple line graph shows scores plotted on the x axis and frequencies indicated on the y axis.

III. Descriptive Statistics
   A. Measures of central tendency are statistics that tell us where our scores tend to center.
      1. The mean is the average of a distribution of scores.
         a. The mean of a set of scores is their total divided by the number of scores in the set.
         b. The mean of a set of numbers is symbolized by X, read X bar.
         c. The uppercase Greek letter sigma, $\sum$, stands for "take the sum of whatever follows."
         d. X represents an individual score from a set of scores.
         e. N stands for the number of scores in the set.
      2. The median is the value of a set of numbers that divides it exactly in half.
         a. It is used when a distribution includes a few extreme cases.
         b. Before choosing the median, the scores must first be placed in order.
      3. The mode is the most frequently occurring value in a set or distribution of scores.
         a. The mode is seldom used as a measure of central tendency.
         b. Computing the mode disregards all of the other values in the distribution.
         c. There is no guarantee that the most frequently occurring number will be at or near the middle.
   B. Measures of variability are statistics that tell us about the extent of dispersion, or the spread of scores within a distribution.
      1. One way to measure the spread of scores in a distribution is to use the range.
         a. The range is found by subtracting the lowest score from the highest.
         b. The range simply disregards all the other scores between the highest and lowest.
      2. The standard deviation (SD) is a kind of average of the extent towhich all the scores in a distribution are different from (deviatefrom) their mean.
         a. Simple calculators often come with a button that yields an SD once the X values are punched in.
         b. An SD tells the extent to which scores in a distribution deviate, or are spread from the distribution's mean.

IV. Inferential Statistics
   A. Inferential statistics tell us about the significance of the results of our experimental or correlational studies, whether the data occurred by chance.
      1. Differences that are not likely to have occurred by chance are called statistically significant differences.
      2. Inferential statistics can be used to judge the statistical significance of any statistic.

3. Significance is usually stated as a proportion.
4. There are three factors that influence a test of significance.
   a. Everything else being equal, the larger the measured difference, the more likely that the difference reflects a real difference.
   b. Everything else being equal, differences based on large numbers of observations are more likely to be significant than the same differences based on fewer observations.
   c. The variability of the data also influences statistical significance.

V. Some Normal Curve Statistics
   A. The normal curve is a frequency distribution that is symmetrical and bell-shaped.
   B. The normal curve is simply a graphical representation of a collection of numbers.
      1. Because the normal distribution is symmetrical, the mean always falls in the middle of the distribution, and is coincident with the median and the mode.
      2. We also know how many scores, or what proportion of scores, fall within standard deviation units around the mean.

**Learning Statistical Appendix Vocabulary**

Write the definition for each of the following key terms on the lines provided at the right. Then fold the paper vertically so you can see only the term and try to say the definition. Practice this until you can say them all correctly.

FREQUENCY DISTRIBUTION ______________________

HISTOGRAM ______________________

CENTRAL TENDENCY ______________________

VARIABILITY ______________________

MEAN ______________________

MEDIAN ______________________

MODE ______________________

RANGE ______________________

STANDARD DEVIATION ______________________

INFERENTIAL STATISTICS ______________________

NORMAL CURVE ______________________

STATISTICALLY SIGNIFICANT DIFFERENCES ______________________

**Matching**

Match the following key terms with the appropriate definitions.

| | | | |
|---|---|---|---|
| ______ | 1. normal curve | ______ | 2. inferential statistics |
| ______ | 3. range | ______ | 4. standard deviation |
| ______ | 5. histogram | ______ | 6. variability |
| ______ | 7. frequency distribution | ______ | 8. central tendency |
| ______ | 9. mode | ______ | 10. mean |
| ______ | 11. median | ______ | 12. statistically significant difference |

a. An ordered listing of all X values, indicating the frequency with which each occurs.
b. A bar graph, a graphic representation of a frequency distribution.
c. A measure of the middle, or average, score in a set.
d. The extent of spread or dispersion in a set or distribution of scores.
e. The sum of all X scores divided by the number of X scores.
f. The score of an ordered set above which and below which fall half the scores.
g. The most frequently occurring X value in a set.
h. The highest score in a distribution minus the lowest score.
i. A type of average of the deviations of each X score from the mean of the distribution.
j. Statistical tests that tell us about the significance of the results of experimental or correlational studies.
k. Differences between descriptive statistics not likely to have occurred by chance if the descriptive statistics were describing the same group.
l. A commonly found, symmetrical, bell-shaped frequency distribution.

**True-False Practice Test**

___ 1. Graphs of frequencies of scores are among the most common types of graphs used in psychology.
___ 2. The mean, median, and mode are all measures of variability.
___ 3. The normal curve is a rare, asymmetrical frequency distribution.
___ 4. The range and the standard deviation are measures of variability.
___ 5. The normal curve could be thought of as a line graph for a frequency distribution.
___ 6. Scores in a distribution that form a normal curve tend to bunch around the standard deviation.
___ 7. In a normal curve, all the measures of central tendency, the mean, median, and the mode, would be the same numerical value.
___ 8. The mean divides the normal curve exactly in half.
___ 9. Mean IQ is 115.
___ 10. All normal curves have the same amount of variability.

**Fill-In Practice Test**

1. A ______________ ________________ lists all the numbers or scores and indicates the frequency with which each occurs.
2. A graphical representation of a frequency distribution is called a/an ______________.
3. The __________ is the middle score in a distribution.
4. The _______ is the central tendency measure that is most often used in statistics.
5. The most frequently occurring value in a data set is the ________.
6. The ____________ _____________ is a measure of variability that tells us the average amount by which scores deviate from their mean.
7. ______________ statistics are tests that tell us about the significance of the results of experiments.
8. A commonly found, symmetrical bell-shaped frequency distribution is called the _________ _______.
9. Differences between descriptive statistics not likely to have occurred by chance are said to be ________________ ______________.
10. A measure of variability based on the highest and lowest values in the distribution is the ________.

**Statistical Appendix Multiple Choice Practice Test**

1. Statistics can best be described as
   a. tools
   b. lies
   c. another form of mathematics
   d. much ado about nothing
2. Which of the following is NOT a measure of central tendency?
   a. mean
   b. median
   c. mode
   d. standard deviation
3. Averages are referred to as measures of
   a. variability
   b. correlation
   c. reliability
   d. central tendency
4. To determine how much dispersion is in a particular set of scores, researchers focus on
   a. variability
   b. correlation
   c. reliability
   d. central tendency
5. The range is a measure of variability that has the weakness of
   a. being a large number
   b. only considering two values in the set
   c. causing the overestimation of variability
   d. causing the underestimation of variability
6. Formulas that allow the researcher to calculate the likelihood that particular experimental or correlational results arose by chance are referred to as
   a. descriptive statistics
   b. inferential statistics
   c. advanced statistics
   d. measures of central tendency
7. Results that seem unlikely to have occurred by chance are said to be
   a. positively correlated
   b. nonstatistical
   c. negatively correlated
   d. statistically significant
8. Which of the following is/are factors that influence a test of significance?
   a. size of the mean difference
   b. sample size
   c. variability
   d. all of the above
9. In a normal curve, the symmetry allows us to know that ______ percent of the values in the distribution fall between one standard deviation below the mean and one standard deviation above the mean.
   a. 34
   b. 50
   c. 68
   d. 84
10. If mean IQ is 100 and the standard deviation is 15, what percent of people will have IQs between 85 and 100?
    a. 10
    b. 28
    c. 34
    d. 50

**Check Your Knowledge of the Learning Objectives**

The following questions are examples of what you should know when you have finished studying this chapter. Write the answers to these questions. Use your book to verify the answers. Page references are provided.

1. Define a frequency distribution and a histogram, and explain what each is used for. p. 522

2. List and define three measures of central tendency. p. 523-525

3. Define standard deviation. p. 526

4. Explain what is meant by "test of statistical significance." p. 528

5. Explain the normal curve and the percentage of cases at each standard deviation. p. 529-531

## Dr. G's Best Study Tips #16

**Use It or Lose It**

Below you will find a list of the fifteen study strategies that have been presented in the previous chapters. Perhaps they will not all be equally helpful to you. It is certain, that none will be helpful unless tried and evaluated. After you have given each strategy a fair trial, write a one sentence evaluation in the space provided. Try to identify several strategies that have helped you the most and make them part of your regular study routine.

1. Time management.
2. Dealing with distractions.
3. Getting to know your textbook.
4. How to read a textbook.
5. Using the Premack Principle to reinforce studying.
6. Getting along with your professor.
7. Using mnemonic strategies.
8. Using 3 x 5 cards.
9. Being a star in class.
10. Suggestions for taking notes.
11. Taking objective tests.
12. Taking essay exams.
13. Stressed about the test.
14. Studying with other people.
15. Adding some color to your studying.

# ANSWER KEY

**Chapter 1 Matching**

| | | | | | | | | | |
|---|---|---|---|---|---|---|---|---|---|
| 1. M | 2. J | 3. G | 4. D | 5. Z | 6. B | 7. Q | 8. P | 9. I | 10. X |
| 11. L | 12. V | 13. S | 14. N | 15. O | 16. T | 17. U | 18. R | 19. W | 20. Y |
| 21. F | 22. H | 23. E | 24. C | 25. K | 26. A | | | | |

**Chapter 1 True-False Practice Test**

| | | | | | | | | | |
|---|---|---|---|---|---|---|---|---|---|
| 1. F | 2. T | 3. T | 4. F | 5. F | 6. F | 7. T | 8. F | 9. T | 10. T |
| 11. T | 12. F | 13. F | 14. F | 15. T | 16. T | 17. T | 18. F | 19. T | 20. F |

**Chapter 1 Fill-in Practice Test**

| | | |
|---|---|---|
| 1. John Locke | 2. interactive dualism | 3. philosophy, science |
| 4. affect | 5. cognition | 6. behavior |
| 7. operational | 8. Wilhelm Wundt | 9. William James |
| 10. John Watson | 11. psychoanalysis | 12. whole |
| 13. correlation | 14. positive | 15. experiment |
| 16. independent | 17. extraneous | 18. treatment |
| 19. random assignment | 20. debriefing | |

**Chapter 1 Multiple Choice Practice Test**

1. D. It is generally acknowledged that psychology began with the opening of Wilhelm Wundt's laboratory at the University of Leipzig in 1879.
2. A. The functionalists introduced the study of animals to psychology.
3. B. John Watson argued that psychology should focus on the study of behavior.
4. C. Humanism is the psychological approach that focuses on the individual and concern for the self.
5. C. Gestalt is the German word for "whole." The Gestalt psychologists believed that the whole is more than the sum of its parts.
6. B. An educational psychologist would most likely teach smoking cessation classes.
7. C. Marital counseling would be provided by a counseling psychologist.
8. B. The subject matter of psychology is the ABCs: affect, behavior, and cognition.
9. D. A developmental psychologist would be most likely to help with delays in speech development.
10. A. Clinical psychologists would typically see more severe problems than a counseling psychologist.
11. D. Psychoanalysis is the psychological approach that emphasizes the role of the unconscious and instincts.
12. A. The behaviorists insisted on the use of measurable observations.
13. B. Max Wertheimer founded the Gestalt approach to psychology.
14. D. Naturalistic observation involves watching behaviors as they occur naturally, without interference from the observer. This is what Diane Fossey did.
15. A. Observer bias can be a problem in naturalistic observation.
16. B. Surveys help us gather data about large numbers of people.
17. B. Correlation coefficients range in value from -1 to +1.
18. D. Positive correlations tell us that high scores on one variable (cholesterol) are associated with high scores on the other variable (risk for heart disease).
19. A. Most of our knowledge in the field of psychology has been learned by doing experiments.
20. B. Independent variables are those manipulated by the experimenter. Exposing the subjects to different levels of fear is the manipulation of the independent variable.
21. D. A baseline design is a way of controlling for the differing past experiences of the subjects by using the same subjects twice (once with blood-doping and once without).
22. D. Guarantee of subject's confidentiality, voluntary participation, and advised consent are all ethical considerations that psychologists should make when conducting experiments.

# Chapter 2

## Chapter 2 Matching

| | | | | | | | | | |
|---|---|---|---|---|---|---|---|---|---|
| 1. J | 2. T | 3. P | 4. K | 5. Z | 6. D | 7. I | 8. V | 9. X | 10. A |
| 11. N | 12. R | 13. B | 14. G | 15. F | 16. O | 17. Q | 18. Y | 19. W | 20. C |
| 21. E | 22. H | 23. L | 24. M | 25. S | 26. U | | | | |

## Chapter 2 True-False Practice Test

| | | | | | | | | | |
|---|---|---|---|---|---|---|---|---|---|
| 1. F | 2. F | 3. T | 4. F | 5. T | 6. F | 7. T | 8. T | 9. T | 10. T |
| 11. F | 12. T | 13. T | 14. F | 15. T | 16. T | 17. F | 18. T | 19. F | 20. T |
| 21. T | | | | | | | | | |

## Chapter 2 Fill-in Practice Test

| | | |
|---|---|---|
| 1. gene | 2. dominant gene | 3. neuron |
| 4. nucleus | 5. axon | 6. myelin |
| 7. myelin | 8. axon terminals | 9. neural impulse |
| 10. ions | 11. resting potential | 12. synapse |
| 13. neurotransmitters | 14. endorphins | 15. memory |
| 16. central nervous system | 17. hormones | 18. spinal cord |
| 19. spinal reflexes | 20. cross-laterality | 21. limbic system |
| 22. hippocampus | 23. cerebrum | 24. corpus callosum |
| 25. split-brain procedure | | |

## Chapter 2 Multiple Choice Practice Test

1. A. Gregor Mendel studied selective breeding (genetics) of pea plants.
2. C. A dominant gene always transmits its characteristic to the individual.
3. A. Dendrites are the part of the neuron that receive neural impulses.
4. B. Myelin speeds the transmission of neural impulses, insulates the nerve cell, and acts as a protective covering for the axon. It does not aid in the production of neurotransmitters.
5. A. We possess the greatest number of neurons at birth because neurons do not replace themselves or regenerate. They begin dying at birth and so we have less and less throughout the lifespan.
6. A. Neurotransmitters are contained in the vessicles of the neurons.
7. D. Neurotransmitters can either inhibit or enhance the firing of the neurons.
8. B. Acetylcholine is the neurotransmitter involved in memory.
9. B. Endorphins are the neurotransmitters that help control pain.
10. D. The peripheral nervous system serves the skeletal muscles and sense organs.
11. A. The endocrine system is related to motivation and emotion.
12. B. The sympathetic nervous system activates the flight or fight response that would cause the pounding heart, the rapid breathing, and the rush of adrenaline.
13. A. The cerebellum controls smooth muscle movements, such as golf swings.
14. B. Sleeping is not monitored by the hypothalamus, but eating, shivering, and feeling thirsty are.
15. A. Split-brain surgery really helped in the acquisition of knowledge about the two hemispheres of the brain.
16. B. The left hemisphere controls speech for most right-handed people because of cross-lateralization.
17. D. The first split-brain surgery was done to relieve epilepsy.
18. B. The medulla controls reflexes.
19. D. Alcohol affects the cerebellum, producing the staggering walk displayed by drunks.
20. C. The reticular activating system controls level of arousal and activity.
21. D. The left parietal lobe is where the sensation would be processed if someone tickled your right foot. The parietal lobes register sensations from the extremities of the body and cross-dominance accounts for the left lobe registering a sensation from the right foot.
22. C. The left hemisphere would control speaking, arithmetic, and language, but drawing would be controlled by the right hemisphere.

23. B. The hypothalamus is involved in homeostasis, keeping our bodies in balance in terms of temperature and certain other functions. So when the child gets too cold, the hypothalamus will trigger shivering to warm her.

## Chapter 3

### Chapter 3 Matching

| | | | | | | | | | |
|---|---|---|---|---|---|---|---|---|---|
| 1. C | 2. H | 3. A | 4. G | 5. D | 6. P | 7. S | 8. U | 9. I | 10. B |
| 11. E | 12. F | 13. O | 14. K | 15. M | 16. R | 17. J | 18. N | 19. L | 20. Q |
| 21. W | 22. T | 23. V | 24. X | | | | | | |

### Chapter 3 True-False Practice Test

| | | | | | | | | | |
|---|---|---|---|---|---|---|---|---|---|
| 1. F | 2. T | 3. T | 4. T | 5. F | 6. T | 7. F | 8. T | 9. T | 10. T |
| 11. T | 12. F | 13. F | 14. T | 15. T | 16. T | 17. T | 18. F | 19. T | 20. T |
| 21. F | 22. T | 23. F | 24. F | 25. F | 26. T | 27. F | 28. T | 29. T | 30. F |

### Chapter 3 Fill-in Practice Test

| | | |
|---|---|---|
| 1. conception | 2. zygote | 3. prenatal |
| 4. implantation | 5. embryonic | 6. fetus |
| 7. viability | 8. fetal alcohol syndrome | 9. neonate |
| 10. vision | 11. visual cliff | 12. schema |
| 13. assimilation | 14. accommodation | 15. conservation |
| 16. growth spurt | 17. puberty | 18. formal operations |
| 19. identity crisis | 20. adolescent egocentrism | 21. personal fables |
| 22. integrative | 23. induction | 24. middle adulthood |
| 25. stagnation | 26. Havighurst | 27. ageism |
| 28. old-old | 29. denial | 30. acceptance |

### Chapter 3 Multiple Choice Practice Test

1. B. The stage of the embryo is considered a critical period, during which there is the most risk of birth defects.
2. D. Smoking mothers do risk having more miscarriages, more stillbirths, and having babies that die soon after birth. It is NOT true that smoking only affects the baby if it is two packs of cigarettes or more per day.
3. A. Cephalocaudal sequencing means top to bottom, so the child gaining control of the head first provides evidence for this sequence of motor development.
4. A. Object permanence develops at about the age of eight months, during the sensorimotor stage of cognitive development.
5. B. You cannot fool an eight-year-old in this way because he is in the concrete operational stage of cognitive development and is able to judge that one piece of gum broken is not the same as two pieces of gum. You might be able to fool a five-or six-year-old, who would be preoperational.
6. D. Erikson's theory of psychosocial development was the first major theory to acknowledge that there might be noteworthy changes in adulthood.
7. D. Kohlberg's theory of moral development is supported by research, and it is true that not many people operate at the higher levels. It is also true that children may be able to operate at higher levels than Kohlberg suggested. However, it is NOT true that answers to the Kohlberg dilemmas can predict criminal behavior.
8. D. Carol Gilligan suggests that female moral development is different in nature from that of male due to the differences in socialization and the difference in sex roles.
9. C. Fetal alcohol syndrome causes retarded physical growth, poor coordination and muscle tone, and intellectual retardation. It does NOT cause heart defects.
10. B. Depth perception develops as a product of experience and visual acuity.
11. C. The ability to manipulate concepts and organize things into categories appears during the concrete operational stage of development.
12. D. The ability to reason about hypothetical situations appears during the formal operational stage of cognitive development.

13. B. Preconventional moral development is focused on punishments and rewards.
14. C. Early maturing girls are more likely to be approached for dates and have more sexual encounters. They also have more problems with self-image and are rated low on leadership ability. However, they have an advantage on measures of intellectual functioning.
15. D. Erik Erikson proposed the idea of identity crisis as a major problem in adolescence.
16. B. A study by Shedler and Block found that adolescents who had experimented with drugs but did not become users were more well-adjusted than either users or abstainers.
17. C. During middle adulthood, individuals turn their attention to social concerns and civic responsibilities.
18. D. The final stage of death and dying is marked by quiet acceptance.

## Chapter 4

### Chapter 4 Matching A

| | | | | | | | | | |
|---|---|---|---|---|---|---|---|---|---|
| 1. C | 2. I | 3. R | 4. M | 5. A | 6. F | 7. K | 8. D | 9. N | 10. Q |
| 11. B | 12. G | 13. E | 14. J | 15. H | 16. L | 17. P | 18. O | | |

### Chapter 4 Matching B

| | | | | | | | | | |
|---|---|---|---|---|---|---|---|---|---|
| 1. N | 2. K | 3. V | 4. R | 5. DD | 6. U | 7. M | 8. S | 9. E | 10. J |
| 11. G | 12. BB | 13. X | 14. W | 15. HH | 16. O | 17. P | 18. T | 19. A | 20. H |
| 21. F | 22. GG | 23. Q | 24. CC | 25. EE | 26. Y | 27. Z | 28. AA | 29. FF | 30. C |
| 31. I | 32. D | 33. L | | | | | | | |

### Chapter 4 True-False Practice Test

| | | | | | | | | | |
|---|---|---|---|---|---|---|---|---|---|
| 1. T | 2. F | 3. F | 4. T | 5. T | 6. T | 7. T | 8. F | 9. F | 10. F |
| 11. T | 12. F | 13. T | 14. F | 15. T | 16. T | 17. T | 18. F | 19. T | 20. T |
| 21. F | 22. F | 23. F | 24. F | 25. T | 26. T | 27. F | | | |

### Chapter 4 Fill-in Practice Test

| | | |
|---|---|---|
| 1. wavelength | 2. psychophysics | 3. subliminal perception |
| 4. difference threshold | 5. sensory adaptation | 6. dark adaptation |
| 7. decreases | 8. nanometer | 9. iris |
| 10. retina | 11. cones | 12. light |
| 13. yellow | 14. cornea | 15. monochromatic |
| 16. amplitude | 17. decibels | 18. timbre |
| 19. white noise | 20. pinna | 21. ossicles |
| 22. taste | 23. smell | 24. pheromones |
| 25. cutaneous | 26. vestibular | 27. kinesthetic |
| 28. placebo | 29. endorphins | 30. pain |

### Chapter 4 Multiple Choice Practice Test

1. D. Psychophysics is the study of sensory thresholds.
2. A. A lower threshold indicates that a person could hear things that other people cannot hear. Lower threshold equals greater sensitivity.
3. C. Sensory adaptation suggests that people become accustomed to a stimulus that they are exposed to over a long period of time and eventually fail to notice it. Thus people living near the airport would eventually become accustomed to the sound of the planes.
4. C. A change in a stimulus is the best way to get that stimulus noticed.
5. D. The trichromatic color theory suggests that we have three distinct receptor areas for the three primary colors of light.
6. C. The fovea and the blindspot are both features of the retina.
7. A. The rods and cones function differently and the rods outnumber the cones twenty to one.
8. B. The just noticeable difference would be the concern of someone trying to match colors or patterns.

9. D. The principles of sensory adaptation suggest that stimuli get noticed if there is a change, so speaking louder, faster, or in a whisper would produce a noticeable change and get the audience's attention.
10. A. Changes in the shape of the lens produce problems such as nearsightedness and farsightedness.
11. A. Vision is most acute in the fovea.
12. B. The rods are involved in vision when light is very dim.
13. A. The wavelength of light produces the psychological experience of hue or color.
14. D. Although we study the parts of the eye, vision actually takes place in the brain.
15. D. The amplitude of sound is measured in decibels.
16. A. Pheromones carry message related to sexual availability.
17. B. Motion sickness is the result of a disturbance in the vestibular senses which are responsible for balance.
18. C. According to gate-control theory, pain actually occurs in the central nervous system.
19. B. The brain produces neurotransmitters called endorphins that help reduce pain.
20. C. Timbre is the quality of purity of sound.
21. A. The oval window marks the transition from the middle ear to the inner ear.
22. B. Sweet tastes are experienced on the tip of the tongue, sour tastes on the sides of the tongue, and bitter tastes on the back of the tongue. But salty tastes are NOT experienced in the center of the tongue, they are at the front.
23. D. The joints serve as the receptors for the kinesthetic sense.
24. D. The techniques described involve counterirritation, the placebo effect, and cognitive training, all of which are effective in reducing pain.

## Chapter 5

### Chapter 5 Matching A

| | | | | | | | | | |
|---|---|---|---|---|---|---|---|---|---|
| 1. D | 2. E | 3. K | 4. I | 5. M | 6. Q | 7. A | 8. G | 9. N | 10. O |
| 11. P | 12. J | 13. B | 14. H | 15. L | 16. C | 17. F | | | |

### Chapter 5 Matching B

| | | | | | | | | | |
|---|---|---|---|---|---|---|---|---|---|
| 1. K | 2. H | 3. N | 4. C | 5. J | 6. F | 7. M | 8. P | 9. L | 10. Q |
| 11. A | 12. E | 13. G | 14. O | 15. B | 16. I | 17. D | | | |

### Chapter 5 True-False Practice Test

| | | | | | | | | | |
|---|---|---|---|---|---|---|---|---|---|
| 1. F | 2. T | 3. F | 4. T | 5. T | 6. F | 7. F | 8. T | 9. F | 10. F |
| 11. T | 12. T | 13. T | 14. F | 15. T | 16. T | 17. F | 18. T | 19. T | 20. T |
| 21. F | 22. T | | | | | | | | |

### Chapter 5 Fill-in Practice Test

| | | |
|---|---|---|
| 1. perception | 2. motion | 3. Gestalt |
| 4. closure | 5. binocular | 6. retinal disparity |
| 7. illusion | 8. phi phenomenon | 9. autokinetic |
| 10. shape constancy | 11. size | 12. illusion |
| 13. accommodation | 14. insomnia | 15. delta |
| 16. REM | 17. NREM | 18. Freud |
| 19. atonia | 20. psychoactive | 21. tolerance |
| 22. withdrawal | 23. psychological | 24. stimulants |
| 25. alcohol | | |

### Chapter 5 Multiple Choice Practice Test

1. A. Proximity refers to events that occur close together in space or time.
2. B. Common fate suggests that as long as the snake is not moving, it is sharing a common fate with its background and cannot be seen. The movement destroys this common fate and allows Charlie to see the snake.

3. D. Retinal disparity allows us to view 3-D movies that are filmed with two cameras, one with a green lens and one with a red lens. When we wear the 3-D glasses, the disparate images seen by our two eyes are combined to create the three-dimensional effect.
4. C. Accommodation is a distance cue that is limited to arm's length.
5. A. When two lines appear to merge or come together in the distance, as railroad tracks do, this is called linear perspective.
6. D. The phi phenomenon explains the appearance of lights as moving back and forth or moving in sequence as on a theater marquee.
7. B. Lightness constancy assures us that our white shirt has really not turned to gray as it appears when we enter a dark place.
8. D. We have perceptual constancy for shape, size, and lightness, but not for dimension.
9. C. A Cyclops has only one eye, so it could experience the monocular cues of size constancy, accommodation, and linear perspective, but not the binocular cue of convergence.
10. B. Texture gradient explains the differences in the appearance of the bricks that are close and those that are far away.
11. D. Motion parallax is the phenomenon that explains why faraway objects like the moon appear to follow us while nearby objects appear to move in the opposite direction as we move.
12. D. The autokinetic effect explains the apparent movement of a stationary light.
13. A. Lightness constancy would not develop in a kitten that is raised in the dark. Remember that some of our visual abilities are based on experience.
14. B. REM rebound refers to the fact that subjects deprived of REM sleep will "make up" what they lost.
15. A. Hypnosis can be used to alleviate pain, but it cannot improve memory, or make a person do anything that he/she would not normally do. However, there is no truth to the statement that avid readers make good hypnotic subjects.
16. D. The feeling of relaxation that smokers enjoy can be explained by the effects of nicotine on the central nervous system.
17. D. Being legally drunk is defined as having a blood alcohol level of 1/10 of one percent.
18. C. LSD is a hallucinogenic drug, whereas heroin, nicotine and alcohol are not.
19. C. Marijuana is associated with bronchitis, chromosomal abnormalities in offspring, and adverse effects on the immune system, but not with hallucinations.
20. C. The instrument that measures and records the electrical activity of the brain is called an electroencephalogram.
21. B. Sexual arousal occurs during REM sleep.
22. C. Depressants reduce a person's awareness of external stimuli, slow bodily functions, and decrease levels of overt behavior, but depressants do not cause a person to feel sorrow or sadness.
23. A. The most dangerous drug is alcohol.
24. C. Death from heroin use is often associated with increased dosages that cause breathing to stop.
25. A. Hallucinogens have the most unpredictable effect on consciousness.

## Chapter 6

**Chapter 6 Matching A**

| | | | | | | | | | |
|---|---|---|---|---|---|---|---|---|---|
| 1. J | 2. E | 3. D | 4. H | 5. B | 6. F | 7. K | 8. N | 9. A | 10. I |
| 11. C | 12. M | 13. G | 14. L | | | | | | |

**Chapter 6 Matching B**

| | | | | | | | | | |
|---|---|---|---|---|---|---|---|---|---|
| 1. V | 2. R | 3. K | 4. S | 5. M | 6. T | 7. F | 8. J | 9. A | 10. H |
| 11. C | 12. I | 13. U | 14. D | 15. O | 16. N | 17. L | 18. B | 19. Q | 20. E |
| 21. P | 22. G | | | | | | | | |

**CHAPTER 6 True-False Practice Test**

| | | | | | | | | | |
|---|---|---|---|---|---|---|---|---|---|
| 1. T | 2. T | 3. F | 4. T | 5. F | 6. T | 7. F | 8. F | 9. T | 10. F |
| 11. F | 12. T | 13. F | 14. T | 15. T | 16. T | 17. F | 18. T | 19. F | 20. F |
| 21. T | 22. F | 23. F | 24. T | 25. T | | | | | |

**Chapter 6 Fill-in Practice Test**

1. conditioning
2. reflex
3. acquisition
4. extinction
5. salivation
6. spontaneous recovery
7. suppressed
8. discrimination
9. Watson
10. habituation
11. cognitive
12. operant
13. consequences
14. Thorndike
15. Skinner box
16. base rate
17. shaping
18. acquisition
19. spontaneous recovery
20. reinforcement
21. primary
22. secondary
23. intermittent

**Chapter 6 Multiple Choice Practice Test**

1. B. The response between the unconditioned response and the unconditioned stimulus in Pavlovian conditioning is reflexive.
2. C. Extinction occurs when a conditioned stimulus is repeatedly presented without being paired with the unconditioned stimulus.
3. A. Sharon has generalized the fear so that she is now afraid of all large dogs, and not just the one that was the original stimulus. This is stimulus generalization.
4. B. Children have few natural fears, most are learned. Watson produced the fear response in Little Albert by using the reflexive relationship between fear and loud noises.
5. D. The eye blink in response to a puff of air is an unconditioned response.
6. C. The correct order of stimuli and responses during the acquisition stage is CS-UCS-UCR.
7. C. Spontaneous recovery will usually occur after a rest period.
8. B. Rescorla's recent research has demonstrated that every stimulus cannot become a conditioned stimulus.
9. D. Watson's research with Little Albert would be considered harmful to the child and thus, by today's standards, unethical.
10. A. In classical conditioning, the first response made to the neutral stimulus is called the orienting reflex.
11. D. The fixed ratio, fixed interval, and variable ratio reinforcement schedules all produce responses that are resistant to extinction.
12. C. Punishment is most effective when administered consistently and immediately after a response. Punishment does not give the organism any information about appropriate behavior. However, punishment decreases behavior in general, not just the punished response.
13. A. Albert Bandura's study using the BoBo doll demonstrated that children do learn behaviors from watching television.
14. B. Reinforcement and punishment play a significant role in observational learning.
15. D. Skinner is the founder of operant conditioning, Pavlov is the founder of classical conditioning.
16. B. An operant chamber is designed to control the environment.
17. B. When reinforcement is withheld, extinction will occur.
18. D. In positive reinforcement, the stimulus is presented after a response and in negative reinforcement, a stimulus is removed after a response.
19. B. Having the fine removed is an example of negative reinforcement.
20. A. Tokens are secondary reinforcers.
21. D. Fixed ratio reinforcement involves reinforcing a set number of responses, thus extra credit is awarded after the completion of each lab project.
22. A. Vicarious reinforcement involves learning about the consequences of behavior by observing the consequences of someone else's behavior.
23. A. The learning that a college student does is cognitive.
24. C. Since the headache is removed, this is negative reinforcement.
25. D. Token economies are seen as bribery by some people.

## Chapter 7

### Chapter 7 Matching A

| | | | | | | | | | |
|---|---|---|---|---|---|---|---|---|---|
| 1. M | 2. F | 3. D | 4. H | 5. E | 6. I | 7. A | 8. J | 9. L | 10. K |
| 11. C | 12. G | 13. B | | | | | | | |

### Chapter 7 Matching B

| | | | | | | | | | |
|---|---|---|---|---|---|---|---|---|---|
| 1. J | 2. O | 3. E | 4. H | 5. I | 6. M | 7. D | 8. A | 9. N | 10. B |
| 11. G | 12. L | 13. F | 14. C | 15. K | | | | | |

### Chapter 7 True-False Practice Test

| | | | | | | | | | |
|---|---|---|---|---|---|---|---|---|---|
| 1. F | 2. T | 3. F | 4. F | 5. T | 6. T | 7. F | 8. T | 9. T | 10. T |
| 11. F | 12. T | 13. T | 14. F | 15. F | 16. T | 17. T | 18. F | 19. T | 20. T |
| 21. T | 22. F | 23. T | 24. F | 25. T | | | | | |

### Chapter 7 Fill-in Practice Test

| | | |
|---|---|---|
| 1. encoding | 2. sensory | 3. working |
| 4. chunk | 5. maintenance | 6. elaborative |
| 7. procedural | 8. semantic | 9. episodic |
| 10. recall | 11. recognition | 12. recall |
| 13. implicit | 14. explicit | 15. procedural |
| 16. procedural | 17. flashbulb | 18. schemas |
| 19. mnemonic devices | 20. narrative chaining | 21. schema |
| 22. overlearning | 23. retroactive | |

### Chapter 7 Multiple Choice Practice Test

1. D. The correct sequence for the process of memory is encoding-storing-retrieving.
2. B. The practical problem with sensory memory is that duration is limited.
3. B. Short-term memory is referred to as working memory.
4. D. Repeating a phone number over and over is an example of maintenance rehearsal.
5. A. Information is stored in short-term memory by sound.
6. B. Loftus and Loftus believe that long-term memories are largely reconstructions from the original information.
7. C. Elaborative rehearsal is the best technique for storing information in long-term memory.
8. D. Most "how to" memories, such as swimming, are recorded in procedural memory.
9. B. Today, memory is seen as a more active processor of information.
10. B. Working a math problem in your head would involve sensory memory, short-term memory, and long-term memory.
11. A. Chunking can increase the capacity of short-term memory.
12. B. Memory of a first kiss would be stored in episodic memory.
13. C. Essay test items require recall, not recognition.
14. B. Our ability to retrieve information is largely influenced by the relationship between how the information was encoded and how we are searching for it.
15. D. The best place to study would be in the classroom where the test will be administered. That way the room itself becomes a cue for memory.
16. C. Words that describe tangible, concrete concepts lend themselves better to the use of mental images.
17. A. Geraldine has formed a schema, an organized, general knowledge of what a teacher does in class.
18. B. Distributed practice is studying for several short periods separated by rest periods.
19. C. Going to sleep would prevent interference.
20. A. Retroactive inhibition refers to new learning (sociology) interfering with the old learning (psychology).

## Chapter 8

### Chapter 8 Matching

| | | | | | | | | | |
|---|---|---|---|---|---|---|---|---|---|
| 1. L | 2. K | 3. V | 4. I | 5. W | 6. X | 7. Y | 8. J | 9. H | 10. A |
| 11. E | 12. G | 13. B | 14. F | 15. P | 16. D | 17. O | 18. M | 19. N | 20. Q |
| 21. U | 22. T | 23. R | 24. S | 25. C | | | | | |

### Chapter 8 True-False Practice Test

| | | | | | | | | | |
|---|---|---|---|---|---|---|---|---|---|
| 1. T | 2. F | 3. F | 4. F | 5. F | 6. T | 7. F | 8. F | 9. T | 10. T |
| 11. F | 12. T | 13. F | 14. T | 15. T | 16. F | 17. T | 18. T | 19. F | 20. F |
| 21. T | 22. F | 23. T | 24. T | 25. T | 26. T | 27. F | 28. T | 29. F | 30. T |
| 31. T | | | | | | | | | |

### Chapter 8 Fill-in Practice Test

| | | |
|---|---|---|
| 1. representation | 2. strategy | 3. algorithm |
| 4. heuristic | 5. mental set | 6. convergent |
| 7. divergent | 8. babbling | 9. holophrastic |
| 10. overregularization | 11. psychological test | 12. reliability |
| 13. test-retest | 14. correlation | 15. validity |
| 16. concurrent | 17. content | 18. norms |
| 19. Alfred Binet | 20. verbal | 21. WAIS-R |
| 22. Army Alpha | 23. 100 | 24. intellectually |
| 25. 130 | 26. Terman | 27. Termites |
| 28. developmentally delayed | 29. Down's syndrome | 30. phenylketonuria |

### Chapter 8 Multiple Choice Practice Test

1. B. Choosing a college major is an example of an ill-defined problem because there are many variables that are difficult to define. Many college students don't know what all the options are and do not have enough information about themselves to make good choices.
2. C. When we are unable to use a familiar object in a new and unique way, we say that we are fixated (or stuck) on the familiar functions of that object, thus the term "functional fixedness."
3. B. The driver is suggesting that he was fixed (or stuck) on the use of the kitty litter only for its familiar purpose, therefore he would not have thought of the more creative use of pouring the kitty litter under the tire to provide traction on the ice.
4. B. Convergent thinking involves taking many ideas and reducing them to just one possible solution, just as the famous Mr. Holmes did when taking many clues and reducing them to the solution of a crime.
5. B. Again, putting many things together (the trees) to create one concept (the forest) exemplifies convergent thinking.
6. A. Divergent thinking involves starting with one idea and generating a number of new alternatives. Thus, thinking of all the uses of a paper towel demonstrates divergent thinking.
7. C. Working a crossword puzzle is an example of a well-defined problem. The squares give a very specific notion of the number of letters in the word and clues give the location of the word and a hint about its meaning. These specifics provide a well-defined structure to help solve the problem.
8. C. Joe is past the initial state and has set a goal so he has completed that state as well. He appears to be stuck without strategies or ideas as to how to actually attain the goal.
9. A. A psychological test can only measure behaviors. Feelings, aptitudes, and abilities cannot be measured; they are inferred from measurements of behavior.
10. B. A test is said to be standardized when all who take it are given the same testing conditions, the same time limits, and the same instructions.
11. D. A good psychological test must measure what it says it will measure (validity), must make that measure consistently (reliability), and must provide a standard of comparison (norms).
12. B. The test is attempting to measure whether a person will become a good pickle packer in the future. Tests that adequately predict future behavior are said to have predictive validity.

13. D. A history test would lack content validity in a psychology class. Psychology students generally expect to be tested over psychology.
14. A. The WAIS-R is the appropriate test for an adult. The OLSAT and AFQT are group tests and the Stanford Binet is more commonly used with children.
15. D. The PSAT is the Preliminary Scholastic Aptitude Test and is designed specifically to give juniors a trial run for the SAT.
16. B. When psychological tests are used to make predictions about future behaviors, they are called aptitude tests. In their construction and administration, aptitude tests are similar to tests of general intelligence.
17. C. Terman did not exclude black children, but he has been criticized for failing to control for socioeconomic factors, for too narrowly defining intelligence, and for excluding children with psychological disorders.
18. B. The AAMD definition of mental retardation includes the phrase "is associated with impairment in adaptive behavior."
19. C. The greatest hope in dealing with mental retardation is in prevention through learning more about the prenatal environment, because so much of retardation begins there. Many of the causes of mental retardation are incurable once they are well established in the individual.
20. C. PKU is a disorder that causes a failure to produce an enzyme that normally breaks down chemicals found in many foods. It is treated by diet.
21. D. Cognitive processes involve all three: perception, learning, and memory.
22. C. We usually notice the appearance of a child's first words at about the age of one year.
23. A. Learning theory would be supported if parents corrected the grammar or usage in a child's language, but parents tend to correct content rather than form and children learn grammar anyway.
24. A. The term intellectually gifted is reserved for the top three percent of the population as identified by a general intelligence test such as the Wechsler test or the Stanford-Binet.

## Chapter 9

### Chapter 9 Matching

| | | | | | | | | | |
|---|---|---|---|---|---|---|---|---|---|
| 1. I | 2. Q | 3. A | 4. K | 5. R | 6. B | 7. L | 8. F | 9. M | 10. O |
| 11. E | 12. C | 13. J | 14. N | 15. H | 16. G | 17. P | 18. D | | |

### Chapter 9 True-False Practice Test

| | | | | | | | | | |
|---|---|---|---|---|---|---|---|---|---|
| 1. T | 2. F | 3. F | 4. T | 5. T | 6. T | 7. F | 8. T | 9. T | 10. F |
| 11. T | 12. T | 13. F | 14. T | 15. F | 16. F | 17. T | 18. T | 19. T | 20. T |

### Chapter 9 Fill-in Practice Test

| | | |
|---|---|---|
| 1. arousal | 2. instincts | 3. McDougall |
| 4. secondary | 5. primary | 6. hierarchy |
| 7. safety | 8. incentives | 9. set point |
| 10. sensation seeker | 11. cognitive dissonance | 12. bulimia |
| 13. Thematic Apperception Test | 14. fear of success | 15. affiliation |
| 16. opponent process | 17. Zajonc | 18. parasympathetic |
| 19. sympathetic | 20. homosexuals | 21. genital herpes |
| 22. AIDS | | |

### Chapter 9 Multiple choice Practice Test

1. B. Trying to explain behavior by referring to instincts simply renamed or relabeled the behaviors and didn't explain. However, psychologists who argued in favor of this explanation did contribute to our knowledge by pointing out that many behaviors are basically physiological and are more inherited than learned.
2. C. Asking for shoes is a secondary drive because wearing shoes is a learned need. Primary drives described by answer choices A, B, and D are based on unlearned, physiological needs.
3. B. Explaining behavior in terms of incentives is like operant conditioning because the incentives are like reinforcements.

4. D. Set point theory suggests that a person who lost weight while ill would gain the weight back as part of the body's effort to maintain equilibrium.
5. A. Cannon postulated a theory of emotion and a theory concerning homeostasis, but did not work on achievement motivation. All the other pairs are correct matches.
6. C. The drive itself would let us know that we are thirsty, but learning from experience would determine preferences such as Coke or Pepsi for quenching the thirst.
7. A. Although some people are stimulated to eat by the sight and smell of food, these external cues are not as important as the hypothalamus and the liver. Even people without stomachs have been known to feel hunger.
8. C. Almost 50% of anorexia patients relapse within a year of being released from treatment.
9. B. Despite LeVay's new research that suggests strong biological influence, no one really knows for sure the cause of homosexuality.
10. B. Genital herpes cannot be cured at all.
11. C. The exchange of bodily fluids such as blood or semen is required for the spread of AIDS.
12. B. Someone with a high nAch would choose a job that was challenging, but could be done well with effort because a job that is too easy would not provide a sense of satisfaction and a job that is too difficult might result in failure.
13. D. Teaching is a profession that would meet the need for achievement.
14. B. One problem with Maslow's theory is that there appear to be exceptions to the hierarchical structure or ordering of needs; for instance, a person might go on a hunger strike to support a higher principle.
15. D. Other physiological drives are largely controlled by internal influences such as hormones, but the sex drive in humans responds a great deal to external cues such as the attractiveness of the sex partner.
16. C. There is no evidence that socioeconomic status is a factor in eating disorders, but all the other choices do appear to be related.
17. B. The involvement of the patient's family seems to be the best predictor of the success of therapy for anorexics.
18. A. Objective feeling is not a component of emotional reactions. Our emotions are quite subjective.
19. A. The James-Lange theory of emotion differs from the common sense interpretation of emotion in terms of the ordering of the experience of the emotion and the behavioral response.
20. C. James and Lange suggested that we see the stimulus, we respond, and then we experience emotion as we become aware of the physiological results of our response.
21. B. In an emotional situation, blood is actually transported away from the center of the body and toward the limbs and brain.
22. D. The cerebral cortex is involved in the cognitive aspects of emotion.
23. B. Drives based on learned needs are called secondary drives.
24. C. Drives based on biological needs are called primary drives.
25. B. Shivering when you are cold is an example of homeostasis.

## Chapter 10

**Chapter 10 Matching**

| | | | | | | | | | |
|---|---|---|---|---|---|---|---|---|---|
| 1. S | 2. A | 3. M | 4. B | 5. E | 6. D | 7. T | 8. K | 9. Q | 10. P |
| 11. V | 12. N | 13. C | 14. H | 15. R | 16. U | 17. L | 18. O | 19. F | 20. I |
| 21. G | 22. J | | | | | | | | |

**Chapter 10 True-False Practice Test**

| | | | | | | | | | |
|---|---|---|---|---|---|---|---|---|---|
| 1. T | 2. F | 3. F | 4. F | 5. T | 6. F | 7. T | 8. T | 9. T | 10. F |
| 11. T | 12. T | 13. T | 14. F | 15. T | | | | | |

**Chapter 10 Fill-in Practice Test**

| | | | | | |
|---|---|---|---|---|---|
| 1. | theory | 2. | personality | 3. | psychoanalysis |
| 4. | conscious | 5. | basic instincts | 6. | eros |
| 7. | thanatos | 8. | defense mechanisms | 9. | Carl Jung |
| 10. | archetypes | 11. | habits | 12. | trait |
| 13. | common traits | 14. | role-playing | 15. | interview |

**Chapter 10 Multiple Choice Practice Test**

1. C. Personality includes affects, behaviors, and cognitions, but does not include preferences.
2. A. Consciousness is marked by awareness, and information that is available is said to be in the preconscious.
3. D. Thanatos refers to a death wish or tendency to be self-destructive.
4. B. The ego is the reality-based structure of our personality.
5. A. Alfred Adler developed the idea of the inferiority complex.
6. D. Karen Horney is not associated with the collective unconscious, but Carl Jung is.
7. C. Karen Horney was the neo-Freudian who believed that people move away, move toward, or move against other people.
8. D. Maslow developed the theory of the hierarchy of needs, not factor analysis. Factor analysis was developed by Cattell.
9. B. Psychoticism is not one of the "Big Five" dimensions of personality. The "Big Five" are extroversion/introversion, agreeableness/hostility, conscientiousness, stability/instability, and intelligence.
10. A. Freud's major contributions were stressing the role of early childhood experiences, introducing the notion of the unconscious, and attending to the impact of sexuality. The focus on aggression is not seen as a major contribution.
11. A. The psychoanalytic approach was criticized for relying too heavily on the notion of biological drives and untestable concepts.
12. B. Genetic planning would not be a valid reason for personality assessment.
13. A. When interpreting the TAT, a psychologist looks for emerging themes or stories that provide insights about the subject.
14. A. The MMPI is considered a criterion-referenced test because items were included only if they differentiated among diagnosed groups.
15. D. Behavioral observation is the personality assessment technique you would likely use at a party.
16. D. Freud based his theory on great works of philosophy, observations of patients, and self-examination, but not on observation of his children.
17. C. One of the goals of psychoanalysis is to help a person get in touch with the unconscious.
18. C. The id operates on the pleasure principle, the ego operates on the reality principle, and the superego operates on the idealistic principle. There is no principle associated with the conscience. It is not even a Freudian concept.
19. D. Alfred Adler, Carl Jung, and Karen Horney all had their beginnings in psychoanalytic theory, all were neo-Freudians, and all offered alternate ideas to psychoanalytic theory.
20. A. Karen Horney was one of the first psychologists to accuse Freud of male chauvinism.
21. B. Carl Rogers was the humanistic psychologist that believed people strive to be fully functioning.
22. C. The behavioral-learning approach relies on concepts that are observable and measurable.
23. A. The humanistic approach differs from the psychoanalytic approach in that it is not deterministic. Humanists believe that people can choose and can change.
24. B. The psychologist who used factor analysis to examine traits was Cattell.
25. B. Regression is a return to childish behavior in the presence of stress.

## Chapter 11

### Chapter 11 Matching

| | | | | | | | | |
|---|---|---|---|---|---|---|---|---|
| 1. H | 2. D | 3. A | 4. B | 5. E | 6. C | 7. F | 8. I | 9. G |

### Chapter 11 True-False Practice Test

| | | | | | | | | | |
|---|---|---|---|---|---|---|---|---|---|
| 1. T | 2. T | 3. F | 4. T | 5. T | 6. F | 7. F | 8. T | 9. T | 10. T |
| 11. F | 12. T | 13. T | 14. T | 15. F | | | | | |

### Chapter 11 Fill-in Practice Test

| | | |
|---|---|---|
| 1. stressor | 2. frustration | 3. approach-approach |
| 4. avoidance-avoidance | 5. change | 6. hassles |
| 7. Holmes | 8. cognitive reappraisal | 9. anxiety |
| 10. frustration | 11. type A | 12. exhaustion |
| 13. multiphasia | 14. aggression | 15. prevention |

### Chapter 11 Multiple Choice Practice Test

1. C. Life events, frustration, and conflict are sources of stress, but aggression is caused by stress.
2. D. Environmental frustration would be considered external, whereas personal frustration would be considered internal.
3. C. Ashley wants the ice cream (approach), but does not want to walk (avoidance).
4. D. Lazarus believes that it is the little hassles in life rather than the big disasters that cause stress.
5. D. Relaxation, exercise, and cognitive reappraisal all reduce stress, but focusing on a smaller hassle probably will not.
6. D. The frustration-aggression hypothesis says that aggression is always caused by frustration, but frustration does not always cause aggression.
7. A. Avoidance-avoidance conflict creates the most stress because there is no desirable choice.
8. B. Being too short to play basketball would be a personal frustration.
9. A. "Out of the frying pan and into the fire" refers to two undesirable options. Most people would want to avoid both of these; thus it is an avoidance-avoidance conflict.
10. C. According to the SRRS, the single most stressful life event is the death of a spouse.
11. B. In coping with stress, the opposite of change is fixation, which refers to being stuck on the same solution, repeating it over and over even though it isn't working.
12. C. Relaxation, exercise, and cognitive reappraisal are all adaptive ways of dealing with stress. Aggression would be a maladaptive coping strategy.
13. B. If you are vulnerable to physical illness and infection to a greater degree than normal, and, although the sympathetic response seems to have returned to normal, the physiological systems continue to mobilize bodily reserves, you are in the resistance stage of the general adaptation syndrome.
14. C. Changing any behavior using humanistic principles is not a basic assumption of health psychologists. Behavioral changes are made using behavioral principles.
15. D. Logan Wright suggests that the characteristics of type A behavior pattern related to coronary heart disease are time urgency, chronic activation, and multiphasia.

## Chapter 12

### Chapter 12 Matching

| | | | | | | | | | |
|---|---|---|---|---|---|---|---|---|---|
| 1. L | 2. G | 3. R | 4. M | 5. B | 6. N | 7. V | 8. T | 9. Q | 10. S |
| 11. O | 12. A | 13. K | 14. U | 15. I | 16. H | 17. P | 18. J | 19. F | 20. E |
| 21. D | 22. C | | | | | | | | |

**Chapter 12 True-False Practice Test**

| | | | | | | | | | |
|---|---|---|---|---|---|---|---|---|---|
| 1. T | 2. T | 3. F | 4. F | 5. T | 6. F | 7. F | 8. T | 9. T | 10. F |
| 11. T | 12. T | 13. T | 14. T | 15. F | 16. T | 17. T | 18. F | 19. F | 20. T |
| 21. T | 22. F | 23. F | 24. T | 25. F | 26. T | 27. F | | | |

**Chapter 12 Fill-in Practice Test**

| | | |
|---|---|---|
| 1. diagnosis | 2. DSM-III-R | 3. insanity |
| 4. anxiety | 5. anxiety | 6. fear |
| 7. generalized anxiety | 8. compulsions | 9. posttraumatic stress |
| 10. somatoform | 11. hypochondriasis | 12. conversion |
| 13. psychogenic fugue | 14. psychotic | 15. mood |
| 16. mania | 17. bipolar disorder | 18. schizophrenia |
| 19. unipolar | 20. neologisms | 21. process |
| 22. reactive | 23. dopamine | 24. catatonic |
| 25. disorganized | | |

**Chapter 12 Multiple Choice Practice Test**

1. C. Statistically speaking, about one in five or 20 percent of people are likely to suffer from a psychological disorder sometime in their lives.
2. B. Behavior must be maladaptive in addition to being bizarre in order to be considered abnormal.
3. A. When the first classification system was done, mental illness was believed to have biological causes.
4. A. Classification does not explain the disorders, it only labels them. The true disadvantages of classification are that it is dehumanizing, it focuses on the individual, and the labeling creates lasting stigmas.
5. D. The person most likely to seek treatment for a phobia is the one who fears open places. Many phobias simply do not interfere enough with a person's normal daily functioning to warrant treatment.
6. A. Panic disorder is characterized by sudden, unprovoked attacks of intense anxiety.
7. B. Obsessive-compulsive disorder is commonly diagnosed in adolescence.
8. C. Compulsive behaviors such as gambling or eating are pleasureable.
9. D. The likelihood of recovery from posttraumatic stress disorder is related to the extent to which there are complicating factors such as alcoholism, the extent of psychological problems suffered before the event, and the extent to which social support is available to the victim.
10. C. The two disorders that are most likely to coexist are agoraphobia and panic disorder.
11. A. Freud developed psychoanalysis in order to treat patients with conversion disorder.
12. A. Psychogenic fugue and psychogenic amnesia may be the results of attempts to avoid stress.
13. C. Multiple personality disorder is associated with unusually high incidence of child abuse, sexual abuse, and drug abuse.
14. B. As opposed to anxiety-based disorders, personality disorders involve a long-standing history of symptoms.
15. C. Overreacting and attention-seeking are characteristic of a histrionic personality.
16. D. Psychotic disorders are characterized by a loss of contact with reality. However, they are not the same as neuroses. They are discussed in the DSM-III-R, and people who suffer from them do often require hospitalization.
17. B. Aaron Beck is a well-known cognitive psychologist.
18. A. Schizophrenics are usually colorless, socially withdrawn, and not at all dangerous.
19. C. Excess dopamine, normal brain configuration, severe disruptions in family life, and a relatively good response to treatment are representative of positive schizophrenia.
20. B. Someone who has an identical twin who has been diagnosed with schizophrenia is at very high risk for acquiring the disease.

## Chapter 13

### Chapter 13 Matching

| | | | | | | | | | |
|---|---|---|---|---|---|---|---|---|---|
| 1. B | 2. D | 3. T | 4. S | 5. K | 6. V | 7. U | 8. G | 9. P | 10. R |
| 11. J | 12. O | 13. L | 14. I | 15. C | 16. F | 17. E | 18. H | 19. A | 20. N |
| 21. Q | 22. M | | | | | | | | |

### Chapter 13 True-False Practice Test

| | | | | | | | | | |
|---|---|---|---|---|---|---|---|---|---|
| 1. T | 2. T | 3. T | 4. T | 5. F | 6. T | 7. T | 8. T | 9. F | 10. F |
| 11. F | 12. T | 13. T | 14. F | 15. T | 16. T | 17. T | 18. T | 19. F | 20. T |
| 21. F | 22. T | 23. T | 24. F | 25. F | 26. F | 27. T | 28. T | | |

### Chapter 13 Fill-in Practice Test

| | | |
|---|---|---|
| 1. clinical psychologist | 2. Hippocrates | 3. middle ages |
| 4. 18th | 5. Bedlam | 6. Pinel |
| 7. 20th | 8. psychosurgery | 9. lobotomy |
| 10. shock treatments | 11. psychoactive drugs | 12. schizophrenia |
| 13. research | 14. medicine | 15. latent |
| 16. transference | 17. countertransference | 18. client-centered |
| 19. behavior | 20. contingency management | 21. contingency contracting |
| 22. cognitive | 23. cognitive restructuring | 24. depression |
| 25. group | | |

### Chapter 13 Multiple Choice Practice Test

1. A. The first insane asylum was St. Mary of Bethlehem Hospital in London.
2. D. The unchaining of the inmates in a French asylum by Pinel was a turning point in the treatment of the mentally ill.
3. C. Moniz was the first person to perform a lobotomy and was awarded the Nobel Prize for doing so.
4. A. The irreversibility of lobotomy was not considered to be a problem.
5. C. Only a psychiatrist or a clinical psychologist can become a psychoanalyst.
6. B. Patients best suited for ECT are those that are suffering from both depression and psychotic symptoms.
7. C. Most antipsychotic drugs are used to treat schizophrenia.
8. D. There are patients who cannot use antipsychotic drugs, and there are numerous side effects. However, although symptoms may return if the drug is discontinued, it is not likely that the symptoms will worsen because of the drugs.
9. A. Lithium is used to treat bipolar disorder and chlozapine is used to treat schizophrenia.
10. B. Antidepressant drugs are more likely to bring about long-term cures, whereas antipsychotic drugs just help to reduce symptoms rather than cure the disease.
11. D. Because antianxiety drugs are so effective, patients are often unmotivated to deal with the source of their anxiety.
12. C. According to Carl Rogers, a good therapist is well-adjusted, warm, empathic, and supportive.
13. B. Client-centered therapy is associated with unconditional positive regard and a nondirective approach.
14. C. Albert Ellis is the father of rational-emotive therapy.
15. B. Taking a child who is fearful of water to a pool and not letting him out is an example of flooding. An important element in this technique is support by the therapist. Notice that the boy's father stays in the water with him to comfort him. He does NOT just throw him in to sink or swim.
16. C. Having a chain-smoker smoke until he is ill is an example of aversion therapy.
17. D. Albert Bandura is associated with modeling.
18. D. A major concern of family therapy is to improve communication among family members.
19. B. The bottom line of therapy is to bring about a relatively permanent change in affect, behavior, and/or cognition.
20. A. Saving money is one advantage of group therapy.

## Chapter 14

### Chapter 14 Matching

| | | | | | | | | | |
|---|---|---|---|---|---|---|---|---|---|
| 1. H | 2. I | 3. P | 4. O | 5. F | 6. A | 7. U | 8. G | 9. L | 10. C |
| 11. K | 12. D | 13. B | 14. E | 15. J | 16. N | 17. T | 18. Q | 19. M | 20. R |
| 21. V | 22. S | | | | | | | | |

### Chapter 14 True-False Practice Test

| | | | | | | | | | |
|---|---|---|---|---|---|---|---|---|---|
| 1. F | 2. T | 3. T | 4. F | 5. F | 6. T | 7. T | 8. T | 9. T | 10. T |
| 11. T | 12. F | 13. T | 14. F | 15. T | 16. T | 17. T | 18. F | 19. T | 20. T |
| 21. F | 22. T | 23. T | 24. T | 25. F | | | | | |

### Chapter 14 Fill-in Practice Test

| | | |
|---|---|---|
| 1. individual | 2. social influence | 3. stereotype |
| 4. norms | 5. attitude | 6. persuasion |
| 7. distraction | 8. internal | 9. external |
| 10. fundamental attribution | 11. reinforcement | 12. attachment |
| 13. reciprocity | 14. conformity | 15. autokinetic effect |
| 16. obedience | 17. Milgram | 18. debriefed |
| 19. bystander apathy | 20. notice | 21. audience inhibition |
| 22. pluralistic ignorance | 23. psychosocial | 24. social loafing |
| 25. social facilitation | | |

### Chapter 14 Multiple Choice Practice Test

1. A. Social psychology is the study of how people influence the thoughts, feelings, and behaviors of an individual.
2. C. An attitude is a relatively stable and general evaluative disposition toward some object, consisting of beliefs, feelings, and behaviors.
3. B. Since beliefs about foreign products are thoughts, rather than emotions or actions, this would represent the cognitive component of attitudes.
4. C. Satisfied customers who give testimonials about products serve as models for the rest of us to observe with the expectation that we will copy their behavior and use the endorsed product.
5. A. A celebrity selling a product related to his fame is likely to be seen as an expert and thus be the most persuasive.
6. D. Getting what is deserved is thinking that exemplifies the "just world hypothesis."
7. A. The self-serving bias involves attributing positive outcomes to one's own abilities and negative outcomes to external sources.
8. A. Social exchange theory suggests that Ben is weighing the costs of the relationship (whatever they might be) against the perceived benefits, one of which is the land.
9. C. The tendency to choose partners similar to oneself in terms of physical attractiveness is referred to as the matching phenomenon.
10. D. Generosity is NOT a determinant of interpersonal attraction, but perhaps more of us should consider it. The three determinants are proximity, similarity, and reciprocity.
11. C. Social psychologists are interested in the influence of the group on the individual.
12. A. A confederate is knowledgeable about the purpose and procedure of the research and assists the researcher.
13. A. Asch studied conformity and Milgram studied obedience.
14. A. Milgram's initial interest in obedience stemmed from the cruelty of the Nazis during WWII, therefore his initial research intent was to determine if ethnic groups differed in the degree to which they would inflict pain.
15. C. Milgram's studies are not likely to be replicated because today's ethical standards will not allow it.
16. B. The person most likely to render aid in an emergency is a single bystander who has experience in similar emergencies. This eliminates the problem of diffusion of responsibility and audience inhibition that occur when many people are present.

17. B. The fact that Scottie skates better when racing another skater than when racing against the clock is best explained by social facilitation. His performance is helped by the presence of the other people.
18. B. Each juror's greater assurance after deliberation with the group is the result of groupthink.

## Chapter 15

### Chapter 15 Matching

| | | | | | | | | | |
|---|---|---|---|---|---|---|---|---|---|
| 1. E | 2. P | 3. F | 4. C | 5. G | 6. B | 7. H | 8. A | 9. I | 10. J |
| 11. N | 12. M | 13. O | 14. K | 15. D | 16. L | | | | |

### Chapter 15 True-False Practice Test

| | | | | | | | | | |
|---|---|---|---|---|---|---|---|---|---|
| 1. T | 2. T | 3. T | 4. T | 5. F | 6. F | 7. T | 8. T | 9. T | 10. T |
| 11. F | 12. T | 13. T | 14. F | 15. T | 16. T | 17. F | 18. T | 19. F | 20. F |
| 21. T | 22. T | 23. F | 24. T | 25. F | | | | | |

### Chapter 15 Fill-in Practice Test

| | | |
|---|---|---|
| 1. job analysis | 2. performance criteria | 3. interview |
| 4. situational testing | 5. validity | 6. AT&T |
| 7. in-basket | 8. training | 9. Goldstein |
| 10. needs assessment | 11. expectancy | 12. equity |
| 13. job satisfaction | 14. personnel | 15. engineering |
| 16. health | 17. Type A | 18. smoking |
| 19. environmental | 20. personal space | 21. intimate |
| 22. social | 23 territoriality | 24. primary |
| 25. population density | 26. neurotoxins | 27. Skinner |
| 28. Sport | 29. Rachel Carson | 30. mental |

### Chapter 15 Multiple Choice Practice Test

1. A. An industrial psychologist is interested in the ABC's of psychology as they apply to work settings.
2. B. The two steps in writing a job analysis are making a complete description of what the person is expected to do and translating the duties into measurable criteria.
3. D. The application is believed to be most helpful in providing biographical data.
4. D. Training can have a positive impact on quality of work, quantity of work, and accident reduction.
5. B. Psychological tests are used to find psychological traits associated with job success.
6. A. Employee training programs are the techniques most commonly used to increase productivity.
7. D. In order to evaluate a training program, one must ask participants how they feel about training, measure the behavioral changes that follow the training, and measure increases in profit or productivity.
8. D. The effectiveness of goal-setting depends on the goal being clear to the employee and the employee believing that the goal is worth the effort.
9. C. Periodical feedback must be a part of the process if goal-setting is to be successful.
10. B. A middle-aged white woman with a high-status job is the most likely to experience a high level of job satisfaction.
11. A. Quality of work life is related to sense of respect from supervisors, income adequacy, job security, and self-esteem among others.
12. C. Absenteeism is related to job satisfaction. The more satisfied an employee, the lower the absenteeism.
13. D. Most people who quit smoking permanently do so on their own without any special program.
14. D. Health psychologists are likely to investigate the relationships between psychological variables and disease (as in the CHD and type A behavior studies), use psychological methods to help ease the symptoms of physical illness, and help people change behaviors in order to prevent health problems.
15. D. Who the intruder is, your age, and your sex will all influence your personal space more than your ethnicity.

16. C. Social distance is the amount of space with which you are most likely to be comfortable in an IRS audit.
17. C. A park pavilion would be public territory.
18. D. The various territories that people devise provide us with a sense of structure and continuity, help us claim some sense of identity, and regulate and reinforce our need for privacy.
19. B. City life is considered worse by those who don't have other options.
20. A. Predictability and control are two important factors.in determining whether noise disrupts our performance.
21. C. Research supports the idea that high temperatures are associated with more aggressive behavior and displays of violence.

## Statistical Appendix

**Appendix Matching**

1. L 2. J 3. H 4. I 5. B 6. D 7. A 8. C 9. G 10. E
11. F 12. K

**Appendix True-False Practice Test**

1. T 2. F 3. F 4. T 5. T 6. F 7. T 8. T 9. F 10. F

**Appendix Fill-in Practice Test**

1. frequency distribution
2. histogram
3. median
4. mean
5. mode
6. standard deviation
7. inferential
8. normal curve
9. statistically significant
10. range

**Appendix Multiple Choice Practice Test**

1. A. Statistics can best be described as tools.
2. D. Standard deviation is a measure of variability. The mean, median, and mode are all measures of central tendency.
3. D. Averages are measures of central tendency.
4. A. Variability refers to how much dispersion exists in a particular set of scores.
5. B. The weakness of the range as a measure of variability is that it considers only two values.
6. B. Inferential statistics tells the researcher if a particular outcome occurred by chance.
7. D. Statistically significant results are not likely to have occurred by chance.
8. D. A test of significance is influenced by the size of the mean difference, the sample size, and the variability.
9. C. Sixty-eight percent of the values in a normal curve fall between one standard deviation above and below the mean.
10. C. Thirty-four percent fall between 100 and 15 if these values represent the mean and the standard deviation respectively.

# FLASH CARDS

interactive dualism/1/

introspection/1/

psychology/1/

affect/1/

humanistic psychology/1/

hypothesis/1/

behavior/1/

phenomenology/1/

A technique in which one examines one's own mental experiences and reports them in the most fundamental, basic way.

Descartes' position that a separate body and mind influence each other and are thus knowable.

The feelings of mood that accompany an emotional reaction.

The scientific study of behavior and mental processes.

A tentative proposition or explanation that can be tested or rejected.

An approach to psychology emphasizing the person or self as a central matter of concern.

The study of events as they are experienced by the individual; that experience is reality.

What an organism does; an action of an organism that can be measured.

| | |
|---|---|
| science/1/ | British empiricists/1/ |
| publicly verifiable/1/ | gestalt/1/ |
| scientific methods/1/ | cognitions/1/ |
| behaviorism/1/ | psychoanalysis/1/ |

Philosophers who claimed that the contents of the mind come from experience.

An organized body of knowledge gained through the application of scientific methods.

Whole, totality, configuration; where the whole is seen as more than the sum of its parts.

The agreement of observers that an event did or did not take place.

The mental processes of knowing, perceiving, thinking, remembering, and so on.

Systematic procedures of discovery that include observation, description, control, and replication.

A Freudian approach to psychology emphasizing the influence of the unconscious and instincts.

An approach to psychology emphasizing the overt, observable, measurable behavior of organisms.

| | |
|---|---|
| gestalt/1/ | scientific methods/1/ |
| cognitions/1/ | operational definition/1/ |
| naturalistic observation/1/ | observer bias/1/ |
| survey/1/ | sample/1/ |

Systematic procedures of discovery that include observation, description, control, and replication.

Whole, totality, configuration; where the whole is seen as more than the sum of its parts.

A definition of a concept given in terms of the methods used to measure that concept.

The mental processes of knowing, perceiving, and thinking.

When one's own motives, expectations, and past experiences interfere with the objectivity of one's observations.

The method of observing and noting behaviors as they occur naturally.

The portion of a larger population chosen for study.

A means of collecting observations from a large number of subjects, usually by interview or questionnaire.

| | |
|---|---|
| case history/1/ | correlation/1/ |
| correlation coefficient/1/ | experiment/1/ |
| independent variables/1/ | dependent variables/1/ |
| extraneous variables/1/ | experimental group/1/ |

| | |
|---|---|
| A largely statistical technique used to determine the nature and extent of the relationship between two measured responses. | An intensive , retrospective, and detailed study of some aspects of one (or a few) individual(s). |
| A series of operations used to investigate relationships between manipulated events (independent variables) and measured events (dependent variables), while other events (extraneous variables) are eliminated. | A number that indicates the nature and the strength of the relationship between measured responses. |
| Those responses measured in an experiment whose values are hypothesized to depend on manipulations of the independent variable. | Those events in an experiment that are manipulated by the experimenter and that are hypothesized to produce changes in responses. |
| Those participants in an experiment who receive some treatment or manipulation-there may be more than one in an experiment. | Those factors in an experiment that need to be minimized or eliminated so as not to affect the dependent variable. |

| | |
|---|---|
| control group/1/ | random assignment/1/ |
| baseline design/1/ | debrief/1/ |
| gene/2/ | chromosome/2/ |
| dominant gene/2/ | recessive gene/2/ |

The selection of members of a population in such a way that each has an equal opportunity to be assigned to any one group.

Those participants in an experiment who do not receive any experimental treatment or manipulation.

To fully inform a subject about the intent and/or hypothesis of one's research once data have been collected.

A method in which subjects' performance with an experimental treatment is compared with performance without that treatment (the baseline).

Literally, "colored body," that thin, threadlike structure found in 23 pairs in human cells that carry genes.

The basic mechanism of hereditary transmission; that which gets passed from one generation to the next.

A gene that carries a trait that will be expressed only if it is paired with another similar recessive gene.

A gene that carries a trait that will be expressed regardless of the gene it is paired with.

| | |
|---|---|
| neuron/2/ | cell body/2/ |
| dendrites/2/ | axon/2/ |
| myelin/2/ | axon terminals/2/ |
| neural impulse/2/ | ion/2/ |

The largest mass of a neuron, containing the cell's nucleus, and receiving neural impulses.

A nerve cell, the basic building block of the nervous system, that transmits neural impulses.

The long, taillike extension of a neuron that carries an impulse away from the cell body toward the synapse.

Branchlike extensions from a neuron's cell body where most neural impulses are received.

The series of branching end points of an axon where one neuron communicates with the next in a series.

A white fatty covering found on some axons that serves to insulate and protect them, while increasing the speed of impulses.

An electrically charged (either + or -) chemical particle.

A sudden and reversible change in the electrical charges within and outside the membrane of a neuron, which travels from the dendrite to the axon end of a neuron.

| | |
|---|---|
| resting potential/2/ | action potential/2/ |
| synapse/2/ | vesicles/2/ |
| neurotransmitters/2/ | synaptic cleft/2/ |
| central nervous system/2/ | peripheral nervous system/2/ |

The short-lived burst of a change in the difference in electrical charge between the inside and the outside of a neuron when it fires.

The difference in electrical charge between the inside of a neuron and the outside when it is at rest.

The small containers, concentrated in axon terminals, that hold neurotransmitter molecules.

The general location where an impulse is relayed from one neuron to another by means of neurotransmitters.

The space between the membrane of an axon terminal and the membrane of the next neuron in a sequence.

Chemical molecules released at the synapse that will, in general, either excite or inhibit neural impulse transmission.

Those neurons not found in the brain or spinal cord, i.e., those found in the periphery of the body.

Those neurons in the brain and spinal cord.

| | |
|---|---|
| somatic nervous system/2/ | autonomic nervous system/2/ |
| sympathetic division/2/ | parasympathetic division/2/ |
| endocrine system/2/ | hormones/2/ |
| spinal reflex/2/ | brain stem/2/ |

Those neurons of the PNS that activate the smooth muscles and glands.

Sensory and motor neurons outside the CNS that serve the sense receptors and the skeletal muscles.

Those neurons involved in the maintenance of states of calm and relaxation.

Those neurons involved in states of emotionality.

A variety of chemical compounds, secreted by the glands of the endocrine system, many of which have effects on behavior or mental states.

A network of glands that secrete hormones directly into the bloodstream.

The lowest part of the brain, just above the spinal cord, comprised of the medulla and the pons.

An automatic, involuntary response to a stimulus that involves sensory neurons carrying impulses to the spinal cord, interneurons within the spinal cord, and motor neurons carrying impulses to muscles.

| | |
|---|---|
| medulla/2/ | nuclei/2/ |
| cross-laterality/2/ | pons/2/ |
| cerebellum/2/ | tremors/2/ |
| reticular activating system/2/ | limbic system/2/ |

Small collections or bundles of neural cell bodies.

An area of the brain stem that monitors breathing and heart rate, and where most cross-laterality occurs.

A brain stem structure forming a bridge between the brain and the spinal cord that monitors the sleep-wake cycle.

The process of nerve fibers crossing over the brain stem so that the left side of the body sends impulses to and receives impulses from the right side of the brain, and vice versa.

Involuntary, trembling, jerky movements.

A spherical structure at the lower rear of the brain involved in the coordination of bodily movements.

A collection of structures, including the amygdala and septum, which are involved in emotionality, and the hippocampus, involved in forming long-term memories.

A network of nerve fibers extending from the brain stem to the cerebrum that is involved in maintaining levels of arousal.

hypothalamus/2/

thalamus/2/

cerebral cortex/2/

cerebral hemispheres/2/

frontal lobes/2/

temporal lobes/2/

occipital lobes/2/

parietal lobes/2/

The last sensory relay station; it sends impulses to the appropriate area of the cerebral cortex.

A small structure near the limbic system in the center of the brain, associated with feeding, drinking, sex, and aggression.

The two halves of the cerebral cortex, separated by a deep fissure running from front to back.

The large, convoluted outer covering of the brain that is the seat of cognitive functioning and voluntary action.

The lobes of the cerebrum, located at the temples.

The largest of the cerebral lobes, found in front of the central fissure and above the lateral fissure.

The lobes of the cerebrum found behind the frontal lobes, in front of the occipital lobes, and above the temporal lobes.

The cerebral lobes at the very back of the brain.

sensory areas/2/

motor areas/2/

association areas/2/

corpus callosum/2/

split-brain procedure/2/

conception/3/

zygote/3/

prenatal period/3/

The strips at the back of the frontal lobes that control voluntary movement.

Those areas of the cerebral cortex that receive impulses from our sense receptors.

A network of nerve fibers that interconnect the two hemispheres of the cerebrum.

Those areas of the frontal, parietal, and temporal lobes in which higher mental processing occurs.

The moment when the father's sperm cell unites with the mother's ovum to produce a zygote.

A surgical technique of severing the corpus callosum, allowing the two hemispheres to operate independently.

That period of development from conception to birth.

The one-cell product of the union of sperm and ovum at conception.

| | |
|---|---|
| viability/3/ | fetal alcohol syndrome/3/ |
| neonate/3/ | schema/3/ |
| assimilation/3/ | accommodation/3/ |
| sensorimotor stage/3/ | object permanence/3/ |

A cluster of symptoms associated with a child born to a mother who was a heavy drinker of alcohol during pregnancy.

The ability to survive without interference or intervention.

One's organized mental representations of the world.

The newborn, from birth to age 2 weeks.

The process of altering or revising an existing schema in the light of new information.

The process of adding new material or information to an existing schema.

The appreciation that an object no longer in view can still exist and reappear later.

In Piaget's theory, from birth to age 2 years, when a child learns by sensing and doing.

| | |
|---|---|
| egocentric/3/ | preoperational stage/3/ |
| concrete operations stage/3/ | conservation/3/ |
| formal operations stage/3/ | puberty/3/ |
| adolescence/3/ | growth spurt/3/ |

In Piaget's theory, from age 2 years to 6 years. when a child begins to develop symbolic representations but cannot manipulate them; also characterized by egocentricity.

To be characterized by self; by "me" and "mine" and "my point of view."

In Piaget's theory, an appreciation that changing the physical properties of an object does not necessarily change its essence.

In Piaget's theory, from age 7 years to 12 years, when concepts can be manipulated, but not in an abstract fashion.

The stage of physical development at which one becomes capable of sexual reproduction.

In Piaget's theory, ages older than 12 years, when one can generate and test abstract hypotheses, and think as an adult, where thinking follows rules.

A marked increase in both height and weight that accompanies the onset of adolescence.

The developmental period between childhood and adulthood, often begun at puberty and ending with full physical growth, generally between the ages of 12 and 20.

| | |
|---|---|
| menarche/3/ | identity crisis/3/ |
| ageism/3/ | sensation/4/ |
| psychophysics/4/ | absolute threshold/4/ |
| subliminal perception/4/ | difference threshold/4/ |

The struggle to define and integrate one's sense of self and what one's attitudes, beliefs, and values should be.

A female's first menstrual period, often taken as a sure sign of the beginning of adolescence.

The process of receiving information from the environment and changing that input into nervous system activity.

Discrimination or negative stereotypes about someone formed solely on the basis of age.

The physical intensity of a stimulus that one can detect 50 percent of the time.

The study of the relationship between physical attributes of stimuli and the psychological experiences they produce.

The minimal difference in some stimulus attribute, such as intensity, that one can detect 50 percent of the time.

The process of responding to, or perceiving, stimuli that are presented at levels below one's absolute threshold.

| | |
|---|---|
| just noticeable difference/4/ | signal detection theory/4/ |
| sensory adaptation/4/ | dark adaptation/4/ |
| light/4/ | wave amplitude/4/ |
| brightness/4/ | wavelength/4/ |

The view that stimulus detection is a matter of decision-making, of separating a signal from background noise.

The minimal change in some stimulus attribute, such as intensity, that can be detected.

The process by which our eyes become more sensitive to light as we spend time in the dark.

The process in which our sensory experience tends to decrease or diminish with continued exposure to a stimulus.

A characteristic of wave forms (the height of the wave) that indicates intensity.

A radiant energy that can be represented in wave form with wavelength between 380 and 760 nanometers.

A characteristic of wave forms that indicates the distance between any point on a wave and the corresponding point on the next cycle of the wave.

The psychological experience associated with a light's intensity or wave amplitude.

| | |
|---|---|
| nanometer/4/ | hue/4/ |
| monochromatic/4/ | saturation/4/ |
| white light/4/ | cornea/4/ |
| pupil/4/ | iris/4/ |

The psychological experience associated with a light's wavelength.

One millionth of a millimeter-the unit of measurement for the wavelength of light.

The psychological experience associated with the purity of a light wave, where the most saturated lights are monochromatic and the least saturated are white light.

Literally one colored; a pure light made up of light waves all of the same wavelength.

The outermost structure of the eye that protects the eye and begins to focus light waves.

A light of the lowest possible saturation, containing a mixture of all visible wavelengths.

The colored structure of the eye that reflexively opens or constricts the pupil.

The opening in the iris that changes size in relation to the amount of light available and emotional factors.

| | |
|---|---|
| lens/4/ | ciliary muscles/4/ |
| accommodation/4/ | aqueous humor/4/ |
| vitreous humor/4/ | retina/4/ |
| photoreceptors/4/ | rods/4/ |

Small muscles attached to the lens that control its shape and focusing capability.

The structure behind the iris that changes shape to focus visual images in the eye.

Watery fluid found in the space between the cornea and the lens that nourishes the front of the eye.

The process in which the ciliary muscles change the shape of the lens in order to focus a visual image.

Layers of cells at the back of the eye that contain the photosensitive rod and cone cells.

The thick fluid behind the lens of the eye that helps keep the eyeball spherical.

Photosensitive cells of the retina that are most active in low levels of illumination and do not respond differentially to different wavelengths of light.

Light-sensitive cells of the retina that convert light energy into neural energy.

| | |
|---|---|
| cones/4/ | optic nerve/4/ |
| fovea/4/ | blindspot/4/ |
| loudness/4/ | decibel scale/4/ |
| hertz/4/ | pitch/4/ |

The fiber made of many neurons that leaves the eye and carries impulses to the occipital lobe of the brain.

Photosensitive cells of the retina that operate best at high levels of illumination and are responsible for color vision.

The small region of the retina, containing no photoreceptors, where the optic nerve leaves the eye.

The region at the center of the retina, comprised solely of cones, where acuity is best in daylight.

A scale of our experience of loudness in which 0 represents the absolute threshold and 140 is sensed as pain.

The psychological experience correlated with the intensity, or amplitude, of a sound wave.

The psychological experience that corresponds to sound wave frequency and gives rise to high (treble) or low (bass) sounds.

The standard measure of sound wave frequency that is the number of wave cycles per second.

| | |
|---|---|
| timbre/4/ | white noise/4/ |
| pinna/4/ | eardrum/4/ |
| malleus, incus, stapes/4/ | cochlea/4 |
| basilar membrane/4/ | hair cells/4/ |

A sound composed of a random assortment of all wave frequencies from the audible spectrum.

The psychological experience related to wave purity by which we differentiate the sharpness, clearness, or quality of a tone.

The outermost membrane of the ear that is set in motion by the vibrations of a sound; and transmits vibrations to the ossicles.

The outer ear that collects and funnels sound waves into the auditory canal toward the eardrum.

Part of the inner ear where sound waves become neural impulses.

Three small bones that transmit and intensify sound vibrations from the eardrum to the oval window.

The receptor cells for hearing, located in the cochlea, stimulated by the vibrating basilar membrane; they send neural impulses to the temporal lobe.

A structure within the cochlea that vibrates and thus stimulates the hair cells of the inner ear.

taste buds/4/

pheromones/4/

vestibular sense/4/

kinesthetic sense/4/

gate-control theory/4/

placebo/4/

perception/5/

contrast/5/

Chemicals that produce an odor that is used as a method of communication between organisms.

The receptors for taste located on the tongue.

The position sense that tells us the position of different parts of our bodies and what our muscles and joints are doing.

The position sense that tells us about balance, where we are in relations to gravity, acceleration, or deceleration.

An inactive substance that has its effect because a person has come to believe that it will be effective.

The theory of pain sensation that argues that there are brain centers that regulate the passage of pain messages from different parts of the body to the brain.

The extent to which a stimulus is in some physical way different from other surrounding stimuli.

The cognitive process of selecting, organizing, and interpreting stimuli.

| | |
|---|---|
| mental set/5/ | gestalt/5/ |
| figure-ground relationship/5/ | proximity/5/ |
| similarity/5/ | continuity/5/ |
| common fate/5/ | closure/5/ |

Whole, totality, configuration, or pattern; the whole being perceived as more than the sum of its parts.

A predisposed way to perceive something; an expectation.

The Gestalt principle of organization that claims that stimuli will be perceived as belonging together if they occur together in space or time.

The Gestalt psychology principle that states that stimuli are selected and perceived as figures against a ground or background.

The Gestalt principle of organization that claims that a stimulus or a movement will be perceived as continuing in the same smooth direction as first established.

The Gestalt principle of organization that claims that stimuli will be perceived together if they share some common characteristics.

The Gestalt principle of organization that claims that we tend to perceive incomplete figures as whole and complete.

The Gestalt principle of organization that claims that we group together into the same figure elements of a scene that move together in the same direction at the same speed.

subjective contours/5/

retinal disparity/5/

convergence/5/

accommodation/5/

illusion/5/

phi phenomenon/5/

autokinetic effect/5/

consciousness/5/

The phenomenon in which each retina receives a different view of the same three-dimensional object.

The perception of a contour that is not there, but is suggested by other aspects of a scene.

The process in which the shape of the lens is changed by the ciliary muscles to focus an image on the retina.

The tendency of the eyes to move toward each other as we focus on objects up close.

The visual illusion of the apparent motion of stationary lights that are flashing on and off.

A perception that is at odds with what we know as physical reality.

Our awareness or perception of the environment and of our own mental processes.

The visual illusion of apparent motion in which a stationary pinpoint of light in an otherwise dark environment appears to move.

| | |
|---|---|
| insomnia/5/ | electroencephalogram/5/ |
| electromyogram/5/ | alpha activity/5/ |
| /REM sleep/5/ | atonia/5/ |
| hypnosis/5/ | psychoactive drug/5/ |

An instrument used to measure and record the electrical activity of the brain.

The chronic inability to get to sleep and to get an adequate amount of sleep.

An EEG pattern associated with quiet relaxation and characterized by slow wave cycles of 8 to 12 per second.

An instrument used to measure and record muscle tensionrelaxation.

Muscular immobility, associated with REM sleep, caused by the total relaxation of the muscles.

Rapid eye movement sleep during which vivid dreaming occurs, as do heightened levels of physiological functioning.

A chemical that has an effect on psychological processes and consciousness.

An altered state of consciousness characterized by an increase in suggestibility, attention, and imagination.

| | |
|---|---|
| dependence/5/ | tolerance/5/ |
| withdrawal/5/ | addiction/5/ |
| drug abuse/5/ | stimulants/5/ |
| depressants/5/ | hallucinogens/5/ |

In drug use, a state where more and more of the drug is required to produce the same effect.

A state in which drug use is either necessary or believed to be necessary to maintain functioning at some desired level.

An extreme dependency, usually accompanied by symptoms of tolerance and painful withdrawal.

A negative, painful reaction that may occur when one stops taking a drug.

Those drugs (such as caffeine, cocaine, and amphetamines) that increase nervous system activity.

A state characterized by a lack of control, a disruption of interpersonal relationships or difficulties at work, and a history of maladaptive drug use for at least one month.

Those drugs (such as LSD) whose major effect is the alteration of perceptual experience and mood.

Those drugs (such as alcohol, opiates, heroin, and barbiturates) that slow or reduce nervous system activity.

learning/6/

reflex/6/

classical conditioning/6/

unconditioned stimulus/6/

unconditioned response/6/

orienting reflex/6/

habituation/6/

conditioned stimulus/6/

An unlearned, automatic response that occurs in the presence of specific stimuli.

Demonstration of a relatively permanent change in behavior that occurs as the result of practice or experience.

In classical conditioning, a stimulus that reliably and reflexively evokes a response.

Learning in which an originally neutral stimulus comes to elicit a new response after having been paired with a stimulus that reflexively elicits that same response.

The simple, unlearned response of orienting toward, or attending to, a new or unusual stimulus.

In classical conditioning, a response reliably and reflexively evoked by a stimulus.

In classical conditioning, an originally neutral stimulus that, when paired with a UCS, comes to evoke a new response.

A simple form of learning in which an organism comes to ignore a stimulus of no consequence.

conditioned response/6/

acquisition/6/

extinction/6/

spontaneous recovery/6/

generalization/6/

discrimination/6/

operant conditioning/6/

law of effect/6/

The process in classical conditioning in which the strength of the CR increases with repeated pairings of the CS and the UCS.

In classical conditioning, the learned response evoked by the CS after conditioning.

The phenomenon in classical conditioning in which a previously extinguished CR returns after a rest interval.

The process in classical conditioning in which the strength of the CR decreases with repeated presentations of the CS alone.

The phenomenon in classical conditioning in which an organism learns to make a CR in response to only one CS, but not to other stimuli.

The phenomenon in classical conditioning in which a CR is elicited by stimuli different from, but similar to, the CS.

The observation that responses that lead to satisfying states of affairs tend to be repeated, while those that do not, are not.

Changing the rate of a response on the basis of the consequences that result from that response.

| | |
|---|---|
| shaping/6/ | acquisition/6/ |
| extinction/6/ | spontaneous recovery/6/ |
| reinforcement/6/ | reinforcers/6/ |
| positive reinforcer/6/ | negative reinforcer/6/ |

The process in operant conditioning in which the rate of a reinforced response increases.

A procedure of reinforcing successive approximations of a desired response until that desired response is made.

The phenomenon in operant conditioning in which a previously extinguished response returns after a rest interval.

The process in operant conditioning in which the rate of a response decreases as reinforcers are withheld.

Stimuli that increase the rate or probability of the responses they follow.

A process that increases the rate or probability of the response that it follows.

A stimulus that increases the rate of a response when that stimulus is removed after the response is made.

A stimulus that increases the rate of a response when that stimulus is presented after the response is made.

primary reinforcer/6/

secondary reinforcers/6/

continuous reinforcement schedule/6/

intermittent reinforcement schedule/6/

punishment/6/

generalization/6/

discrimination/6/

latent learning/6/

Stimuli that increase the rate of a response because of their having been associated with other reinforcers; also called conditioned, or learned, reinforcers.

Stimuli that increase the rate of a response with no previous experience required.

A reinforcement schedule in which responses are not reinforced every time they occur.

A reinforcement schedule in which each and every response is followed by a reinforcer.

The process by which a response that was reinforced in the presence of one stimulus appears in response to other, similar stimuli.

The administration of a punisher, which is a stimulus that decreases the rate or probability of a response that precedes it.

Hidden learning that is not demonstrated in performance until that performance is reinforced.

The process of differential reinforcement wherein one stimulus is reinforced while another stimulus is not.

| | |
|---|---|
| cognitive map/6/ | social learning theory/6/ |
| vicarious reinforcement/6/ | memory/7/ |
| encoding/7/ | storage/7/ |
| retrieval/7/ | sensory memory/7/ |

| | |
|---|---|
| The theory that learning takes place through observation and imitation of models. | A mental representation of the learning situation or physical environment. |
| The cognitive ability to encode, store, and retrieve information. | Increasing the rate (with reinforcement) or decreasing the rate (with punishment) of responses due to observing the consequences of someone else's behaviors. |
| The process of holding encoded information in memory. | The active process of representing, or putting information into memory. |
| The type of memory that holds large amounts of information registered at the senses for very brief periods of time. | The process of locating, removing, and using information that is stored in memory. |

| | |
|---|---|
| short-term memory/7/ | maintenance rehearsal/7/ |
| chunk/7/ | long-term memory/7/ |
| elaborative memory/7/ | procedural memory/7/ |
| semantic memory/7/ | episodic memory/7/ |

A process of rote repetition to keep information in short-term memory.

A type of memory with limited capacity and limited duration.

A type of memory with virtually unlimited capacity and very long, if not limitless, duration.

A somewhat imprecise concept, referring to a meaningful unit of information as represented in memory.

In long-term memory, where learned stimulus-response associations and skilled patterns of responses are stored.

A mechanism for processing information into long-term memory that involves the meaningful manipulation of the information to be remembered.

In long-term memory, where life events and experiences are stored.

In long-term memory, where vocabulary, facts, simple concepts, rules, and the like are stored.

| | |
|---|---|
| recall/7/ | recognition/7/ |
| relearning/7/ | encoding specificity principle/7/ |
| state-dependent memory/7/ | flashbulb memories/7/ |
| meaningfulness/7/ | mnemonic devices/7/ |

A measure of retrieval in which an individual is required to identify material previously learned as familiar.

A measure of retrieval in which an individual is provided with the fewest possible cues to aid retrieval.

The hypothesis that we can only retrieve what we have stored and that retrieval is enhanced to the extent that retrieval cues match encoding cues.

A measure of memory in which one notes an improvement in performance when learning material for a second time.

Particularly clear and vivid memories that are easily retrieved, but not necessarily accurate in all detail.

The hypothesis that retrieval can be enhanced by the extent to which one's state of mind at retrieval matches one's state of mind at encoding.

Strategies for improving retrieval that take advantage of existing memories in order to make new material more meaningful.

The extent to which information evokes associations with information already in memory.

| | |
|---|---|
| narrative chaining/7/ | peg word method/7/ |
| method of loci/7/ | schema/7/ |
| overlearning/7/ | retroactive interference/7/ |
| proactive interference/7/ | problem/8/ |

The mnemonic device of forming interactive visual images of materials to be learned and items previously associated with numbers.

The mnemonic device of relating words together in a story, thus organizing them in a meaningful way.

A system of organized, general knowledge, stored in long-term memory, that guides the encoding and retrieval of information.

The mnemonic device that mentally places information to be retrieved in a series of familiar locations.

The inhibition of retrieval of previously learned material caused by material learned later.

The practice or rehearsal of material over and above what is needed to learn it.

A situation in which there is a discrepancy between one's current state and one's desired, or goal state, with no clear way of getting from one to the other.

The inhibition of retrieval of recently learned material caused by material learned earlier.

| | |
|---|---|
| strategy/8/ | algorithm/8/ |
| heuristic/8/ | mental set/8/ |
| functional fixedness/8/ | divergent thinking/8/ |
| convergent thinking/8/ | language/8/ |

A problem-solving strategy in which all possible solutions are generated and tested and an acceptable solution is guaranteed.

In problem-solving, a systematic plan for generating possible solutions that can be tested to see if they are correct.

A tendency to perceive or respond to something in a predetermined, set way.

A problem-solving strategy in which hypotheses about problem solutions are generated and tested in a time-saving and systematic way, but that does not guarantee an acceptable solution.

The creation of many ideas or potential problems solutions from one idea.

The phenomenon in which one is unable to see a new use or function for an object because of experience using the object in some other function.

A large collection of arbitrary symbols that have significance for a language-using community, and that follow certain rules of combination.

The reduction or focusing of many different ideas into one possible problem solution.

babbling/8/

holophrastic speech/8/

overregularization/8/

intelligence/8/

psychological test/8/

reliability/8/

test-retest reliability/8/

validity/8/

The use of one word to communicate a number of different meanings.

Speech sounds produced in rhythmic, repetitive patterns.

The capacity to understand the world and the resourcefulness to cope with its challenges; that which an intelligence test measures.

The excessive application of an acquired language rule in a situation where it is not appropriate.

Consistency or dependability; in testing, consistency of test scores.

An objective, standardized measure of a sample of behavior.

In testing, the extent to which a test measures what it claims to be measuring.

A check of a test's consistency determined by correlating the results of a test taken by the same subjects at two different times.

| | |
|---|---|
| predictive validity/8/ | concurrent validity/8/ |
| content validity/8/ | norms/8/ |
| g/8/ | mental retardation/8/ |
| /Down's syndrome/8/ | phenylketonuria (PKU)/8/ |

The extent to which the scores on a test are correlated with other assessments made at about the same time.

The extent to which a test can be used to predict future behaviors.

Results of a test taken by a large group of subjects whose scores can be used to make comparisons or give meaning to new scores.

The extent to which a test provides an adequate and fair sample of the behaviors being measured.

A condition indicated by an IQ below 70 that began during the developmental period and is associated with impairment in adaptive functioning.

A measure of one's overall, general intellectual abilities, commonly thought of as "IQ."

A genetically caused disorder that produces mental retardation and that is now detectable and preventable.

A condition of many symptoms, including mental retardation, caused by an extra (47th) chromosome.

| | |
|---|---|
| motivation/9/ | arousal/9/ |
| instincts/9/ | need/9/ |
| drive/9/ | incentives/9/ |
| homeostasis/9/ | set point/9/ |

One's level of activation or excitement; indicative of a motivational state.

The process of arousing, maintaining, and directing behavior.

A lack or shortage of some biological essential resulting from deprivation.

Unlearned, complex patterns of behavior that occur in the presence of particular stimuli.

External stimuli that an organism may be motivated to approach or avoid.

A state of tension resulting from a need that arouses and directs an organism's behavior.

A normal, optimum level (or value) of equilibrium or balance among physiological or psychological reactions.

A state of balance or equilibrium among internal, physiological conditions.

hypothalamus/9/

syphilis/9/

sexually transmitted diseases/STDs/9/

need to achieve/9/

/Thematic Apperception Test/9/

need for power/9/

need for affiliation/9/

acquired immune deficiency syndrome (AIDS)/9/

An STD caused by a bacterial infection, which may pass through four stages, ultimately resulting in death.

A small brain structure involved in many drives, including thirst, hunger, sex, and temperature regulation.

The learned need to meet or exceed some standard of excellence in performance.

Contagious diseases that are usually transmitted through sexual contact.

The learned need to be in control of events or persons, usually at another's expense.

A projective personality test requiring a subject to tell a series of short stories about a set of ambiguous pictures.

A deadly disease caused by a virus (HIV) that destroys the body's natural immune system, and which can be transmitted by sexual behaviors.

The need to be with others and to form relationships and associations.

homosexuals/9/

chlamydia/9/

gonorrhea/9/

emotion/9/

psychoanalytic approach/10/

neo-Freudians/10/

life instincts (eros)/10/

libido/10/

A very common STD; a bacterial infection of the genital area.

Persons who are sexually attracted to and aroused by members of their own sex.

A reaction involving subjective feeling, physiological response, cognitive interpretation, and behavioral expression.

An STD caused by a bacterial infection of moist tissues in the genital area.

Personality theorists (including Adler, Jung, and Horney) who kept many of Freud's basic psychoanalytic principles, but differed from a strict Freudian view, adding new concepts of their own.

The approach to personality associated with Freud and his followers that relies on instincts and the unconscious as explanatory concepts.

The energy that activates the life (sexual) instincts (largely of the id).

Those inborn impulses proposed by Freud that compel one toward survival, including hunger, thirst, and sex.

| | |
|---|---|
| death instincts (thanatos)/10/ | id/10/ |
| pleasure principle/10/ | ego/10/ |
| reality principle/10/ | defense mechanisms/10/ |
| superego/10/ | idealistic principle/10/ |

That instinctive aspect of personality that seeks immediate gratification of impulses; and operates on the pleasure principle.

Those inborn impulses proposed by Freud that compel one toward destruction, including aggression.

That aspect of personality that encompasses the sense of "self"; it is in contact with the real world; and operates on the reality principle.

The impulse of the id to seek immediate gratification to reduce tensions.

Unconsciously applied techniques that protect the self (ego) from feelings of anxiety.

The force that governs the ego; arbitrating between the demands of the id, the superego, and the real world.

Governs the superego; opposed to the id, seeks adherence to standards of ethics and morality.

That aspect of personality that refers to ethical or moral considerations; and operates on the idealistic principle.

| | |
|---|---|
| inferiority complex/10/ | phenomenological/10/ |
| repression/10/ | denial/10/ |
| rationalization/10/ | fantasy/10/ |
| projection/10/ | regression/10/ |

Emphasizes one's perception and awareness of events as being more important than the events themselves.

The Adlerian notion that as children we develop a sense of inferiority in dealing with our environment that must be be overcome for us to reach maturity.

Refusing to acknowledge the presence of stressors.

"Motivated forgetting" in which stressful events are forced from awareness into the unconscious and can no longer be remembered directly.

An escape from stress through imagination andor daydreaming.

Generating excuses to explain one's behaviors rather than facing the real (anxiety-producing) reasons for those behaviors.

A return to earlier, childish patterns of previously reinforcing behaviors as an escape from stress.

Seeing in others those very characteristics and motives that cause stress in one's self.

| | |
|---|---|
| displacement/10/ | traits/10/ |
| behavioral observation/10/ | interview/10/ |
| /Minnesota Multiphasic Personality Inventory (MMPI)/10/ | projective technique/10/ |
| /Rorschach inkblot test/10/ | /Thematic Apperception Test (TAT)/10/ |

Distinguishable, relatively enduring ways in which individuals may differ.

Directing one's motives at some substitute person or object rather than expressing them directly.

The personality assessment technique involving a conversational interchange between the interviewer and subject to gain information about the subject.

The personality assessment technique of drawing conclusions about one's personality on the basis of observations of one's behaviors.

A personality assessment technique requiring subjects to respond to ambiguous stimuli, thus projecting their "self" into their responses.

A paper-and-pencil inventory of 567 true-false questions used to assess a number of personality dimensions, some of which may indicate the presence of a psychological disorder.

A projective personality test requiring a subject to tell a series of stories about a set of ambiguous pictures.

A projective technique in which the subject is asked to say what is seen in a series of inkblots.

frustration/11/

conflict/11/

frustration-aggression hypothesis/11/

general adaptation syndrome/11/

health psychology/11/

type A behavior pattern (TABP)/11/

abnormal/12/

diagnosis/12/

A stressor in which some goals can be satisfied only at the expense of others.

A stressor; the blocking or thwarting of goal-directed behavior.

A pattern of physiological reactions to stress, producing alarm to resistance and exhaustion.

The view that all aggression stems from frustration.

A collection of behaviors often associated with coronary heart disease.

The field of applied psychology that studies psychological factors affecting physical health and illness.

The act of recognizing a disorder on the basis of the presence of particular symptoms.

Statistically uncommon, maladaptive cognitions, affect, andor behaviors that are at odds with social expectations and that result in distress or discomfort.

insanity/12/

anxiety/12/

phobic disorder/12/

prognosis/12/

agoraphobia/12/

panic disorder/12/

generalized anxiety disorder/12/

obsessions/12/

A general feeling of apprehension or dread accompanied by predictable physiological changes.

A legal term for diminished capacity and inability to tell right from wrong.

The prediction of the future course of an illness or disorder.

An intense, irrational fear that leads a person to avoid the feared object, activity, or situation.

A disorder in which anxiety attacks suddenly and unpredictably incapacitate; there may be periods free from anxiety.

A phobic fear of open places, of being alone, or of being in public places from which escape might be difficult.

Ideas or thoughts that involuntarily and persistently intrude into awareness.

Persistent, chronic, and distressingly high levels of unattributable anxiety.

| | |
|---|---|
| compulsions/12/ | somatoform disorders/12/ |
| hypochondriasis/12/ | conversion disorder/12/ |
| dissociative disorder/12/ | psychogenic amnesia/12/ |
| psychogenic fugue/12/ | multiple personality disorder/12/ |

Psychological disorders that reflect imagined physical or bodily symptoms or complaints.

Constantly intruding, stereotyped, and essentially involuntary acts or behaviors.

The display of a severe physical disorder for which there is no medical explanation; often accompanied by an apparent lack of concern on the part of the patient.

A mental disorder involving the fear of developing some serious disease or illness.

A psychologically caused inability to recall important personal information.

A disorder in which one separates from or dissociates from aspects of one's personality.

The existence within one individual of two or more distinct personalities, each of which is dominant at a particular time.

A condition of amnesia accompanied by unexplained travel or change of location.

| | |
|---|---|
| personality disorders/12/ | posttraumatic stress disorder (PTSD)/12/ |
| mood disorders/12/ | schizophrenia/12/ |
| process schizophrenia/12/ | reactive schizophrenia/12/ |
| psychosurgery/13/ | lobotomy/13/ |

An anxiety disorder in which disruptive recollections, distressing dreams, flashbacks, and felt anxiety occur well after the experience of a traumatic event.

Enduring patterns of perceiving, relating to, and thinking about the environment and one's self that are inflexible and maladaptive.

Complex psychotic disorders characterized by impairment of cognitive functioning, delusions and hallucinations, social withdrawal, and inappropriate affect.

Disorders of affect or feeling; usually depression; less frequently mania and depression occurring in cycles.

Schizophrenia in which the onset of the symptoms is comparatively sudden.

Schizophrenia in which the onset of the symptoms is comparatively slow and gradual.

A psychosurgical technique in which the prefrontal lobes of the cerebral cortex are severed from lower brain centers.

A surgical procedure designed to affect one's psychological or behavioral reactions.

electroconvulsive therapy (ECT)/13/

antipsychotic drugs/13/

antidepressant drugs/13/

antianxiety drugs/13/

psychotherapy/13/

psychoanalysis/13/

free association/13/

resistance/13/

Chemicals, such as chlorpromazine, that are effective in reducing psychotic symptoms.

A treatment (usually for the symptoms of depression) in which an electric current passed through a patient's head causes a seizure and loss of consciousness.

Chemicals, such as meprobamates and benzodiazepines, that alleviate the symptoms of anxiety.

Chemicals, such as MAO inhibitors and tricyclics, that reduce andor eliminate the symptoms of depression.

The form of psychotherapy associated with Freud, aimed at helping the patient gain insight into unconscious conflicts.

The treatment of mental disorders through psychological means, effecting change in cognitions, affect, andor behavior.

In psychoanalysis, the inability or unwillingness to freely discuss some aspect of one's life.

The procedure in psychoanalysis in which the patient is to express whatever comes to mind without editing responses.

| | |
|---|---|
| transference/13/ | client-centered therapy/13/ |
| empathic/13/ | behavior therapy/13/ |
| systematic desensitization/13/ | flooding/13/ |
| aversion therapy/13/ | contingency management/13/ |

The humanistic psychotherapy associated with Rogers, aimed at helping the client grow and change from within.

In psychoanalysis, the situation in which the patient comes to feel about the analyst in the same way he or she once felt about some other important person.

Techniques of psychotherapy founded on principles of learning established in the psychological laboratory.

Able to understand and share the essence of another's feelings; and to view from another's perspective.

A technique of behavior therapy in which a subject is confronted with the object of his or her phobic fear while accompanied by the therapist.

The application of classical conditioning procedures to alleviate extreme anxiety in which anxiety-producing stimuli are presented while the subject is in a relaxed state.

Bringing about changes in one's behaviors by controlling rewards or punishers.

A technique of behavior therapy in which an aversive stimulus, such as a shock, is paired with an undesired behavior.

contingency contracting/13/

modeling/13/

rational-emotive therapy/13/

cognitive restructuring therapy/13/

family therapy/13/

stereotype/14/

norms/14/

attitude/14/

The acquisition of new responses through the imitation of another who responds appropriately.

Establishing a token economy of secondary reinforcers to reward appropriate behaviors.

A form of cognitive therapy, associated with Beck, in which patients are led to overcome negative self-images and pessimistic views of the future.

A form of cognitive therapy, associated with Ellis, aimed at changing the subject's irrational beliefs or maladaptive cognitions.

A generalized mental representation of someone that minimizes individual differences and is based on limited experience.

A variety of group therapy focusing on the roles, interdependence, and communication skills of family members.

A relatively stable and general evaluative disposition directed toward some object, consisting of feelings, behaviors, and beliefs.

Rules or expectations that guide our behavior in certain social situations by prescribing how we ought to behave.

social psychology/14/

persuasion/14/

cognitive dissonance/14/

attribution/14/

internal attribution/14/

external attribution/14/

fundamental attribution error/14/

just world hypothesis/14/

The process of intentionally attempting to change an attitude.

The scientific study of how others influence the thoughts, feelings, and behaviors of the individual.

The cognitions we generate when we attempt to explain the sources of behavior.

The state of tension or discomfort that exists when we hold inconsistent cognitions; and that motivates us to reduce dissonance.

An explanation of behavior in terms of something outside the person; a situational attribution.

An explanation of behavior in terms of something within the person; a dispositional attribution.

The belief that the world is just and that people get what they deserve.

The tendency to overuse internal attributions when explaining behavior.

| | |
|---|---|
| self-serving bias/14/ | actor-observer bias/14/ |
| mere exposure phenomenon/14/ | matching phenomenon/14/ |
| conformity/14/ | audience inhibition/14/ |
| pluralistic ignorance/14/ | diffusion of responsibility/14/ |

The overuse of internal attributions to explain the behaviors of others and external attributions to explain our own behaviors.

The tendency to attribute our successes to our own effort and abilities, and our failures to situational, external sources.

The tendency to select partners whose level of physical attractiveness matches our own.

The tendency to increase our liking of people and things the more we see of them.

Reluctance to intervene and offer assistance in front of others.

Changing one's behavior so that it is consistent with the behavior of others.

The tendency to allow others to share in the obligation to intervene.

A condition in which the inaction of others leads each individual in a group to interpret a situation as a nonemergency, thus leading to general inactivity.

| | |
|---|---|
| social loafing/14/ | social facilitation/14/ |
| social interference/14/ | group polarization/14/ |
| groupthink/14/ | job analysis/15/ |
| performance criteria/15/ | training/15/ |

Improved performance due to the presence of others.

The tendency for a person to work less hard when part of a group in which everyone's efforts are pooled.

The tendency for members of a group to give more extreme judgments following a discussion than they gave initially.

Impaired performance due to the presence of others.

A complete and specific description of a job, including the qualities required to do it well.

A style of thinking of cohesive groups concerned with maintaining agreement to the extent that independent ideas are discouraged.

A systematic and intentional process of altering the behaviors of employees to increase organizational effectiveness.

Specific behaviors or characteristics that a person should have in order to do a job as well as possible.

expectancy theory/15/

equity theory/15/

job satisfaction/15/

quality of work life (QWL)/15/

environmental psychology/15/

personal space/15/

territoriality/15/

population density/15/

The view that workers are motivated to match their inputs and outcomes with those of fellow workers in similar positions.

The view that workers make logical choices to do what they believe will result in their attaining outcomes of highest value.

A group of factors concerning one's work that influence one's attitude toward one's job.

An attitude; a collection of feelings about one's job or job experiences.

The mobile "bubble" of space around you reserved for intimate relationships into which others may enter only by invitation.

The field of applied psychology that studies the effect of the general environment on organisms within it.

A quantitative measure of the number of persons per unit of area.

The setting off and marking of a piece of territory as one's own.

/crowding/15/

neurotoxins/15/

applied behavioral analysys/15/

sport psychology/15/

frequency distribution/appendix/

histogram/appendix/

central tendency/appendix/

variability/appendix/

Chemicals that affect psychological processes through the nervous system.

The subjective feeling of discomfort caused by a sense of lack of space.

The application of psychological principles to sport and physical activity at all levels of skill development.

An approach, based on operant conditioning, that attempts to find solutions to human environmental problems in the real world.

A bar graph, a graphical representation of a frequency distribution.

An ordered listing of all x values, indicating the frequency with which each occurs.

The extent of spread or dispersion in a set or distribution of scores.

A measure of the middle, or average, score in a set.

mean/appendix/

median/appendix/

mode/appendix/

range/appendix/

standard deviation/appendix/

inferential tests/appendix/

statistically significant differences/appendix/

normal curve/appendix/

The score of an ordered set above which and below which fall half the scores.

The sum of all x scores divided by the number of x scores.

The highest score in a distribution minus the lowest score.

The most frequently occurring x value in a set.

Statistical tests that tell us about the significance of the results of experimental or correlational studies.

A type of average of the deviations of each x score from the mean of the distribution.

A commonly found, symmetrical, bell-shaped frequency distribution.

Differences between descriptive statistics not likely to have occurred by chance if the descriptive statistics were describing the same group.